THE LAW
AND LIABILITY
A GUIDE FOR NURSES

THE LAW AND LIABILITY

A GUIDE FOR NURSES

Second Edition

Janine Fiesta, B.S.N., J.D.
Vice-President, Legal Services
HealthEast, Inc.
Allentown, Pennsylvania

A WILEY MEDICAL PUBLICATION
JOHN WILEY & SONS
New York · Chichester · Brisbane · Toronto · Singapore

Cases were adapted from the National Reporter System. Portions
were reprinted with permission of West Publishing Company, St. Paul,
Minnesota.
Copyright © 1983, 1988 by John Wiley & Sons, Inc.

Library of Congress Cataloging in Publication Data:

Fiesta, Janine.
    The law and liability.

    (A Wiley medical publication)
    Bibliography: p.
    Includes index.
    1. Nurses—Malpractice—United States. 2. Nursing—
Law and legislation—United States. I. Title.
II. Series. [DNLM: 1. Legislation, Nursing—United
States. 2. Malpractice—nurses' instruction.
WY 33 AAl F466L]

KF2915.N83F53 1988   346.7303'32   87-25332
ISBN: 0-471-85854-4   347.306332

Printed in the United States of America

10 9 8 7 6 5 4 3 2

PREFACE

This book is designed to provide nurses with an introduction to the legal issues they are likely to encounter in their profession. The emphasis is on malpractice issues, since these occur most frequently. There is also coverage of issues related to criminal actions, contracts, and wills.

The book makes ample use of the case study method; that is, principles of law are stated, and case histories are given to illustrate the way the law is applied. This method is helpful because it reminds the student that the law is not always black and white. Every case is unique and must be decided based upon the specific facts involved. On the other hand, general principles may be applied to a variety of situations that may not seem the same at first glance. Thus, failure to observe an orthopedic patient may be compared to failure to monitor an obstetric or psychiatric patient.

Although this book cannot provide definitive legal advice, it should give nurses the basic understanding they will need to practice their profession more effectively. Those nurses who have specific legal questions should seek advice from legal counsel.

The second edition continues the use of the case study method. Nurses utilizing the first edition have consistently communicated their enthusiasm for this approach.

The line of case law involving nursing liability has continued to develop. This text includes dozens of new cases involving issues of law previously addressed as well as evolving new issues. Information about recent ethical questions, as well as AIDS, has been included. A new chapter addressing nurses by specialty has been written. An attempt has been made to include legal cases involving nurses from every state. An index to the cases by state appears at the end of the book.

It is the author's wish that nurses will continue to enjoy reading this work as well as finding it to be of value in providing guidance and counsel as they contemplate the complex legal and ethical issues facing society and the health care profession today.

I would like to thank Steven L. Salman, J.D., for his consulting services on the first edition of this book. Many of his original comments continue to be a part of the second edition.

Janine Fiesta

CONTENTS

THE LAW
AND LIABILITY
A GUIDE FOR NURSES

INTRODUCTION

Although the intent of this book is to provide an overview of nursing law, nursing liability is emphasized. This emphasis is deliberate and reflects the author's finding, during many presentations and classes on nursing law, that the majority of questions deal with the material in these chapters.

Case examples have been used generously. Such examples serve to peak the interest of the student, to identify these issues as real problems, and in some instances, to allow the student to learn about cases decided in his or her own state.

The reader may question why some cases seem incomplete. In many malpractice cases, a final judgment or decision is not rendered because the parties reach a settlement before the time of the decision.

The majority of the nursing malpractice cases described in this book are reported cases only because they have been heard by a court of appeals; that is, a trial court has heard the case and has given an opinion, and the losing party has disagreed with the opinion and has appealed the decision. If the case is not appealed, it is usually not reported (published) in the legal reporting system. This has two implications. First, hundreds of cases are not appealed. Therefore, many trial court decisions are not available for purposes of research and review. Second, and perhaps even more significant to this book, if the case is appealed, it is appealed only on points of law. The appeals court is not a finder of fact and must rely on the lower court's findings of fact and credibility.

The appellate court determines procedural issues. Many times the issue is simply a decision as to whether the case was sufficient to be brought to the jury. The question may be posed as follows: "Is there sufficient evidence of malpractice for the jury to decide if malpractice has occurred?" If the answer is "yes," the case may be sent back to the lower court for retrial, or the decision of the lower court may be simply affirmed. If the case is sent back for retrial, the subsequent decision may not be published, and thus we will not know the ultimate determination of the case. For this reason, sometimes the author has said in concluding the case: "The court held that the jury should determine whether negligence has occurred." This means the case has been sent back to the lower court, and the subsequent decision was not published.

Through the study of these cases, the nurse can gain an understanding of how the legal system views the practice of nursing. Because the law is constantly evolving and may differ somewhat from state to state, the guidance provided in this book cannot be viewed as definitive. In any individual case, the nurse should always consult an attorney for specific advice.

CHAPTER 1

THE LEGAL PROCESS

SOURCES OF LAW

The law cannot be defined simply nor is there any comprehensive way to define the law. In the United States, however, there are four primary sources of the law. These are (1) the Constitution, (2) statutes, (3) administrative law, and (4) common law. Parallel systems exist at the federal and state levels. The Constitution is the basic framework established by the founders of our government and provides the basis on which our government is built. It grants the authority for the other three sources of the law. The Constitution, however, has little direct involvement in the area of malpractice.

Statutes are the written laws enacted by the legislature. They are passed by the House of Representatives and the Senate and are the basic rules for society. They become effective when signed by the president or the governor. There were a minimal number of statutes dealing with malpractice before the malpractice crisis of the mid-1970s. Today there are few federal statutes dealing with malpractice; however, there are many such state statutes.

Administrative law is a form of law made by administrative agencies appointed by the executive branch of government, the president or the governor. These agencies make rules in their limited areas of expertise. Examples of administrative agencies that make laws are the National Labor Relations Board, the Interstate Commerce Commission, and the Civil Aeronautics Board. These rules are made under the authority established by acts of the legislature. Some of these administrative agencies operate in areas that have no effect on malpractice; however, the effect is limited.

The final source of the law is common law. This is court-made law. Most law in the area of malpractice is court-made law. Also, the courts are responsible for interpreting the statutes. They may look at the language of the legislative pronouncements, or they may look beyond at the intent of the legislature. Most malpractice law is not addressed by statute but is established by the courts.

In the United States, there are two levels of court. The first level of court is the trial court. The trial court hears all the evidence and makes decisions as to facts, usually through a jury. However, sometimes cases are presented to a judge only, without a jury.

The two parties at trial are the plaintiff, the individual initiating the law suit, and the defendant. who in civil law is the party being sued. Issues of the law are decided by the judge. Most trial cases are not published beyond the county in which they take place. They have no binding effect on other counties or states. The second level of court is the appellate court. There are no juries at the appelate court level. All cases are heard by a judge or panel of judges. The only cases that are heard by the appellate court are those questioning a point of law decided by the trial court. Therefore, there are no witnesses asked to testify at the appellate level. Appellate judges write opinions that are published in books available to all courts in all states. These published opinions become the common law or case law that forms the bulk of the law in the United States.

Since trial court opinions are usually not published, many malpractice decisions are not available for review. The malpractice cases that are available are the appellate opinions that discuss primarily the point of law in dispute. Frequently, these decisions do not specify all the details of the trial court's decisions. For instance, the opinion may not state the precise dollar amount of the trial court's verdict. Therefore, the reader of these opinions is often left with unanswered questions regarding the lower court's handling of specific issues.

If the appellate court renders an opinion indicating that the case must be retried because of an error in the application of law at the trial level, these cases will go back for a new trial but may not again be reported unless a new error of law is made.

LEGAL PRECEDENT

The appellate court opinions become legal opinions or precedents that should be followed by other courts in the same jurisdiction. Precedent refers to a case furnishing an example for a similar case arising subsequently.

Malpractice cases are frequently settled either before the trial or during the actual case presentation. These settlements are not reported or published as opinions. Therefore, the cases that are settled out of court are not available for review and do not become legal precedents.

Although each case is decided based on its own merits with the appropriate application of legal principles, it is possible to find common threads in cases dealing with similar issues and facts. For example, many courts have evaluated malpractice cases involving patients who have fallen while in the hospital. Through an analysis of these cases and the court's response to the nurse, we become aware of how these cases are viewed by the judicial system. This understanding leads to an ability to predict how a future case might be decided based on past decisions. This is the value of case law precedent.

The value of a familiarity with case law should be readily apparent to the nurse. Malpractice cases that have already been decided serve as a guide to future decisions. These cases also help the nurse understand the legal process and how the courts apply these laws to professional liability cases.

It is also important for the nurse to be aware of specific malpractice cases that have been litigated in his or her own jurisdiction, that is, the state in which the nurse practices his or her profession. When a malpractice case is being decided, the court will look with particular interest to cases already decided in its own state. In some instances, these cases will serve as a precedent and guide the court in its decision. This will be true if the highest court of the state, usually the state Supreme Court, has decided a case dealing with the same issue. If no such decision exists, the court may look to other jurisdictions for direction. California cases are well-recognized trend-setters in the law and are frequently used as examples for other jurisdictions. Thus, an understanding of the overall scope of malpractice case law is important.

The judicial system evaluates the law on constitutional terms. This is the primary function of the United States Supreme Court. It must ensure that all laws formulated are in accord with basic constitutional rights. The Supreme Court fulfills this function by accepting for review only those cases involving a right guaranteed by the Constitution. Therefore, malpractice cases are not heard by the U.S. Supreme Court on appeal. The "right" to health care is not a basic right guaranteed by the Constitution.

As courts decide specific cases, a body of law develops known as case law or common law. Decided cases become a source of guidance for current cases before the court. Sometimes these cases are more than a source of guidance and the court must follow these prior cases without any discretion to differ. This is true, for example, where the United

States Supreme Court has ruled in a specific case dealing with a constitutional issue, and this rule must now be applied throughout the United States.

An example of this was *Griswold v. Connecticut*. The Supreme Court determined that a basic right of privacy exists for all citizens of the United States.

A married couple was prohibited by law in Connecticut from purchasing contraceptives. This law was held to be unconstitutional. The Supreme Court indicated that a constitutional right of privacy operates to protect the individual against intrusion by the government in certain areas of conduct.
    Griswold v. Connecticut, 381 U.S. 479 (1965).

Since *Griswold* was decided by the Supreme Court, it must be followed by all other courts.

LEGAL PROCEDURE

When all efforts to prevent malpractice have failed and the elements of the negligence action have been met, the usual outcome is that the injured party (the plaintiff) pursues a legal action. In many situations, with a good risk management program in effect, a settlement will take the place of a legal action. Risk management is a systematic approach to the prevention of malpractice claims. If the plaintiff has a true injury, that is, an injury serious in nature and caused by the negligence of a professional, compensation should be given. There is no reason why the expense of litigation should be paid when a true claim occurs. All parties, named defendants (usually physician, hospital, and nurse, if appropriate) as well as insurance companies and attorneys, should work toward a fair settlement if the above conditions are met.

If the plaintiff has not been satisfied by the initial efforts of the hospital/risk manager, then the next step is usually a visit to an attorney. The patient will request an interview to discuss his potential claim. The attorney will then, with the patient's written authorization, request a copy of the medical record.

At this point, the documentation on the medical record plays a vital role (see Chapter 11). Often a case is initiated because of poor documentation. Sometimes the attorney finds in the medical record evidence pointing to a different basis for claim than the incident that the patient has described. The following case is a hypothetical example.

An injured patient visited the attorney to discuss the fact that he was unhappy with the results of his hospitalization. He had had a surgical procedure performed during which he had needed a blood transfusion. Following the transfusion, he had experienced an adverse reaction. The attorney reviewed the patient's medical record. He realized that the blood was the proper type, that all policy and procedure had been properly followed, and that the policy itself had set a reasonable standard. Despite the due care exhibited by the institution, the patient had a reaction. There was no negligence involved. However, he noted on the record two additional factors. One was the absence of a consent form for the surgical procedure. The second was the omission of a dose of medication with the inappropriate documentation on the record: "incident report filed." Based on these two factors, he brought a lawsuit.

Whether or not the plaintiff recovers damages, both parties will spend a great deal of time, money, and emotional energy before the outcome is known. Had there been a valid surgical consent documented, no case would have been brought. If the nurse who omitted the one dose of medication had not charted "incident report filed," the situation may have been quite different.

Many claims have been brought to court that simply should not have been initiated. The first such situation is when there is an obviously valid claim on which the defendant should make an honest attempt to reach a fair settlement out of court. The second occurs when the claim is specious; that is, there is no justification, from a legal viewpoint, for the initiation of the action.

Many plaintiff's attorneys, on receipt of the medical record, will immediately forward it for review to a qualified physician. This is done to determine if there is a medical basis for alleging a deviation from proper standards of care, as well as to prove causation and damages. This is a proper procedure, and attorneys should be encouraged to begin their evaluation of the case in this manner. In most instances, attorneys do not have medical expertise to provide this initial determination. Some law firms, particularly large malpractice firms, are now employing nurses to perform this first evaluation. The attorney who fails to do this runs the risk of being sued for malpractice himself or herself for failing to bring a claim that might be valid.

When this request is received by the medical records department, it should be routinely reviewed by the risk manager. This may be the first notice received by the hospital that a suit is being contemplated by a particular patient. If the risk management process has not been notified of this earlier, this is the time that an in-hospital investigation should take place as well as communication with the hospital's insurance carrier. The physician involved in the case should also be notified and given an opportunity to review the record. *It is vital that no changes be made in the medical record.* If, at this point, a determination is made that the record is incomplete or inaccurate, this should be clarified in an addendum to the record with the date documented (see Chapter 11). It is extremely difficult to explain and defend in court a change that has been made subsequent to the request for the record.

Once the attorney reviews the record and determines that the basis for the claim is appropriate and timely, a complaint will be filed. A complaint is a legal document that is put on file in the courthouse and presented to the defendants. It is a summary, in legal terms, of what the injured party is going to try to prove. The complaint is filed with the court, and a copy is served on the defendant personally. A summons is also served with the complaint. The summons notifies the defendant of the date by which an answer to the complaint must be filed. The defendant then has a designated number of days to answer the complaint. In most jurisdictions, the complaint goes to a lower level judge. In jurisdictions having an arbitration system, it is the arbitration panel that receives the complaint. The arbitration panel will initially hear the case (see Chapter 12). The case may then be appealed to the designated court.

The filing of the complaint begins the time known as the discovery period; that is, the parties will now be given opportunities to elicit evidence and attempt to understand the facts of the case. Depositions, testimonies taken down in writing under oath, will be scheduled for plaintiff, defendants, and witnesses. A court stenographer will record all depositions. This gives all the attorneys involved an opportunity to question the parties. Some attorneys will use interrogatories, lists of written questions provided to the parties, in order to determine the evidence that is available. The plaintiff's attorney may request from the hospital all records, policies and procedures, and committee minutes pertaining to the plaintiff's case. In many instances, these documents are protected from discovery under Peer Review Acts. These statutes are legislative enactments designed to encourage physicians to engage in peer review and to protect such material from review by attorneys pursuing malpractice claims. Each jurisdiction will have different statutes governing what may be made available to opposing counsel. The purpose of discovery is to ensure that each party is fully aware of all the facts involved in the case and of the contentions of the parties regarding these facts. Another purpose of discovery is to encourage the settlement of suits when it is appropriate.

After the period of discovery has terminated, the parties will be ready to appear in court. In many complex malpractice cases, the discovery period may last 1 or 2 years. In court, both plaintiff and defendants will have the opportunity to testify as well as any witnesses. Witnesses will include those persons who have knowledge of the actual incident, expert witnesses, as well as perhaps family members who may attest to the pain and suffering of the plaintiff.

A nurse may be asked to serve as a witness in a malpractice case. The witness is placed under oath. Testimony is based on firsthand knowledge, not assumptions. If a nurse is asked to testify as an expert witness, an opinion will be sought.

In cases heard initially in a court, rather than by an arbitration panel, the case is brought before a jury made up of members of the community. The purpose of the jury in a medical malpractice case is to decide issues of fact. In almost every malpractice case, there are contradictory statements made by the parties involved. The following is a hypothetical example.

The injured party testified that she was injured while she was a patient at a hospital. She stated that she had to go to the bathroom and called the nurse for assistance. She stated that the nurse did not answer her call button. The nurse, however, testified that she had responded by telling the patient not to get out of bed alone and that she would be right with her. The patient went to the bathroom alone, fell, and fractured her hip.

The jury must now weigh the credibility of the two persons testifying, listen to all the other evidence, and decide which of the two parties to believe. In many instances, it is not a question of truth-telling but rather of what is remembered by the parties involved after a long period has elapsed.

The judge's role, in a malpractice case, is to monitor the testimony, decide legal questions regarding how the evidence is presented, and to determine questions of law.

After all the testimony has been presented, the judge discusses with the jury how the law should be applied, and they will then make their determination. The jury decides, in most cases, whether negligence has occurred and what damages should be awarded. It should be remembered that at any point before this decision by the jury, the parties themselves may decide to settle the case and remove it from the province of the jury. Settlements do not usually receive the publicity that large jury verdicts produce. Therefore, if a poor case is being defended, a knowledgeable attorney can protect his client from adverse publicity by settling out of court.

GRAY AREAS

As the previous discussion indicates, the legal process takes into account the unique facts of each malpractice case. Although it is extremely helpful to be familiar with already developed case law, often clear-cut answers to a particular situation will not be found. An attorney will be able to apply past case law to the present situation. However, many issues related to the legal aspects of medicine have yet to be decided. In fact, it is questionable whether the courts should render decisions on all questions related to medicine. The following case is a hypothetical example.

A young man was hospitalized with a bone marrow aplasia. His only hope for possible recovery was a bone marrow transplant. A brother, his only matching relative, refused to donate. The patient sued wanting to force the donation. The court held that this could not be compelled by the law.

There is some controversy, with regard to cases such as the one cited above, as to whether a court of law should consider questions that involve the application of ethical principles rather than legal principles. While in many cases a discussion of legal and ethical principles will result in the same conclusion, this is not always the situation. The following case is a hypothetical example.

A father practicing the religion of Jehovah's Witness refused a blood transfusion for himself. The court held that the blood transfusion should be given despite the patient's wishes, because his minor child could conceivably become a ward of the state if the parent died. Therefore, the state's interest prevailed.

This court imposed a legal standard where the ethical consideration might have emphasized the patient's right to control his own life and freely practice his religious beliefs.

Another example of the court's willingness to step into the medical area is evident in recent decisions where courts have acted to impose a judicial standard in a particular medical situation.

In Washington an ophthalmologist was held negligent for not administering a simple diagnostic test for the diagnosis of glaucoma. This was despite the fact that evidence clearly indicated the usual standard of care was not to provide this test in patients of the plaintiff's age group.
Helling v. Carey, 519 P.2d 981 (Wash. 1974).

The court, in the above case, imposed a national standard. Despite the fact that courts have sometimes, as indicated previously, moved into medical areas to make judicial determinations, it is more common to find courts recognizing their limitations and expressing reluctance in these specialized areas. This has resulted in many "gray" areas of law, that is, cases that are not black and white, are difficult to understand and apply or require legal interpretations and sometimes medical judgments as well.

Unfortunately, many of these very cases involve nursing, particularly the question of accountability. The gray areas of the law presently existing in regard to medicine often meet head on with the gray areas of nursing and the question of nursing accountability. It will be up to the nursing profession internally to clarify gray areas and to outline the scope of accountability. Nurses establish the standards for the nursing profession. This will, in turn, provide the legal system with guidelines with which to delineate more clearly the limits of what the law can consider to be the practice of professional nursing.

SUMMARY

There are basically two legal systems in the United States—the federal system and the state system. All four sources of the law exist at the federal level and at the state level. The United States Supreme Court's opinions must be followed by the state courts; however, within the states, the decisions of the highest court available, usually the state Supreme Court, must be followed by the lower court within the states. The state Supreme Court's position in one state has no binding effect on the courts of another state.

Most malpractice law is state law. Thus, it becomes vitally important to know the laws on a particular issue established in your state. It may be the complete opposite of that in another state.

Nurses need to familiarize themselves with the legal process. An understanding of the law, both sources and procedural aspects, will form the foundation for the nurse's ability to become comfortable with the law and its application to nursing. The need to study case law is particularly significant since this analysis provides some direction for the nurse in regard to how future cases may be decided.

CHAPTER 2

DEVELOPMENT OF THE LEGAL STATUS OF THE NURSE

HISTORICAL ANALYSIS

The role of the nurse is changing. In no other profession is there as much uncertainty as to its own status. Nurses themselves still seriously consider the age-old question of whether nursing is a profession that falls within the realm of art or science. The medical and legal professions, on the other hand, are somewhat more well defined in scope.

In the medical profession, a clear emphasis on scientific aspects has emerged in response to our modern technological society. Although some would argue that the decreasing emphasis on the "art" of medicine has led in many instances to the increasing medical malpractice problem in our society, few would deny themselves the benefits of these technological advances or the need for specialists with the knowledge necessary to implement these advances.

The legal profession, on the other hand, lends itself to falling within the definition of an art. The law seems to rely more on the ability of a person to look at society and to respond to the problems of society with a broad background of experience and interest.

Nursing is unique within this context; it draws on the best of both worlds. The modern nurse is educated in programs that rely equally on science and liberal arts courses. The depth of knowledge required of a nurse in the scientific area is rapidly approaching the level that we used to expect from a general practitioner of medicine. For the profession to survive, nurses must constantly work to redefine their position in society.

The majority of nurses, because of the equal emphasis on the art of professional nursing, is able to cope with advances and yet retain an awareness of the patient as a unique person.

Liberal arts courses that are directed toward nursing enable nurses to study communications, psychology, sociology, history, and philosophy. When this knowledge is implemented in the hospital and the community as part of the nursing curriculum. the students are provided with an opportunity to demonstrate their skills and receive reinforcement for their efforts.

The emphasis of the nursing curriculum on the uniqueness of the individual patient requires this broad-based, multifaceted approach. It readily becomes apparent that the practicing nurse has more knowledge and experience than most would expect. However, the legal standard of care for nursing makes it obvious that both the legal and, in many instances, the medical profession, gravely underestimate the knowledge and ability of nurses.

Courts, however, are beginning to respond to the changing role of the nurse. As case law illustrates, recognition of the increased standard of care that the nursing profession is providing has led to increased numbers of nurses named as defendants in malpractice cases. If nurses are held liable for the acts that they should be responsible for, and if the courts recognize this responsibility, the result will be an increased awareness on the part of society and an increased use of nurses to perform these services.

Nurses will not necessarily suffer as the result of this increased legal responsibility. Nurses already have this level of responsibility, and accept their ethical accountability. What they do not have, however, are the status and income levels to reflect the contribution that they make to the public.

WHEN IS A NURSE A DEFENDANT?

Historically, nurses have not been named individually as defendants in malpractice cases, since the law did not recognize, through case analysis, the role of the nurse as a health care provider. Either the hospital or the physician was named as a defendant for the acts of the nurse. The nurse was not recognized as a "person" in the eyes of the law. Whether the hospital or the physician was held liable depended on the nature of the particular activity in question. By imposing liability on other professionals for the acts of nurses, courts failed to recognize nursing as a unique profession with its own standards and accountabilities. The nurse was viewed as an employee merely carrying out the orders of either the hospital or the physician.

It appears that during the past 10 years, an increase in the number of malpractice cases in which nurses have been named as defendants has occurred. This is a reflection of the evolving independent status of the professional nurse. The concept of a professional includes legal accountability for a person's own actions. In fact, a basic premise of our legal system is the fact that a person should always be held accountable for his or her own actions. This premise should certainly extend to a professional group such as nursing.

As the legal profession becomes increasingly aware of the education and experience of the professional nurse, as well as the unique role a nurse plays in the health care delivery system, it is anticipated that nurses will become more legally accountable for their actions. This is in keeping with the development of nursing as a profession. The hospital and/or the physician may, as the employer of the nurse, still be held liable in addition to the nurse.

CURRENT STATUS—JOINT LIABILITY

Historically, hospitals were not held liable for the acts of their employees. Their protection arose from the doctrine of *charitable immunity*, which basically stated that a charitable organization such as a hospital could not be sued. The rationale for this doctrine was the belief that hospitals provided a large amount of charitable care. Before the development of health insurance programs and federally funded programs such as Medicare, this was true. However, by the 1950s, it was apparent that hospitals were crossing an invisible line from the provision of charitable care to the status of a business organization. In many cases, hospitals were operating at a profit, and many patients who were true victims of negligence could not be compensated. It became increasingly evident that the doctrine was not working for the best interests of the patient. In 1965 the Illinois case, *Darling v. Charleston Community Memorial Hospital*, the court did not accept charitable immunity as a defense to recovery.

An 18-year-old boy broke his leg while playing in a college football game. He was brought to the hospital, a cast was applied, and the patient was admitted to the hospital. Not long after application of the cast, he was in great pain, and his toes became swollen and dark in color. Three days later, the cast was split, and in the course of cutting, the plaintiff's leg was cut on both sides. The leg eventually had to be amputated. Evidence indicated that the nurses had not adequately observed the toes for changes of color, temperature, and movement. The amputated limb contained a considerable amount of dead tissue that could have resulted from interference with the circulation of blood in the limb caused by swelling or hemorrhaging of the leg against the cast.

The hospital was held liable for $110,000.

Darling v. Charleston Community Memorial Hospital, 33 Ill. 2d 326, 211 N.E. 2d 253, 14 A.L.R.3d 869 (1965), cert. denied, 383 U.S. 946 (1966).

This case eliminated charitable immunity in the Illinois jurisdiction. Many other states began to consider and ultimately apply the *Darling* rationale to cases within their jurisdiction. A limited number of states have held steadfast to the doctrine of charitable immunity, but exceptions have been made in order to hold the hospital negligent in some specific situations, such as the selection or retention of nurses.

The patient had a back operation. The head nurse gave the patient an injection and the needle broke. It was evident that prompt action to remove the needle was necessary. The nurse, however, did not report the incident or tell the patient. The imbedded needle caused a severe infection and was difficult to remove.

The court found the conduct of the nurse in failing to report the incident to be far below the standard of care required of a head nurse. The jury was permitted to decide if the hospital was negligent in placing her in a supervisory position, even though North Carolina hospitals were protected from suit by the doctrine of charitable immunity

Helms v. Williams, 166 S.E.2d 852 (N.C.1969).

As a result of these decisions, hospitals are now usually held liable for the acts of their employees when negligence is established. The concept of an individual being held liable for the acts of another is known as vicarious liability. Vicarious liability is almost an automatic accountability; if the nurse is found liable, the hospital is automatically held liable for its employee's actions. If the nurse is successfully defended, under the principle of vicarious liability, the hospital is also automatically defended. However, the hospital may still be held liable under the theory of corporate liability which will be discussed later in this chapter.

This legal principle makes it quite clear that it will always be to the hospital's benefit to vigorously defend the actions of its employees. In doing so, the hospital is also defending itself.

RESPONDEAT SUPERIOR

One form of vicarious liability is known as *respondeat superior*, a Latin term meaning that the master is responsible for the acts of his servants. This is applied to the situation where an employer is liable for the acts of the employees. In no other area of the law has this term been applied as readily as that of nursing law. Until very recent times, *respondeat superior* was consistently applied to hold either the hospital or physician, whichever was the employer of the nurse or under whose control the nurse was working, liable for nursing acts. The underlying justifications for this theory are the right of the employer to select employees, pay their wages, control their conduct, as well as the employer's ability to pay an injured patient.

One of the greatest conflicts in case law centered around the issue of exactly who was responsible for the acts of the nurse, the physician or hospital. The answer to this dilemma often depended on the specific facts of the case. Because of the complexity of some of these situations, courts began to resort to elaborate systems to assist their evaluation of these difficult cases.

One such line of decisions evolved from the New York judicial system and their determination as to whether an act was *administrative* or *medical*. The premise was that if the nurse performed an act that fit into the criteria of a medical act, the physician would be held liable for the actions. However, if the act could be described as administrative, liability would be imposed on the hospital. This doctrine was originally established in the case described below.

A woman was suffering from a disorder of the stomach. She was admitted to the hospital, and her physician discovered a lump. The physician informed the patient that the character of the lump needed to be determined. She gave permission for this but stated she wanted no organ surgically removed without further discussion. The surgeon, however, removed the organ.

The nurse had prepared the patient for surgery. The Court stated that the nurse was not acting under the direction of the hospital. Therefore, the physician was held liable.

Schloendorff v. Society of New York Hospital, 211 NY 125, 105 N.E. 92 (1914).

Nurses employed by the hospital, when not performing duties related to the administrative conduct of the hospital but in performing those acts of preparation immediately preceding an operation under the orders of the physicians, were not acting as servants of the hospital.

Many years of decision followed with an attempt to categorize decisions as medical or administrative.

Placing an improperly capped hot water bottle on a patient's body was administrative.
> Iacono v. New York Polyclinic Medical School and Hospital, 296 N.Y. 502, 68 N.E.2d 450.

Keeping a hot water bottle on a patient's body too long was medical.
> Sutherland v. New York Polyclinic Medical School and Hospital, 298 N.Y. 682, 82 N.E.2d 583.

Administering blood to the wrong patient was administrative.
> Necolayff v. Genesee Hospital, 296 N.Y. 936, 73 N.E.2d 117.

Administering the wrong blood to the right patient was medical.
> Berg v. New York Society for Relief of Ruptured and Crippled, 1 N.Y.2d 499, 154 N.Y.S.2d 455, reversing 286 App. Div. 783, 146 N.Y.S.2d 548.

Using an improperly sterilized needle was administrative.
> Peck v. Charles B. Towns Hospital, 275 App. Div 302, 89 N.Y.S.2d 190.

Improperly administering a hypodermic injection was medical.
> Bryant v. Presbyterian Hospital, 304 N.Y. 538, 110 N.E.2d 391.

Finally in 1957, this method of evaluation was recognized as an artificial system for categorizing how nurses function. The application of a medical versus an administrative rationale was abandoned.

A patient was severely burned during the course of surgery for correction of a fissure of the anus. The nurses and the anesthetist painted the patient's back with Zephiran, an inflammable antiseptic. They were aware that it was potentially dangerous and acknowledged that they had been instructed not only to exercise care to see that none of the fluid dropped on the linen but also to inspect it and remove any linen that became stained or contaminated. However, they made no inspection, and the sheets originally placed under the patient remained on the table throughout surgery.

The surgeon was not present during this procedure. Fifteen minutes later, he took a heated electric cautery tool and touched it to the fissure to mark it. There was a smell of singed linen, and the surgeon doused the area with water

and then proceeded with the surgery. Subsequent examination of the patient revealed severe burns as well as several holes in the sheet under her.

The legal issue was the question of whether this act of the nurses was a medical or an administrative act. The court held that this distinction should be eliminated and the over-all test of *respondeat superior* should prevail. The hospital was held liable for the acts of the nurse.

Bing v. Thunig, 163 N.Y.S.2d 3, 2 N.Y.2d 656 (1957).

The courts recognized that the medical versus administrative rule often resulted in nonliability for the hospital and was at variance with modern health care and the role of the hospital. Because an act was classified as medical was not a sound reason for eliminating the hospital as a defendant.

CAPTAIN-OF-THE-SHIP DOCTRINE

The captin-of-the-ship doctrine is another theory based on the concept of vicarious liability. This theory was primarily applied in the operating room and imposed liability on the surgeon for the acts of any people working within the room. It must be clearly understood that these physicians are usually not employed by the hospital but are appointees to the medical staff. This theory effectively removed the hospital from any responsibility for the acts of their own employees as long as they were acting under the control of the surgeon. These hospital employees, according to the courts, become the "borrowed servant" of the physicain.

Pennsylvania was the primary jurisdiction for the application of this theory. The landmark case occurred in 1949.

A surgeon was held liable for the actions of an intern who put an excessive quantity of silver nitrate in an infant's eye causing blindness. The child lost the sight of both eyes.

McConnell v. Williams, 65 A.2d 243 (Pa.1949).

Because of charitable immunity, and without the captain-of-the-ship theory, if the physician was not held liable for the acts of the intern, resident, or nurse, there would be no recovery of damages for the injured patient. This doctrine expanded from care provided within the operating room to include care provided for the surgical patient postoperatively.

A surgeon was held liable for the negligence of an intern and resident who failed to note the patient's allergy to penicillin on the chart and of a nurse-anesthetist who failed to act on her knowledge of the allergy. The patient sustained severe brain damage as the result of subsequent administration of large doses of penicillin.

Yorston v. Penell, 153 A.2d 255 (Pa.1959).

The captain-of-the-ship doctrine imposed liability on the surgeon beyond the walls of the operating room itself. Subsequently, courts sought to limit this type of extension.

An 11-month-old child suffered permanent sciatic nerve injuries from the administration of an injection by a student nurse.

The court refused to apply the captain-of-the-ship doctrine to hold the physician liable for the nurse's negligence in administration of the injection.

Honeywell v. Rogers, 251 Fed.Supp. 841 (1966).

Courts have recently held that staff physicians are not liable for the failure of hospital employees to execute reasonable postoperative procedures for the treatment of patients. It is clearly within the realm of nursing judgment to institute certain measures after surgery such as observing for bleeding on the dressing, taking vital signs, and administering injections as ordered. The physician has the right to assume that hospital employees are competent to follow reasonable orders unless he or she has knowledge to the contrary.

A man was admitted to the hospital for treatment of stab wounds. After surgery, he was to receive intramuscular injections of an antibiotic to control infection. One of the nurses in the intensive care unit, while administering an injection, struck his sciatic nerve and caused damage to his right leg.

An issue discussed by the court was whether the surgeon could be held liable for the acts of the nurse. The court held that since the surgeon had neither selected nor supervised the nurse nor was personally present when the injection was administered, the borrowed servant principle was inapplicable, and the surgeon could not be held liable for the act of the nurse.

Massey v. Heine, 497 S.W.2d 584 (Kentucky 1973).

A patient was being treated for coronary disease and was given an anticoagulant by injection. The patient suffered permanent damage to her leg when she received an injection into the femoral nerve.

The court held the plaintiff was entitled to recover damages from the hospital since the physician had no right to control the nurse. Since the injection was a routine nursing procedure requiring no special skill or knowledge, the physician was not liable for the action of the hospital nurse.

Muller v. Likoff, 225 Pa.Super.111. 310 A.2d 303 (1973).

Pennsylvania has, however, more recently limited its use of this doctrine in two decisions involving nurses.

A Kelly clamp was left in a patient's abdomen following a colectomy. Evidence indicated that no count of these instruments had been taken. The court, in this case, held that both the surgeon and the hospital could be held liable.

Tonsic v. Wagner, 329 A.2d 497 (Pa.1974).

A patient's heart stopped when a nurse-anesthetist failed to properly monitor the administration of anesthesia. The patient suffered serious brain damage and died 2 months later. Both the hospital and anesthesiologist were held liable.

Willinger v. Mercy Catholic Medical Center, 362 A.2d 280 (Pa.Sup.Ct.1976).

Instrument counts have been a major source of litigation and have sometimes yielded inconsistent results.

A hemostat was left in a patient following surgery. The surgeon settled the case and then testified that he was solely liable for the instrument count. Based on this testimony, the hospital was not held liable.

Mossey v. Mueller, 218 N.W.2d 514 (Wisc.1974).

A patient came out of surgery with a scalpel blade in his bladder necessitating later corrective surgery. The hospital contended that the nurse was a borrowed employee of the surgeon while in the operating room. Therefore, when the nurse failed to report a missing surgical instrument, the surgeon should have been liable. The court, however, said that operating room nurses may have two masters, and negligence may be attributed to both. The hospital and the surgeon had a mutual interest in treating the patient, and each would have benefitted by an accurate count of scalpel blades.

City of Somerset v. Hart, 549S.W.2d 814 (Ky.1977).

In a recent case, the court pointed out that the physician or surgeon is hardly expected to be in constant attention at a patient's bedside but may leave to others the duty of carrying out prescribed treatments as well as routine nursing care.

A 22-year-old patient became paralyzed following childbirth. The patient was on a respirator in the recovery room, and nursing personnel failed to note that the equipment was not functioning correctly.

The court held the hospital could be liable, since the physician was not expected to remain in constant attention at the patient's bedside. The physician had a right to assume that nurses employed by the hospital were competent to perform the duties to which they were assigned.

Hill v. Hospital Authority of Clarke County, 137 Ga.App.633, 224 S.E.2d 738 (1976).

It is quite clear that the doctrine of the borrowed servant is being replaced by the concept of joint liability, a recognition of the fact that now physicians and hospitals share in the activities of patient care. The hospital is being held liable through the acts of its employees.

A physician removed a cyst from each of a patient's breasts for examination to see if the cysts were malignant. As they were removed, the cysts were placed in one container and were essentially undifferentiated. The scrub nurse asked if the surgeon wanted the specimens separated. He said no because they were not malignant anyway. One cyst was malignant. The plaintiff had to have both breasts removed. She was awarded $100,000 by the jury against both the surgeon and hospital.

Variety Children's Hospital v. Osle, 292 So2d 382 (Fla.App.1974).

Other jurisdictions recently have dealt with the issue of joint liability.

A healthy young man developed a shoulder separation while playing football. Surgery was indicated. Anesthesia was administered by a nurse-anesthetist employed by the hospital. The surgeon draped the patient including his face. The nurse-anesthetist was, therefore, unable to observe the patient's face when respiratory difficulty occurred. The surgeon also interrupted her monitoring of the movements of the muscles between the patient's ribs and failed to inform her that the patient's blood was becoming darker. Following the operation, the surgeon left without determining whether the patient's breathing was normal. The nurse-anesthetist then noticed that the patient was having trouble breathing. Attempts were made to resuscitate, but the patient died.

The court, in holding the hospital liable for the acts of the nurse and holding the surgeon liable for his own acts, pointed out that the hospital, not the physician, has the power and responsibility to hire and fire nurses.

Foster v. Englewood Hospital Association, 19 Ill.App.3d 1055, 313 N.E.2d 255 (1974).

Some courts have expressly rejected both the captain-of-the-ship doctrine, which held the surgeon alone liable, and the doctrine of joint liability, thereby holding the nurse liable and not the physician.

A surgeon was not held liable for the negligence of an operating room nurse who made an incorrect sponge count. The court stated that the issue should be whether the surgeon had the right to control the assisting nurses in the details of the specific act. Since the sponge count was a procedure established by the hospital, the surgeon was not directing the activity.

The jury found that the nurses who assisted the surgeon were not his borrowed employees and that the surgeon was not personally negligent in failing to remove the sponge. The court found that only the hospital could be held liable.

Sparger v. Worley Hospital, Inc., 547 S.W.2d 582 (Tex.1977).

A patient was undergoing an emergency hysterectomy following the birth of her third child. During surgery, additional transfusions became necessary. The operating room nurse took two units of blood for another patient and administered it to the plaintiff. Following surgery, the plaintiff had postoperative complications.

The court refused to hold the surgeon liable, finding that the nurse was not under his direct control at this time.

Parker v. St. Paul Fire and Marine Insurance Co., 335 So2d 725 (La.App.1976)

The captain-of-the-ship doctrine was also found inapplicable by Colorado's highest court in a case where an injured patient attempted to impose liability on her surgeon for negligence in a postoperative treatment.

A patient suffered paralysis in her foot following hip surgery. The patient claimed that an elastic bandage had been incorrectly applied by hospital personnel.

There was no evidence that the surgeon was aware that any employees in the orthopedic ward were incompetent. They were selected, hired, and paid by the hospital and not the surgeon. The surgeon was not physically present when an elastic bandage was rewrapped on the patient's leg. The captain-of-the-ship doctrine was not applicable with respect to the patient's claims against the surgeon.

Although the court recognized that the surgeon was generally in charge of postoperative care, the court determined he would have no control of hospital employees (nurses) who carry out orders in his absence.

Adams v. Leidholdt, 579 P.2d 618 (Colo. 1978)

The captain-of-the-ship doctrine is clearly yet aother legal doctrine that has contributed to the delayed recognition of the professional status of nursing by holding other professionals responsible for the nurse.

CORPORATE LIABILITY—INDIVIDUAL LIABILITY

INDIVIDUAL RESPONSIBILITY AND PRIMARY ACCOUNTABILITY

In American society the individual is primarily responsible for his or her own actions. Therefore, the individual should have primarv legal accountability also. In malpractice cases the individual who is actually responsible for the harm to the patient will be the primary defendant.

All health care providers have a basic level of accountability for their actions. Whether the health care worker is a professional or a nonprofessional, that basic level of legal accountability exists, particularly in regard to meeting the safety needs of patients.

Because of the complexity of malpractice cases, there may be joint liability in which multiple defendants share the legal responsibility or secondary accountability in which a supervisor or manager is responsible in addition to the primary defendant.

In general, the courts are reluctant to impose secondary liability. The supervisor or manager would be responsible for the acts of their staff only in unusual circumstances. If the staff person is incompetent and the supervisor is not handling the problem appropriately, there may be secondary liability in addition to the liability of the employee.

CORPORATE LIABILITY

A parallel development to the expansion of nursing liability has occurred to the nurses' employer; the hospital, agency or nursing home. This is the expansion of the doctrine known as *corporate liability*.

The employer had previously experienced liability primarily under the doctrine of vicarious liability in which the employer was automatically liable if the employee was found liable. In addition to this doctrine, the corporate employer now bears liability under the currently evolving doctrine of corporate liability.

Corporate liability means that the corporation has a duty, separate and distinct from its duty as an employer, to assure that patients receive safe, quality care. The hospital, for example, is not simply a hotel where patients arrive to be cared for by others. The hospital is also a health care provider and, therefore, has its own separate legal accountability.

While the cases continue to evolve, thus far the courts have identified those issues involving corporate liability areas to include security of hospital premises, environmental hazards, the failure to establish and enforce appropriate policies, and the need for adequate staffing and reasonable types and amounts of equipment, as well as the hospital's liability for the acts of staff physicians who are not employees of the corporation. The hospital assumes some liability for these physicians through the credentialling system, although it does not reach the level of automatic accountability that the employer has under the vicarious liability doctrine.

A surgical patient suffered brain damage while an unsupervised, unlicensed nurse-anesthetist administered anesthesia. The hospital's policies stated that only a qualified physician or certified registered nurse anesthetist was authorized to administer anesthetics.

This nurse had temporary staff privileges that were limited to instances when working under the direct supervision of a CRNA. The hospital attempted to escape liability by claiming that it had no duty to supervise a nurse who was not a hospital employee. Involved here is not the duty to supervise or review the provision of medical treatment, the court pointed out, but rather the hospital's independent duty to enforce its own policies that, if followed, would have precluded the administration of anesthesia by "an unqualified, uncertified, inexperienced nurse."

Williams v. St. Claire Medical Center, 657 S.W. 2d 590 (Ky.Ct.App.1983).

While there are a number of cases in which the hospital has been found to have corporate liability for the acts of physicians within its walls, the courts are reluctant to expand that liability for the care rendered by physicians in their own offices.

In December of 1978, a woman, in her 35th week of pregnancy, was under the care of her private physician. During the following week she became ill and

exhibited the classical symptoms of preeclampsia, namely hypertension, headaches, and edema of the lower extremities. She visited her physician's office on two occasions, and telephoned him on December 8. He prescribed no medicine other than bed rest and aspirin. He did not refer her to another health care provider.

On December 9, 1978, the patient was admitted, comatose, to defendant Hospital. She was admitted to surgery, with a diagnosis of irreversible cerebral death due to intracerebral hemorrhage resulting from eclampsia. Her private physician was neither the admitting nor the treating physician for this hospitalization.

In surgery her child was successfully delivered by emergency cesarean section. After family consent was obtained, respiratory support for the mother was discontinued on December 15, 1978, whereupon she died.

Her husband sued, alleging that the hospital was negligent in that it violated a duty of care owed his wife to grant hospital admitting and treating privileges only to those physicians who are competent.

The court held that a hospital was not liable on the grounds that it granted privileges to a physician who later committed malpractice while in private practice off the hospital premises. The trial court dismissed the husband's claim.

Pedroza v. Bryant, 677 P.2d 166 (Wash.1984)

The implications of corporate liability for the nurse involve the nurse's duty to communicate. All of the examples of liability imposed upon the board of the hospital are situations occurring at the clinical unit level. Whether the issue is one of short-staffing, inadequate equipment, or physician incompetence or impairment, the nurse must bring the situation to the attention of the nurse's immediate supervisor. Failure to consistently and repetitively communicate these examples may impose liability upon the individual nurse for a situation of management or corporate liability.

The nurse will discharge individual legal accountability by communication. With serious problems the nurse may decide to document this communication. The documentation of such management problems should not be done in patients' medical records but rather in a management documentation vehicle or system established by the hospital. In addition to utilizing the chain-of-command communication system, the nurse may communicate with the Risk Management and Quality Assurance departments.

FUTURE PROMISE—ACCOUNTABILITY

During the last 10 years, nurses have attempted to alleviate some of their frustrations with the nursing profession by turning to new fields where their skills could be better used and where they could find a sense of accomplishment and self-fulfillment. Some nurses have achieved this by turning outward into other professions. Others have moved into the expanded roles for nurses such as the nurse-practitioner, the patients' rights advocate, and the private nurse practitioner, all of which bring increasing responsibilities to the nurse. And still others are remaining within the classification of nursing and are expanding the profession within its traditional boundaries. Staff nurses, for instance, are assuming new responsibilities.

As the profession expands and as courts become more aware of what the professional practice of nursing involves in terms of knowledge and judgment, it is obvious that nurses will become more accountable legally for their actions. The nursing profession has always held itself to the highest of standards. The legal recognition of these standards is the promise of the future for nursing.

SUMMARY

As the role of the professional nurse becomes better defined, nurses will be held to a higher level of accountability.

The nurse's unique role in the health care delivery system is now recognized. Earlier doctrines such as the captain-of-the-ship theory, which held other professionals solely liable for the actions of nurses, are no longer applicable. Today, through *respondeat superior*, the hospital as the employer of the nurse is legally accountable for the acts of the nurse. As the nurses' role as a professional health care provider expands, nurses will be held more accountable for their acts. Joint liability, where the nurse and physician or the nurse and the hospital are both held liable, is a more accurate reflection of the current position of the nurse.

The increased accountability of the nurse is an indication of the increased recognition of the professional status of nursing. The corporation employing the nurse also has expanded accountability through the evolving doctrine of corporate liability.

CHAPTER 3

STANDARD OF CARE

MALPRACTICE VERSUS NEGLIGENCE

The terms *malpractice* and *negligence* are often used interchangeably. *Negligence* is a more general term referring to a deviation from the standard of care that a reasonable person would use in a particular set of circumstances. *Malpractice* is a more specific type of negligence; deviations from a professional standard of care; nurses, doctors, lawyers, and accountants are some types of professionals who may be liable for malpractice.

In order to prove that malpractice or negligence has occurred, these four elements must be established—duty, breach of duty, causation, and damages.

Duty is the particular relationship that has arisen between the plaintiff and defendant. For example, historically hospitals were free to determine who would receive treatment, including emergency cases. Currently, hospitals that maintain emergency facilities are obligated to care for those in need of emergency treatment. Thus, the hospital's duty has been expanded. Courts and legislatures have determined that a legal relationship arises when an injured patient in need of emergency care visits an emergency room.

The criterion of duty is usually easy to satisfy in terms of the nurse-patient relationship and is rarely challenged in legal decisions, since the nurse is an employee of the institution providing care for the patient.

Breach of duty occurs when a standard of care has not been met. Professional health care providers are expected to possess the specific skills and knowledge required for the practice of their professions. How the standard of care is determined for nurses is discussed in subsequent chapters. There are many examples of how nurses breach their duty to patients, including cases involving falls, burns, medications, errors, unidentified complications, and communication failures.

28

Causation is the most difficult criteria of malpractice to understand and often the most difficult to prove. The term *causation* refers to the breach of duty that actually causes the injury. For example, if the patient is seeking damages for an infection, he or she must prove not only that the nurse or physician caused the immediate incident (such as failure to follow sterile technique in the operating room) but also that the failure to follow sterile technique was the cause of the infection. The fourth term, *damages*, means that an actual injury to the patient must have occurred.

DUTY OF THE NURSE

The first element that must be proven in a malpractice case is duty. The plaintiff must prove that the defendant had a duty toward him or her.

With regard to nursing, duty is one of the easier elements to prove, particularly in a hospital. Since the nurse is an employee of the hospital, and the patient is a "captive audience," duty arises. The legal concept of reliance may be applied; that is, the patient has a right to rely on the fact that the nursing staff has a clear duty to act in his best interests. The practical implications for nurses are exemplified in the following scenario.

Many nurses are familiar with the concept of team nursing in which a professional nurse is assigned to split the care of a certain group of patients. In this manner, the patient receives professional care when it is needed, and other routine tasks are performed by those team members less qualified, such as nursing assistants. This is a functional approach to nursing. If a nurse assigned to a particular group of patients walks by the room of another patient, who asks for help and requires immediate assistance, and if assistance is not provided, it is no defense to say that this was not an assigned patient.

In other words, the element of duty has been established despite the fact that an assignment to this particular patient has not been made. The nurse has a duty (even if only a minimal duty to assist a patient when an emergency arises) to all patients in the hospital. The nurse's failure to respond to a patient's request for assistance in an emergency is clearly practicing below a reasonable standard of care.

Postoperatively, a patient had a respiratory arrest. A call for immediate assistance ("Code 54") was made. Evidence indicated that the delay of some 15 minutes occurred between the time the code was issued and the time of response. The patient sustained irreversible brain damage and died 21 days later.

The jury awarded $400,000 in damages. Both the physicians and the hospital on behalf of the nurses were found to be negligent in failing to respond promptly to the patient's emergency call.

Spadaccini v. Dolan, 407 N.Y.S.2d 840, A.D.2d 110 (1978).

The concept of duty was, at one time, discussed much more frequently in medical malpractice cases than now. Many of these cases had to do with the telephone call situation—when a physician had prescribed treatment for a patient by way of the telephone without having seen the patient. The defense that the physician attempted to use was that he had no duty to this particular patient. For a time, courts accepted this argument. However, many cases involving serious injury were precluded by this type of argument. If duty was not proven, the first element of negligence, was not satisfied, and the injured party did not receive an opportunity to present the facts. This was an injustice because it was frequently these cases that resulted in serious negligence problems. Certainly a breach of proper standards of care had occurred. This is no longer true as the majority of courts have found a duty to exist based on the phone call between physician and patient.

A patient walked three blocks to the hospital emergency room with classic symptoms of a heart attack. The physician spoke to the patient on the phone in the emergency room and allegedly told the patient to return in the morning. The patient then asked to be examined by a physician, but the emergency room nurse refused his request. He returned home and died that night.

One of the issues to be considered by the jury was the question of whether a duty had arisen between the patient and physician or the patient and the hospital because of this phone call. The judge, at the trial court level, dismissed the case against the hospital.

The appeals court, however, held that in this situation the element of duty was satisfied and that the jury should be permitted to decide if the nurse had fulfilled her obligation to the patient.

O'Neill v. Montefiore Hospital, 11 A.D.2d 132, 202 N.Y.S.2d 436 (1960).

There are other situations, as illustrated below, where a consideration of the duty question is still appropriate.

The defendant was a medical school professor who, while making rounds, suggested that the patient needed surgery. When the patient had a bad result, the professor defended himself by stating that his duty to the patient had not arisen and that the surgeon was the proper defendant.

The court held that the professor of medicine who did not see or treat the patient but only reviewed the case as a teaching vehicle, did not have any duty of care toward the plaintiff. The court dismissed the case against the professor.

Rainer v. Grossman, 107 Cal.Rptr. 469, 31 Cal.App.3d 539 (1973).

Obviously, imposition of liability in the above situation would be counterproductive as it would stifle efforts to improve medical knowledge. The defendant physicians who examined the patient and performed surgery were more appropriate defendants in the case since they were more familiar with the patient's medical care.

A physician agreed, as a favor, to allow his name to be used in order to have a patient admitted to a hospital for emergency care by the staff. He had not met the patient, examined her, diagnosed her condition, or had any contact with her or her family. He was not to handle the case once the patient had been admitted. He simply allowed his name to be used as a courtesy staff member to assist the patient in admission.

The patient was treated as a drug abuse case but died of meningitis 3 days later.

The court held that allowing the use of his name cannot be said to have resulted in a doctor-patient relationship.

Giallanza v. Sands, 316 So.2d 77 (Fla.App.1975).

A pathologist misdiagnosed material from a biopsy specimen resulting in the patient having her uterus unnecessarily removed. The court stated this could subject him to liability even though he had never seen the patient.

The usual practice of pathology does not involve the actual physical presence of the patient, but the duty of the pathologist is clear.

Lundberg v. Bay View Hospital, 191 N.E.2d 821 (Ohio 1963).

Legal cases focusing on the aspect of duty between the nurse and patient tend to deal with the issue of how far the nurses duty to the patient extends. When does the nurse's legal duty stop and the physician's legal duty begin? What about areas of overlap between the nursing profession and the medical profession? This issue is illustrated in cases charging nurses with the unauthorized practice of medicine.

A nurse midwife was charged with the unlawful practice of medicine. The state argued that Indiana law defined nurse midwifery as the limited practice of medicine and therefore the nurse needed a limited medical license.

The court decided that in the state of Indiana, midwifery is the limited practice of medicine. Because the nurse did not have the appropriate license, she was charged with a criminal offense.

Smith v. State of Indiana, Case No. 2-683-A-204, (February 1984).

NURSING STANDARDS

Duty in nursing usually involves whether a particular function is within the "duty of a nurse." In other words, what is the standard of care for the nursing profession?

Nursing standards are established in a variety of ways. External standards may be applied to determine how the nurse should function. Examples of such external standards include the Nurse Practice Act of each state, guidelines by the Joint Commission of Accreditation of Hospitals (JCAH), and guidelines in textbooks. The Nurse Practice Acts define duty in a particular state, as what the practice of nursing entails. Courts look to this legislation for guidance when a particular case is presented. The court, however, makes the final determination as to how these laws are interpreted and applied.

Where the statute involved defines the limits of licensure prerogatives, an inference of negligence may be created since conduct that exceeds those limits may result in a higher standard of care being imposed on the individual whose conduct is challenged.

A practical nurse administered an inoculation to a child in a state that prohibited individuals not licensed as registered nurses from performing this procedure.

The court held that an inference of negligence could be raised and that evidence of this being custom and practice was itself a violation of the law.

Barker v. Reinking, 411 P.2d 861 (1966).

A hospital was found negligent for failing to prevent the administration of anesthesia to a surgical patient by a student nurse-anesthetist who was not supervised by a physician as required by state law.

Central Anesthesia Assoc. v. Worthy, 333 S.E.2d 829 (Georgia 1985).

Sometimes a nurse's license is suspended for acts of professional negligence.

A nurse's license was suspended for acts committed during a three-year period which included: seventeen allegations of failure to administer medication, treatment and feedings to patients, fourteen allegations of false or incorrect entries on patient records, numerous allegations of sleeping on duty, three charges of removing patient call bells during the night, several allegations of patient abuse, including the forced feeding of one patient and hitting the stump of two amputees against their bedrails, one allegation of failure to recognize that a patient was not yet dead and could be resuscitated.

The nurse's termination was upheld.

Kibler v. State, 718 P.2d 531 (Colorado 1986).

Internal standards also define the role of the nurse. Examples of internal standards include the nurse's job description as well as the policies and procedures of the institution. Courts will review these references to evaluate what standards of performance are required. The hospital's own internal policy in regard to the practice of nursing is often a crucial factor in how the case is decided. Hospital rules are admissible as evidence of standards of care in the community.

For many years nursing has accepted, as part of its responsibility, the duty to formulate a nursing care plan, individualized to each particular patient and based on nursing assessment. The purpose of the assessment and the resulting care plan is the need to provide adaptations of care, particularly emotional support, depending on the age, education, background, experience, habits, and behavior of the patient.

Nursing care plans are another example of a standard that courts may evaluate in determining if a breach of duty has occurred. If the care plan indicates that a nursing judgment has been made that four siderails should always be up on a patient's bed, then the defense that the siderails were not necessary would not be accepted in a malpractice case. Nursing care plans are, on the other hand, an extremely good basis for a solid defense in many cases. They may indicate that a nurse attempted to deal individually with a difficult patient who tried to get out of bed after being told not to. They may show the various approaches and problem-solving techniques the nurse has used. Unfortunately, these care plans, in many institutions, are not made a permanent portion of the medical record and are destroyed. The destruction of this document may result in a lack of documentation necessary to support the testimony of the nurse.

This concept of nursing assessment and the nursing plan play a key role in malpractice cases in establishing what the proper standard of care may be.

In order for a nurse to formulate an assessment and plan for care, nursing judgments must be made. These judgments are based on the nurse's education and experience. Sometimes these judgments are referred to as *nursing diagnoses*. This term is not to be confused with the medical diagnosis that a physician makes based on the patient's signs and symptoms.

Because nurses and physicians both study disease and the treatment of disease, an overlapping knowledge base exists. Therefore, a physician and a coronary care nurse will each understand and interpret various cardiac arrhythmias. Both will know when and how to defibrillate a patient. However, their information is overlapping only in selected areas. The physician will also be able to determine if surgery is necessary and what drugs the patient should take; thereby medically diagnosing the patient's illness. The nurse will be able to formulate a nursing diagnosis that may include meeting the patient's psychologic needs, observing for the side effects of drugs administered, and providing health teaching for the patient.

In a case where a patient has fallen and becomes injured, the court may ask what precautions should have been taken based on a nursing assessment. A common example of this is the nursing decision to use siderails after a patient has been sedated. The systematic assessment by the nurse results in the knowledge that this patient is more likely to fall.

A hospital was liable for injuries to the patient's nose. She fell out of bed while recovering from anesthesia. The head nurse had failed to have siderails attached to the bed.
Ranelli v. Society of New York Hospital, 56 N.Y.S.3d 481, 67 N.E.2d 257 (1946).

As indicated in Chapter 2, the hospital is frequently held liable for the activities of the nurse under the theory of vicarious liability (*respondeat superior*).

Court decisions are a reflection of the perceptions of society, particularly when a jury is involved in the judgment. However, there is often a time lag in how this judgment is made. Because the judicial process moves slowly and cases are sometimes not finally decided for many years, there may be a long gap. Case law has not yet caught up with the new role of the nurse, although there are some indications that nursing judgments are now recognized by at least some courts.

A nurse administered an injection to an obese patient with standard size needle. The patient, therefore, received a subcutaneous rather than an intra-

muscular injection, due to her size. This resulted in necrosis and subsequent plastic surgery. The nurse's defense was that the physician did not tell her to use a longer needle.

The court said this was a nursing judgment. The physician prescribes what is given as well as the amount and mode of administration; however, it is the nurse who determines the method of administration.

Su v. Perkins, 211 S.E.2d 421 (Ga.App.1974).

Rules established by the nursing departments may also be evaluated. Noncompliance with an institution's own rules is strong evidence of breach of duty.

A patient underwent a radical mastectomy for removal of a malignant tumor. A Kelly clamp was left in the patient, undiscovered for 3 weeks. As a result, she suffered permanent injury to the nerves in her left shoulder area, which caused a limitation of motion. About 18 months later the patient died of cancer. Her husband contended that the hospital, through its nurses, had a duty to count all surgical instruments used.

The court found that sponge and needle counts fell within the duty of nursing but that the evidence indicated that instrument counts were the surgeon's responsibility.

Mossey v. Mueller, 218 N.W.2d 514 (Wisc.1974).

The rule of law established by this case has not been the same in every jurisdiction. There is precedent that instruments as well as sponges must be counted during surgical procedures and that the hospital shares this responsibility. As a result, many insurance companies require hospitals to establish such policies.

State regulations would also be admissible in court to indicate the proper standards of care.

A patient was admitted to the hospital and "bathroom privileges with assistance" were ordered. Shortly after the patient's admission, a nurse accompanied her to the bathroom. Later in the day, the patient called a staff nurse and told her she wished to use a bedpan on a chair. The nurse placed the patient on a bedpan on a straight-back chair close to the bed and then left the room to take the temperatures of other patients, stating she would return in a few minutes. While the patient was left sitting on the bedpan, she fainted and fell to the floor. She died as a result of her injuries.

State Department of Health regulations were introduced at the trial in an attempt to prove that proper equipment was not available and that the hospital had failed to adopt or establish a routine, policy, or procedure to provide adequate care for patients.

The jury allowed the plaintiff to recover damages. However, the court, on appeal, felt that the plaintiff failed to show that proper equipment was not available or that the hospital had failed to adopt proper regulations.
Shay v. St. Raphael Hospital, 210 A.2d 664 (Conn.1965).

Hospitals routinely use nursing manuals as an administrative and educational tool. Such manuals define policies and procedures. Administrators should use care and judgment in developing these manuals. For example, policies and procedures should be clearly differentiated. A policy is a statement of purpose. It usually defines the minimum standard for the institution. Care should be taken in the use of such words as *maximum* or *the best*. Since a minimum standard of care is being defined, this wording subjects the personnel to the charge of not acting in accordance with such high standards. The standard should not place an unduly great legal burden on personnel by requiring optimum behavior in every situation. Only reasonable professional standards should be applied.

Procedures define how a task or function should be performed. They should be specific and should include a rationale for each particular avenue taken, as in this example:

Policy
To meet basic safety needs.
Procedure
To provide raised siderails on the beds of elderly patients who are sedated.
Rationale
Studies indicate that the elderly patient is especially sensitive to the disorienting effects of sedation. More falls in the hospital occur to patients older than 60 than to any other age group.

A short, obese hospital patient, in severe pain, was placed in a hospital bed that was on rollers and had no siderails. The patient was sedated, foggy, drowsy, and disoriented. While under the effects of this sedation, she fell from her bed and was injured.

A *Nurses' Procedures Manual* was introduced into court that provided that siderails should always be applied to the bed of a patient who is restless, very obese, or under deep sedation, or in any other case in which siderails would be an added protection. Any omissions of the rails had to be on written order of the physician. The manual also provided that, if the patient was permitted to get up alone, the rollers must be removed. Evidence indicated that the patient was permitted to be out of bed. Therefore, the rollers should have been removed.

The court held that the jury should determine whether the hospital exercised reasonable care in enforcing rules to protect the patient against dangers related to her condition.

Burks v. The Christ Hospital, 249 N.E.2d 829 (Ohio 1969).

The law has recognized that standards of care for nursing include continuing education. With the increase in technology, its use, and complexity, it is clear that in order for a health care practitioner to function both adequately and safely, certain educational standards must be met. For example, because of his or her training and experience, a nurse should be able to recognize the obvious and dangerous signs of medication errors as well as common side effects indicating that a discontinuation of the drug is appropriate. It is probable that as the number and variety of drugs increase, the capability of nursing personnel to become familiar with such symptoms will diminish. However, nurses will continue to be responsible for this knowledge. Although physicians can familiarize themselves with those drugs used in their particular specialty, nurses who must administer medications ordered by different specialists need to be familiar with the proper use of all drugs in the hospital. Every nurse is taught that her responsibility involves not administering a drug that is unfamiliar. Courts have sometimes misinterpreted this standard of care.

The court held that the jury instruction stating that nurses are bound to know the fatal doses of *all* drugs and the danger of any type of drug as well as the proper way to administer the drug was incorrect. The court said the instruction should have dealt more generally with the duty of the nurse to act as a reasonable prudent nurse would have done under the same or similar circumstances rather than the specific requirement relating to all drugs.

The patient was claiming that the nurse was negligent in administering medication.

Doctors Hospital of Mobile, Inc. v. Kirksey, 275 So.2d 651 (Ala.1973).

Courts in future cases should be more apt to hold nurses accountable for the drugs they administer. The standard for nursing is reflected more accurately in the jury instruction requiring the nurse to know the fatal dose of all drugs. Where the potential for death or serious injury is great, the responsibility and accountability of nurses should increase correspondingly.

Courts have held the standard of care for nursing includes the nurse's responsibility to follow instructions regarding drugs.

A 37-year-old woman with a life expectancy of 68.75 years was employed by a factory as a machine operator at a salary of $75 a week. The lens broke on a pair of glasses while at work, and she sustained a cut about one-half inch long on the middle finger of her left hand.

The patient visited the local emergency room, had her wound sutured, and received a penicillin injection. She was also given a sensitivity test to determine her reaction to horse serum, the most common base used in administering a tetanus antitoxin. The antitoxin was then administered. It was alleged by the patient that the nurse failed to wait a sufficient time to determine if the patient was sensitive to the medication.

The patient immediately began experiencing symptoms which subsequently led to a 50 to 55 percent permanent loss of hearing in both ears as well as a noticeable change of personality.

The jury awarded her damages of $80,000 based on testimony that an expected time period to wait for the development of a reaction was 15 minutes, and evidence indicated that no more than 5 minutes had elapsed between the test shot and the tetanus shot. The court pointed out that this totally defeated the purpose of the skin test.

Neely v. St. Francis Hospital and School of Nursing, Inc., 188 Kansas 546, 363 P.2d 438 (1961).

STUDENT NURSE

The standard of care for a student nurse requires the student to perform as a reasonable person with similar background and experience. The student nurse is always held to the same standards as a graduate professional nurse for those activities that have been studied. This protects the patient's interest. There is no reason for the patient to expect any less than the care provided by a professional nurse. Thus, if the student has studied medications in both the academic and clinical settings, the patient has the right to expect that all safeguards will be taken.

A student nurse administered pHisoHex instead of milk of magnesia to a patient. Subsequently, the patient complained of a burning sensation and received treatment for gastritis and esophogitis.

One issue of the case was whether the hospital was negligent in its managerial capacity. At the time of this decision, charitable immunity was still in force to prevent a recovery against the hospital on the basis of negligence for the acts of its employees. Evidence indicated that the hospital had an appropriate regulation requiring that a medication label be read three times before administering the drug.

The court held that the situation of a student nurse who has passed her work, has demonstrated an aptitude for nursing, and who works diligently for self-improvement and is assigned to work under a registered nurse does not constitute managerial negligence destroying the immunity of a charitable hospital.

Habuda v. Trustees of Rex Hospital, Inc., 164 S.E.2d 17 (N.C.1968).

Student nurses have a clear responsibility, just as graduate nurses, to make their superiors aware of their limitations. A student who is assigned to a patient requiring expertise beyond her capabilities has a duty to inform her instructor. In many instances, the misassignment has occurred because of the instructor's lack of familiarity with the patient or due to the patient's changing condition.

The instructor may bear responsibility for the work-related actions of the student and will share in the liability of the student has been negligently supervised.

SUPERVISING NURSE

There is no doubt that supervision of personnel is one of the functions of the professional nurse. Thus, any nurse who oversees another may be responsible for that person's negligent act. Failure to supervise in accordance with the standard expected of a professional nurse may be viewed as negligence. This does not remove responsibility from the individual nurse; rather it extends liability to those in supervisory positions.

One of the duties of the nursing supervisor is to provide an adequate staff. There must be a safe ratio of nursing personnel to patients. Nurses often question their own individual liability when they must work in a short-staffed situation. Courts do not look favorably on the defense of having inadequate staff to care properly for patients. The hospital can be held liable but the individual nurse may not be if it can be proven that nursing supervisors were aware of the problem.

A psychiatric patient was admitted to a hospital. On a cold, blustery December day, he walked out of the hospital wearing only a T-shirt, trousers, and socks. He got on the subway and began to experience stomach cramps, and a police officer took him to another nearby hospital. The officer told the emergency room nurse that he thought the patient had escaped from a psychiatric hospital. The nurse left the patient in a room alone. He walked out and threw himself in front of a subway. His right leg was crushed and had to be amputated.

The argument against the hospital was their failure to use due care. Hospital policy dictated that in the situation described, the nurse should have remained with the patient.

The Court agreed that hospital policy should have been followed and awarded the patient $300,000.

Torres v. City of New York, 396 N.Y.S.2d 34 (1977).

A supervising nurse may be held liable for the negligence of another nurse when duties are delegated that the individual nurse is obviously incompetent to perform without supervision. Liability of the supervisor is based on failure to assign and supervise employees properly. For example, a nurse who does not have additional training to care for patients in intensive care units should not be assigned to these patients unless circumstances indicate no other nurse is available.

PRACTICAL NURSE

The same general rule for students also applies to the practical or vocational nurse. The duty of the practical nurse to the patient is the same as the registered nurse r those functions that are within the scope of employment of the nurse. If the practical nurse has been trained to administer injections and is permitted by state law to do so, the standard of care required is identical to that of the registered nurse.

A practical nurse administered a polio booster to a 2-year-old child. The child moved as the nurse injected, and the needle broke off. Three operations were required before the needle was extricated.

The court held the nurse negligent in not anticipating the sudden movement of the child and guarding against it.

Barber v. Reinking, 411 P.2d 861 (Washington 1966).

The decision in the previous case was based on the issue of what a reasonable nurse would have done in the same or similar circumstances. A registered nurse would have been held to the same standard. Courts do not differentiate between different levels of nursing when a procedure may be administered by a nurse regardless of his or her educational background.

The decedent, 49 years old, died of anaphylactic shock following an injection of penicillin. The allegation was that the licensed practical nurse injected the drug into the patients bloodstream instead of muscle.

The jury awarded $100,000.

Rodriquez v. Columbus Hospital, 326 N.Y.S.2d 438 (New York 1971).

INDUSTRIAL NURSE

Although the standard of care for the industrial nurse is basically the same as for any other professional nurse, the nurse who fills this role usually functions in a less supervised situation. The industrial nurse, as the emergency room nurse, may be the first health care provider to evaluate the patient's medical condition. Because of this unique aspect of the industrial nurse's role, the most important duty may be to use valid judgments in determining the limitations of practice.

A registered nurse, working under the standing orders of a physician in a dispensary, treated a patient who had received a puncture wound on his head when another employee dropped a piece of metal. A carcinoma later developed at the site of the wound.

According to the employee's testimony, the nurse did not examine or probe the wound following the accident. He returned the next day and the following day but the nurse just looked at the wound.

The wound appeared to close but left a little red mark about the shape of the cut. After about 2 or 3 months, the redness began to spread. The employee continued to visit the dispensary and point out that the wound did not seem to be healing.

Ten months later he was referred to a physician who diagnosed cancer. An area of his forehead had to be excised.

The patient was awarded $15,000 because of the nurse's failure to probe the wound.

Cooper v. National Motor Bearing Company, 288 P.2d 581 (Calif.1955).

EXPANDED ROLE OF THE NURSE

The primary care crises that began in the 1960s found many physicians specializing and few practicing primary medicine. New approaches to meet the resulting societal need included an expanded role for nurses as nurse practitioners or nurse clinicians as well as physician assistants.

The expanded role of the nurse brings some new questions to the concept of legal duty. In most jurisdictions, the practice of nursing is controlled by the Nurse Practice Act. This act defines how nurses are to function within a particular state. An important consideration in the new roles of nurse practitioners and the independent nurse clinician is whether these nurses are functioning within the scope of the act. Many jurisdictions have, in recent years, expanded such legislative enactments to cover nursing's growth as a profession. For example, the term *nursing diagnosis* has been added to many state statutes. As discussed previously, a nursing diagnosis is generally defined as the identification of patient needs based on the various aspects of the nursing process.

A 39-year-old woman was admitted to the hospital with asthma. Her physician ordered Demerol for pain, among other medications. When the patient complained of chest pain, the nurse administered the medication. Shortly after the patient stopped breathing and died. The nurse was charged with an improper nursing judgment in administering a medication that can depress respiration.

The jury felt the nurses and physicians were not negligent and pointed out that standard medical practice permits physicians to give nurses, in certain medical situations, the exercise of independent judgment.

Fraijo v. Hartland Hospital, 160 Cal.Rptr. 246, 99 Cal.App.3d 331 (1979).

The court in the previous case confirmed that nurses may exercise independent judgment. This type of court interpretation will provide a basis for the expanded role of nursing.

The duty of the nurse acting in an expanded role will, of necessity, differ from that of the nurse working directly under supervision in the clinical setting. Legal accountability will increase to reflect the increase in duty.

A doctor, clinic and nurse practitioner were sued for failing to inform the mother about amniocentesis or genetic counseling. The child was born with Down's syndrome.

The court found the nurse practitioner not negligent because the parents could not prove that she had failed to advise them about the matter. The doctor was negligent because he had advised against amniocentesis.

Azzolino v. Dingfelder, 322 S.E.2d 567 (North Carolina 1984).

In a recent case a nurse midwife was charged with the unlawful practice of medicine.

The nurse midwife admitted that she had conducted manual, internal vaginal examinations, cervical dilations and assisted in childbirth.

The state found the extensive prenatal care and actual deliveries did constitute the practice of medicine. Since the nurse midwife did not hold either a physician's license or a midwifes license, she was found guilty as charged.

Smith v. State of Indiana, Case No. 2-683-A-204, Court of Appeals, Indiana (1984).

A recent case discussed the distinction between a nursing diagnosis and a medical diagnosis.

Two certified nurse practitioners were providing services in a family planning clinic. The services were provided according to standing orders and protocols agreed upon jointly by the nurse practioners and the physicians.

A written complaint was filed with the Missouri Board of Registration alleging that the nurses were practicing medicine without a license. A criminal prosecution following which found the nurses guilty. This judgment was overturned on appeal.

The court stated that there can be no question that a nurse undertakes only a nursing diagnosis, as opposed to a medical diagnosis, when she or he finds or fails to find symptoms described by physicians in standing orders and protocols for the purpose of administering courses of treatment prescribed by the physician in such orders and protocols.

The court also pointed out that the broadening of the field of practice of the nursing profession authorized by the legislature and here recognized by the court carries with it the profession's responsibility for continuing high educational standards and the individual nurse's responsibility to conduct herself or himself in a professional manner. The hallmark of a profession is knowing the limits of one's professional knowledge. The nurse, either upon reaching the limit of her or his knowledge or upon reaching the limits prescribed for the nurse by the physician's standing orders and protocols, should refer the patient to the physician.

Sermchief v. Gonzales, 660 S.W.2d 683, (Missouri 1984).

LOCALITY RULE

Whether the law is dealing with a physician, nurse, nurse practitioner, or student nurse, the issue of standard of care and duty is phrased in the following manner: How would the reasonable professional (physician, nurse, student, etc.) have acted in this particular situation?

Traditionally, in malpractice, the physician or nurse was held to the standard of care of a professional practicing in the same geographical area. This was called the locality rule. This rule arose because at one time in the United States there were wide variations in the type of care a person would receive depending on the type of setting in which he or she lived—rural versus urban. Historically, the rural practitioners did not have the same means to practice medicine as metropolitan physicians.

Where the locality standard still stands, the hospital and its employees must exercise toward the patient that degree of skill, care, and diligence used by hospitals generally in the community where the hospital is located or in similar communities.

To determine the standard, the court may consider standards and regulations of the state department of health and organizations such as the American Hospital Association. Standards, rules, and regulations of the defendant hospital as well as other hospitals in the same or similar communities may be pertinent evidence.

A patient, a young woman, delivered a child in the defendant hospital. She then developed a severe β-hemolytic streptococcus infection that caused her death the next day.

The patient had told the nurse of her cold and sore throat. When the patient's vital signs deteriorated, the physician was not notified of the change by the intern. An attending nurse testified that good nursing practice would require notifying the attending physician.

The court applied the locality rule allowing recovery, stating that a hospital must guard against known physical and mental conditions of patients as well as conditions as it should have discovered by exercise of reasonable care.
Foley v. Bishop Clarkson Memorial Hospital, 173 N.W.2d 881 (Neb.1970).

In the previous case the court considered the standards of the community to determine whether the average reasonable nurse would have notified the attending physician.

With the use of mass media, seminars, and better transportation systems, it is no longer a defense to a malpractice case for the physician or nurse to indicate unfamiliarity with the use of a particular diagnostic procedure or therapeutic treatment. A certain degree of standardization in the profession exists particularly in the area of primary medical education.

In recognition of this, together with the realization that the so-called

"conspiracy of silence" placed great peer pressure on the locally practicing physician not to testify against his neighbor, courts began to
challenge this rule. The initial move was the expansion to the concept
that specified that a physician or nurse could testify if he or she were
from the same or similar locale. This led to some finely defined criteria
as to what "similar" meant. Courts began to look at population, econo-
my, income of inhabitants, and other qualifications in order to determine what this meant. This finally enabled the injured plaintiff to
procure testimony from a physician, for example, in Los Angeles, as to
what the proper standard of care was for his counterpart in Chicago.
More important was the use of this rule to the samll town plaintiff who
no longer had to fight to obtain the testimol of the only other physician in town.

The trend continues; although this approach solved some problems,
it was not the total answer. The law is moving toward a national standard, which would enable a practitioner from any area in the country to
testify as to the proper standard of care. The community cannot set a
standard that is below the nationally accepted standard.

A specialist is held to the standard of care and skill of the average
member of the specialty, taking into account advances in the profession. Courts have previously recognized that specialists should be held
to a higher standard of care than nonspecialists.

A patient received spinal anesthesia to deliver a baby. The following day she
attempted to get out of bed and fell to the floor. There was testimony that her
condition resulted from an excessive dose of anesthesia. Evidence indicated
that this was a standard dose in this community but not in other areas.

The court said that the anesthesiologist should exercise the degree of skill
and care of the average qualified practitioner taking into account advances in
the profession. The case was sent back for retrial based on this standard.
Brune v. Belinkoff, 354 Mass. 102, 235 N.E.2d 793 (1966).

Standards for nursing have also been held to be national, rather than
local, in scope. In the following case, the court stated that standards for
accredited hospitals should be the same regardless of location.

A 13-year-old girl was admitted to the hospital with a diagnosis of acute
rheumatic fever. The patient's mother was permitted to stay with her. Her
physician saw her at 7 PM and told the parent that if the patient should go into
heart failure, she should have medical treatment immediately. The mother
stayed with her until she died about 6 hours later. The mother testified that at

8 PM her daughter began to cough violently. She testified that she told the nurse of this symptom. By 9 PM the child's heart was "beginning to pound so loudly" that the mattress shook. She requested nurses repeatedly to come into the room, but they refused. By 11 PM the child was turning blue all over, and the mother hoped that the change of shift would provide her with help. When she requested the night nurse to come in, the reply was: "All she needs is a night's rest, and if you will sit down and be quiet, she will get it." The nurse later refused to call the physician at the mother's request. Finally, the mother found the supervisor of nurses who immediately came to her assistance, but the child died a short while later.

The judge dismissed the initial complaint for insufficient evidence, but on appeal the court held that enough evidence existed for the case to go to the jury. The second trial by jury or settlement was not published.

Duling v. Bluefield Sanitarium, Inc. 142 S.E.2d 754 (W.Va.1968).

A subsequent case in a different jurisdiction based judgement on a national standard for accredited hospitals. The court in the following case stated that hospitals are required to use the degree of care and skill expected of reasonably competent hospitals in the same or similar circumstances. Under this standard, advances in the profession as well as availability of special facilities and specialists should be considered.

An infant suffered brain damage from intracranial bleeding at birth. This was complicated by subsequent treatment rendered by several physicians. As a result, the child had to be institutionalized.

The issue before the appeals court was whether a national standard of care should be applied to the physicians and hospital. The court held that the national standards should be applied.

Shilkret v. Annapolis Emergency Hospital Association, 349 A.2d 245 (Maryland 1975).

The initiation of the prospective payment system (DRGs or Diagnosis Related Groups) has resulted in a change in our current national standard of health care. Liability questions will now be decided based upon reasonable medical care in view of this new development in health care.

EXPERT TESTIMONY

In a court of law, a deviation from a professional standard will be shown by the introduction of expert testimony. This is a significant distinction between the ordinary negligence case (e.g., liability in an auto accident) and the malpractice case.

In every negligence or malpractice proceeding, the injured party or plaintiff must prove that the defendant did something that a reasonable person in the same or similar circumstance would not have done or did not do something that a reasonable person would have done. In a malpractice proceeding, it must be proven that a professional has deviated from what a reasonable professional person would have done in the same or similar circumstances. Therefore, an expert is required to give this testimony.

Expert testimony is another area where courts have traditionally failed to recognize the uniqueness of nursing. In a medical malpractice case, only a physician may testify as to the proper standard of care that should have been provided. This enables physicians to control very tightly how medical care is interpreted by the judicial system. However, in nursing cases, courts have often looked to physicians rather than nurses to identify proper nursing care. The following case is an example of a situation in which a physician was permitted to testify as to the proper standard of nursing care.

A patient was admitted to the psychiatric section of the hospital. He was then transferred to the surgical ward for surgery. Family members stayed with the patient during the 2-day period following surgery.

On the third night, as the daughter was leaving, she told the nurses that her father was quite confused and asked for them to watch him and keep the siderails up. Early the next morning, the patient was found on the roof of the emergency tunnel directly below a window of the bathroom he was using. There was a conflict in the testimony as to whether he had jumped or fallen from the window. He sustained serious injuries including several fractures.

Hospital records disclosed that the patient had been given a narcotic and two sedatives that evening. The night nurse had not been told of the patient's particular problems.

A physician from another part of the state reviewed the medical records as well as other significant documents and testified as to the standards of care for nursing in the community. The court held that his testimony was appropriate especially since all hospitals in the state were subject to the state licensing law.

Avey v. St. Francis Hospital, 442 P.2d 1013 (Kansas 1968).

This is another example of a societal attitude reflected by the judiciary system, which does not recognize the professional aspects of nursing. It is also a way in which nursing loses control of its own development of practice. Once the physician testified as to proper standards of care for nursing and this is accepted by the judiciary in a particular case, the interpretation stands as a judicial precedent and may be applied to a subsequent case. There is ample justification for the philosophy that only nurses should be permitted to testify in a case involving nursing malpractice. One essential characteristic of a profession is its ability to control its own growth and development.

In some cases, courts have undermined the role of the nurse as a professional by permitting nonprofessional testimony on the standard of care for the nurse.

An obstetric patient fell out of bed while in the labor room. The state Supreme Court stated that the standard of care did not have to be shown by expert testimony since six of the jurors were women and probably knew more about children than many experts.

Jones v. Hawkes Hospital of Mt. Carmel, 196 N.E.2d 592 (Ohio 1964).

In this case, the lay jury was allowed to act as its own expert. However, a judge's dissenting opinion elucidated some persuasive arguments for the requirement of expert testimony. He suggested that nursing is a profession, and the nurses' acts should be evaluated according to a professional standard of care.

The expert testimony of the nurse must reflect her familiarity with the standards of the care.

A patient was recuperating from surgery and was found to be in a state of shock. He was administered the drug Levophed by intravenous infusion. During the course of the infusion, the medication was found to have infiltrated his arm, resulting eventually in a sloughing of the skin of the arm. New skin was subsequently grafted onto the arm from other parts of the patient's body.

The patient's attorney had a nurse from another state testify as to the proper use of Levophed. This "expert" testified that she did not have any experience with intravenous infusion of this drug. The knowledge she gained was by reading the directions on a newly purchased package of that drug.

Based on this lack of expert testimony and the court's belief that the cause could have been a disoldgement of the needle by physical movement of the patient or a rejection by his body, the plaintiff was not permitted to recover damages.

Hundemer v. Sisters of Charity of Cincinnati, Inc., 258 N.E.2d 611 (Ohio 1969).

A patient claimed that the nurse had improperly administered potassium solution intravenously causing burning and the need for subsequent plastic surgery.

Another nurse was asked to testify as an expert witness. The court initially felt that since the nurse was not licensed to diagnose or prescribe medical treatment, she should not be permitted to testify that the improper aaministration of potassium caused the injury. A judgment for the defendant resulted.

On appeal, however, the higher court held that the nurse was an expert in the field of intravenous therapy and, therefore, competent to testify as to the cause of the plaintiff's physical injury.

Maloney v. Wake Hospital Systems, 262 S.E.2d 680 (North Carolina 1980).

In a more recent case concerning an infusion, the court also permitted the nurse to testify as an expert witness.

The patient claimed she suffered arm injuries because Dopamine had been infused with an infusion pump rather than a drip chamber.

The nurse was permitted to testify as an expert witness although she had experience only with smaller hospitals.

Macon-Bibb County Hosp. Auth. v. Ross, 335 S.E.2d 633 (Georgia 1985).

A nurse's aide is permitted to testify as an expert witness about the general practices in her field.

A patient recoverying from back surgery broke her wrist in a fall. She claimed the hospital was negligent because a nurses aide had failed to assist her in leaving the shower. The jury awarded her $50,000.

On appeal the court held that expert testimony by the aide was admissible.

Biggs v. Cumberland County Hospital System, 317 S.E.2d 421 (North Carolina 1984).

In some situations a nurse may now be permitted to testify as an expert in a physician malpractice case.

A patient alleged that her radial nerve was damaged by her physician's use of an unsterile needle to draw blood.

The nurse-expert testified about the proper procedure for keeping the hypodermic needle sterile.

The court held that as a licensed nurse she was qualified to provide this testimony.

McCormick v. Avret, 267 S.E.2d 759 (Georgia 1980).

SUMMARY

Malpractice refers to a deviation from a profession standard of care. In order to prove that malpractice has occurred, four criteria must be established—duty, breach of duty, causation, and damages.

The nurse-patient relationship, which establishes a duty toward a particular patient, is easily demonstrated when the nurse is an employee of the institution and the plaintiff has been a patient in the institution.

Nursing standards determine whether a particular function falls within the duty of a nurse. Standards of care for nursing are established by external and internal standards. External standards include the Nurse Practice Act of each jurisdiction, guidelines from accrediting agencies, and textbooks. Internal standards include the nurse's job description as well as policies and procedures of the institution. Court cases are an important source of information regarding standards of care for nursing, illustrating how the judicial system interprets nursing and indicating how future cases might be decided.

The standard of care required for a student nurse, a supervising nurse, a practical or vocational nurse, and an industrial nurse is frequently questioned by the nursing profession. The expanded role of the nurse is raising new issues in the legal and medical communities.

The location of the nurse's practice used to be a major determinant of what standards were expected. In recent years, courts have moved from the locality rule to a national standard for both the nursing and medical professions.

The final method of determining the appropriate standard for nursing is the use of expert testimony in court.

CHAPTER **4**

BREACH OF DUTY

In a negligence case against a nurse, once the standard of care has been established and a legal duty shown on the part of the nurse, the injured party must prove that a breach of this duty has occurred.

THE ESTABLISHMENT OF BREACH OF DUTY

In negligence cases, breach of duty often involves the matter of foreseeability.

Forseeability is the legal requirement that the case must be judged on the unique facts as they were at the time of the occurrence, since it is always easier to state what should have been done in retrospect. It is more difficult to judge a situation at the time and then decide what should be done. Certain events may foreseeably cause a specific result. For example, if water is on the floor of a hospital room, a duty is imposed on hospital personnel. It is not enough simply to walk around the water to avoid injury; a reasonably prudent person would take steps to remove the water or at least to warn the patient.

The following case of a patient suicide is an example of a situation where foreseeability is frequently discussed. Courts have established that it is the duty of the hospital and its staff to exercise reasonable care to protect suicidal patients against foreseeable harm.

A patient who was depressed and had suicidal thoughts voluntarily entered a psychiatric unit. He was assigned a status level according to hospital policy and was not allowed to leave the psychiatric unit without a staff escort. About 2 weeks later, the nurses began to allow the patient to leave the ward unescorted even though policy indicated a physician should have changed the order. The patient committed suicide by jumping out a window.

His survivors were awarded $180,000 in damages based on the negligent acts of the hospital employees. Suicide was a foreseeable event.
Abille v. U.S., 482 F.Supp.703 (1980)

Some occurrences that appear to indicate malpractice do not meet the legal standard because foreseeability is absent. It is not foreseeable that the patient who is told that he or she has cancer will commit suicide as a result; therefore special suicide precautions may not be necessary on the part of the nursing staff.

The deceased had a two-year history of Alzheimer's disease and was a patient in a State Hospital. Because of a suspected head injury, the patient was transferred to another hospital for a CAT Scan. She was given 5 milligrams of Valium for sedation. She began to show symptoms of respiratory distress and died 10 days later as the result of pneumonia.

The court held that no evidence existed to show that the health care providers could have foreseen ihe patient's adverse reaction to the medication.
Hodge v. Crafts-Farrow State Hospital, 334 S.E.2d 818 (South Carolina 1985).

As Chapter 3 illustrates, the legal duty of the nurse is established by the standards of the profession. These standards may be external standards (legislative enactments, case law, etc.) or internal standards (job descriptions, institutional policies and procedures, etc). Whether the nurse has breached these standards is often the main issue in a malpractice case.

FALLS

No other type of injury to patients is responsible for as many malpractice suits against hospitals and nurses as falls. These cases present the most common examples of how a nurse may breach a duty to a patient. Almost every jurisdiction in the country has dealt with cases involving patient falls in hospitals. The question of when and how to provide siderails, restraints, and other protections continues to perplex the best minds in hospital administration and to challenge the best judgment of nurses.

A patient was admitted to the hospital for the treatment of severe headaches. On the morning of her last day, she requested the aid of a nurse on duty, complaining that she was suffering from constipation. The nurse brought the patient a suppository. The patient then complained of being unable to have a bowel movement on the bedpan. The nurse brought her a straight-back chair and put the bedpan on it. The patient later testified in court that the chair had a bottom of "pasteboard or paper." While the patient was sitting on the bedpan, the chair's bottom fell through. The patient injured her back while trying to grasp the back of the chair.

The trial judge did not permit the jury to render a verdict, stating that there was insufficient evidence of negligence. However, the appeals court felt the jury should have been permitted to decide the case and sent it back for a new trial. The second opinion was not published.

Williams v. Orange Memorial Hospital, 202 So.2d 859 (Fla. App.1967).

A 55-year old woman entered the hospital with high blood pressure, arthritis, and head and chest pains. She was restless and confused. Siderails were placed on her bed. She then became noisy and disturbed other patients. On the same afternoon, she was transferred to a private room, and private duty nurses were employed. The physician ordered the siderails to be removed, and the private duty nurses were subsequently discontinued. The patient testified that she fell while getting out of bed to go to the bathroom.

In the finding for the hospital, the court stated that "due care did not require that the (night) nurse on duty devote her time to watching a sleeping patient." The court held that expert testimony would have to be introduced to show that the physician was negligent and that, in this case, there was no reason for the nurses to disregard or request a change in the order to remove the siderails. The patient had alleged that the nurses were negligent for complying with the physician's order.

Carrigan v. Roman Catholic Bishop, 178 A.2d 502 (New Hampshire 1962).

The previous case illustrates a court's evaluation that found that the nurses did not have an independent duty to countermand the physician's order. However, in recent decisions, courts tend to look more stringently at the nurse's role. Frequently, courts now recognize an independent duty on the part of the nurse to evaluate the patient professionally.

A patient who was 41 years old had a hysterectomy. Two days later, her surgeon left instructions that she was to exercise with assistance. When two nurses attempted to walk with her, the woman became violently ill and was immediately returned to her bed. The following day, when two nurses undertook to exercise her, she protested, stating she was sick and unable to walk. She collapsed and fell, suffering a ruptured disc.

The appeals court felt that the jury should be given the opportunity to decide whether the nurses were negligent in performing their duties.

At the trial, the patient's claim had been dismissed based on the nurse's compliance with the physician's orders.

Arnold v. James B. Haggin Hospital, 415 S.W.2d 844 (Kentucky 1967).

In the previous case, the jury should have been permitted to determine if the nurses were negligent for complying with the physician's order.

A patient was admitted to the hospital for psychiatric evaluation. The admitting psychiatrist did not take her history or enter it on her chart until after the incident in question. He did, however, leave standing orders for the patient's care; they did not contain any reference to baths.

The hospital regulations contained directions for patient showers at 9:00 p.m. each evening. The patient had complained of dizzy spells all day. When she entered the shower alone, she lost consciousness and fell, lacerating her lip and breaking her jaw. Subsequently, she had to have all her teeth removed.

The court stated that the standard to be applied was reasonable care for patients as their known mental and physical condition would require. The court made it clear that the presence of physician's orders does not necessarily prevent a hospital from being liable for the care rendered by its nurses in compliance with these orders.

Kastler v. Iowa Methodist Hospital, 193 N.W.2d 98 (Iowa 1971).

Sometimes an injury occurs through a nurse's failure to assess properly a patient's situation and take appropriate precautions.

Two nurses were teaching a patient to walk again after she had had a stroke. The two nurses, each holding one of her arms, assisted her into the hospital sunroom. The defendant nurse then released her hold on the patient to step forward to arrange a chair for her, whereupon the patient fell and sustained a fracture.

The court stated that the patient had a right to recover damages since the nurse should have anticipated the need for the chair and arranged it before bringing the patient to the sunroom.

Stevenson v. Alta Bates, 20 Cal.App.2d 313. 66 P.2d 1265 (1937)

While the previous case is one of the older malpractice cases discussing the duty of the nurse, it continues to serve as a timely illustration of the need for nurses to foresee the consequences of their actions and inactions.

A 2-year-old child fell from a hospital bed after climbing over the side. The child's parents had asked the nurse to take extra precautions because their child was very active, but the nurse failed to carry out their request.

The jury found the nurse negligent for failing to provide additional restraint. The hospital was liable for the nurse's actions.

Pierson v. Charles Wilson Memorial Hospital, 273 App.Div.348, 78 N.Y.S.2d 146 (1946).

Not only was it foreseeable in the previous case that a 2-year-old child might climb over the side of the bed, fall, and become injured, but also the parents had clearly warned the nurse of this possibility. The breach of proper standards of nursing care is obvious:

A 3-year-old boy was admitted to the hospital to have his tonsils and adenoids removed. Before surgery, his mother told the nurse that he normally slept in a crib and would fall out of a hospital bed without siderails. The nurse placed siderails on the child's bed. During the night the child wedged his head between the rails and strangled to death.

The court concluded that a higher degree of care is required when the patient is a child, and the parents could recover damages for the death of their child.

St. Luke's Hospital Association v. Long, 240 P.2d 917 (Colo. 1952).

Not all cases involving children result in recovery of damages for the injured child. As with all malpractice cases, some breach of duty must be proven.

A 9-year-old child and her mother went for treatment at a medical clinic. The examining physician diagnosed the child's condition as tonsillitis and sent her to another room for an intramuscular injection of penicillin. The mother was asked to remain with the doctor for treatment of her own medical problems. A registered nurse employed by the doctor administered penicillin to the child by injection and then left the room. The child fainted and fell to the floor, breaking two permanent teeth that later had to be pulled.

Evidence indicated that there were no signs the child felt faint during or after the injection, that the child had never before fainted when receiving a hypodermic injection, and that on this occasion she felt no dizziness until after the nurse had left the room.

Therefore, it was not foreseeable on the part of the nurse that this injury would have occurred.

The court held that the injured child could not recover damages.
Stafford v. Hunter, 401 P.2d 986 (Wash.1965).

A young woman who had been chronically ill since she was 7 years old, when she suffered brain damage resulting in seizures and mental retardation, was a patient in a nursing home. An employee of the home testified that, because of the patient's weight and the possibility of a seizure, two attendants were required to help her move about. While in the bathroom, however, she was accompanied by only one attendant because the room was very small. On this particular occasion, the patient fell in the bathroom and sustained a fractured hip.

The appeals court held there was sufficient evidence for the jury to determine whether or not the attendants were negligent. The trial judge originally had dismissed the case based on insufficient evidence.
Ivy Manor Nursing Home, Inc. v. Brown, 488 P. 2d 246 (Colo. 1971).

An elderly patient was admitted to the hospital for treatment of chronic high blood pressure and symptoms of dizziness, headaches, and instability. She was not told by the hospital staff that she was to call for assistance if she had to go to the bathroom, nor was she told not to leave her bed without assistance. During the night she awoke, needing to use the bathroom. Without calling for assistance or reaching for her bedpan, she got out of bed and, after taking a step or two, fell. Evidence was introduced that, in the community, general nursing practice was to put up siderails for patients over 60 years of age.

The jury held that the patient's fall, as she attempted to leave bed without assistance, was due to the negligence of the nurses in failing to put up siderails.
Mercy Hospital, Inc. v. Larkins, 174 So.2d 408 (Fla.App.1965).

The previous case illustrates that the standard of care for nursing requires the use of siderails for most elderly patients. In addition, the patient should be instructed to call for assistance. If this instruction is not documented on the patient's medical record, the defendant has a more difficult task to establish a defense.

The nurse's failure to provide adequate instruction to the patient may be the basis of a malpractice action.

A woman fractured her hip as a result of stepping into a hole in the street. She was admitted to a hospital, and, on her first day of using crutches, she fell and fractured her wrist. The patient had received only a few words of instruction from the nurse on how to use the crutches.

The court decided that failure to take proper and customary precautions to prevent her falling was a breach of proper standards of care. The patient was permitted to recover damages for her injurv because the nurse failed to supervise her use of the crutches.

Butler v. Lutheran Medical Center, 36 A.D.2d 640,. 319 N.Y.S. 291, 1971).

In the following case involving a fall, the nurse failed to follow the physician's directions and improperly instructed the patient.

The patient's physician prescribed bed rest and bathroom privileges with assistance. The nurse incorrectly instructed the patient to use the bathroom without supervision and explained to patient the procedures to use in collecting urine specimens.

On the day of the fall, the patient had been given a laxative by one of the hospital's employees and was also in a weakened condition.

The jury found in favor of the patient.

Doctor's Hospital of Augusta, Inc. v. J.F. Poole, 241 S.E.2d 2, (Georgia 1977).

In addition to the elderly and the young, it is quite clear that proper standards of nursing care require that siderails be provided for patients who have been sedated and/or are mentally impaired in order to prevent falls.

A patient with a history of heart involvement was hospitalized for bronchitis. The treating physician instructed the hospital staff to administer pain medication as necessary. The patient received pain medication and a sedative for sleep. During the next hour, the patient fell and sustained a fracture of the neck of the femur and a hematoma above the right temple.

The court found that the patient fell out of bed through no fault of her own. The use of siderails would have prevented such a fall, and the hospital was negligent in not having placed siderails on the bed. The physician had properly left the handling of the patient to the hospital and was not negligent in failing to order siderails placed on the bed.

The jury awarded $38,122.20 for damages, medical costs, and personal injuries.

Smith v. West Calcasieu-Cameron Hospital, 251 So.2d 810 (La.1971).

A patient was admitted to the hospital for the treatment of migraine headaches. No siderails were put on her bed, and she fell out of bed. She claimed that she had been heavily sedated.

The court denied recovery of damages and said that the plaintiff must show either that the physician had ordered siderails for the bed or that she was sedated to such an extent that hospital employees should have been on reasonable notice that her condition required the placement of siderails. There was some discrepancy in testimony as to the amount of sedation the patient received.

Thompson v. General Hospital Authority of Upton County, 151 S.E.2d 183 (Ga. 1966).

The previous case states the general principle applied to fall cases on the issue of siderails. The injured patient must prove that the physician ordered siderails or that the patient was sedated to such an extent that hospital employees should have been on reasonable notice that siderails were necessary. In other words, the nurses could have foreseen that the patient might have fallen.

The issue that must be decided is whether the defendant should have foreseen the injury that ultimately occurred. A patient who falls out of bed because the siderails were not up would not, of course, have fallen if the judgment had been made to provide siderails. In retrospect, it is easy to say that the siderails should have been used.

A woman in her early forties who was in a deteriorated physical condition and in a state of mental confusion was admitted to the hospital as an emergency case with her husband and son in attendance. As her family was leaving the hospital that evening, the husband advised the charge nurse that siderails would be needed on his wife's bed. The nurse obtained the doctor's consent, got the siderails, and placed them in the hall outside the patient's room. A short while later the patient fell and was injured.

The court felt that since the nurse had been warned, reasonable care was not exercised. The case was originally dismissed for lack of evidence but on appeal was sent back for a jury trial.

Sanders v. St. John's Hospital, 369 P.2d 165 (Okla. 1962).

When the nurse fails to communicate with the patient by not answering a call for help, liability may occur.

A woman was admitted to the hospital with bursitis in her right knee. On the second day of hospitalization, she put on her call light because she wanted help in getting to the bathroom. When no one answered, she proceeded to get out of bed, fell, and injured her back. It was foreseeable that the patient, not getting a response to her call, might fall while walking.

The patient received a jury award of $30,594.

Newhall v. Central Vermont Hospital, 349 A.2d 890 (Vt.1975)

When to restrain patients or remove restraints is often a difficult decision for nurses. In general the nurse should balance the need for restraints based on safety to the patient or to others against the patient's right not to be restrained. A reasonable nursing judgment should then be made based on the assessment of the individual patient's needs. If the nurse's judgment is reasonable, any injury to the patient will be defensible. However, if the nurse's judgment appears unreasonable, liability may be found.

The patient had abdominal surgery. A few days later he was in cloth restraints when a nurse brought in his supper. She untied the restraint on his right arm, placed the tray in front of him, watched him eat for a short period, and then left the room.

Sometime later the patient undid his left arm restraint, pushed his supper tray out of the way and as both siderails were up, slid off the foot of his bed. Upon reaching the floor while attempting to stand he fell and fractured his hip.

The judge directed a verdict in favor of the hospital that was overturned on appeal.

Cramer v. Theda Clark Memorial Hospital, 172 N.W.2d 427 (Wisconsin 1970).

If the patient is neither young nor old, has no mental impairment, and has given no indication of being unable to keep from falling out of bed, the court will be reluctant to permit recovery of damages for lack of siderails.

A patient had surgery on his leg. He was not delirious or confused when he fell out of his hospital bed 9 days later. His physician testified that he had not observed any condition in the patient that would require siderails.

The hospital was not held liable.

Mossman v. Albany Medical Center Hospital, 311 N.Y.S.2d 131 (N.Y.1970).

A mental patient fell out of bed and fractured his leg. He had been in the hospital for 8 months, had never had siderails on his bed, and had never fallen before.

The court denied recovery of damages saying that the injury was not foreseeable.

Shannon v. State of New York, 289 N.Y.S.2d 462 (1968).

COMMUNICATION FAILURE AS THE CAUSE OF FALLS

Falls may occur in ancillary departments providing patient services. Negligence may be the result of lack of awareness regarding the basic safety needs of patients, or there may be a lack of communication among hospital departments. In the following case, the court discussed the duty of the nurse to communicate information regarding patients to other departments.

A patient fell and was injured in the radiology department of a hospital. The radiologist's defense was that the nurse had not filled out the requisition adequately; therefore, he had had no knowledge of the patient's history of being unable to walk for 6 months.

However, the court held the radiologist liable for negligence in not remaining alert to the reasonable possibility that the patient might faint and fall.

Favalora v. Aetna Casualty Company, 144 So.2d 544 (La.1962).

A District of Columbia court has more recently emphasized the need for communication between the nursing and radiology departments.

Before admission to the hospital, a patient had been suffering from dizziness, blackouts, and weakness. A pyelogram was ordered. The form to be completed by the nurse required a summary of the patient's history and complaints. The nurse wrote "diabetic complications" but made no reference to the patient's dizziness. During the examination, the x-ray table was placed in a vertical position. When the patient stood up, she fell over and broke her cheekbone.

The court held that expert testimony was not needed to prove her case. Since the chart clearly indicated that the patient was prone to fainting spells, the court ruled that the nurse was negligent in not notifying the radiologist of that fact. The court also held that the radiologist, who knew that the patient was a diabetic, should have known that she was quite likely to be unsteady. The court said there was sufficient evidence for the jury to conclude that a reasonably prudent person in the circumstances would have provided this particular patient with some form of safeguard from falling.

Washington Hospital Center v. Butler, 384 F.2d 331, (D.C 1967).

Examples of cases involving deficiencies in communication are frequent in malpractice law. The lack of adequate communication is a recurrent issue that will be discussed in subsequent cases dealing with different types of malpractice.

A hospital patient testified that, while she had been in a weakened condition, the nurse who was attending her put her on a bedpan, negligently permitted her to fall, and then scolded her for falling. The nurse, however, testified in detail that she had exercised exceptional care of and interest in this patient. She also stated that the patient had ignored the order to use the bedpan rather than the bathroom and, while ignoring the order, had fallen in the bathroom. The patient's injury was a broken collar bone.

The jury believed the nurse's testimony and allowed no recovery.

Pittman v. Methodist Hospital of Mississippi, 173 So.2d 923 (Miss.1965).

The plaintiff, a 74-year-old man, was admitted to the hospital with suspected prostate problems. His physician ordered an intravenous pyelogram to be preceded by a cleansing enema.

The patient, contrary to his own request, had been placed in a private room without a bathroom. The licensed practical nurse who administered the enema admitted during her testimony that she was hurrying because it was near the end of her shift. After she administered the enema, the nurse asked if the patient wanted to use the bedpan or go the bathroom. He was unacquainted with the physical surroundings and asked where the bathroom was located. He was told it was "right around the corner to the left." He thought this meant 8 to 10 feet, when in fact, it was 70 feet. The nurse remained in the room and permitted the patient to travel down the hall unescorted in his slippers. The plaintiff slipped in the enema solution and fell.

The patient was permitted to recover damages for his injury. Particularly damaging to the hospital's defense was a textbook passage on the administration of enemas that listed "assist patient on to bedpan or to toilet" as the last step.

Tills v. Elmbrook Memorial Hospital, Inc., 180 N.W.2d 699 (Wisc. 1970).

BURNS

A number of nursing malpractice cases have been based on a burn injury suffered by a patient. Sometimes it is a very simple accident—a patient who spills a hot liquid on himself or herself and is injured. Normally this would not be a basis for a negligence action. However, when a hospitalized patient is involved who is elderly, young, sedated, or confused, liability may be imposed on the hospital for the actions or omissions of the nursing staff.

A hospitalized infant received severe burns when her foot was placed in contact with an electric light bulb in an incubator. The nurse had failed to remove the light bulb or turn it off in accordance with proper procedures. A cover placed over the incubator concealed the light bulb from observation. The infant had to have three-fourths of her foot amputated.

The court held that a cause of action existed against the hospital because of the nurse's negligence but that no cause existed against the physician. Therefore, the case was sent back for trail against the hospital.

Emory University v. Porter, 129 S.E.2d 70 (Ga.1962).

An 11-year-old boy was hospitalized for a tonsillectomy. His doctor ordered a postop diet of milk, ice cream and Jello; cooked cereal and broth were added the following day. The nurse knew that hot tea was not allowed.

The day after surgery, however, for her own convenience, she ordered a complete liquid diet which included hot water for tea. She intended to remove the hot water from the tray, but before she was able to, the child started to eat.

While picking up the Jello dish he knocked over the hot water, burning his ankle.

The court held the physician was not liable for the nurse's negligence because she was acting contrary to his instructions and as an employee of the hospital.

Striano v. Deepdale General Hosp., 387 N.Y.S.2d (New York 1976)

As noted in the previous discussion of cases involving falls, the age of the patient is one factor to consider when liability is imposed. The previous cases illustrate this point in regard to an infant and a child. The following case deals with an elderly patient:

An 83-year-old patient was burned by hot water while in the bathtub at an army hospital. There was evidence that he was feeble, partially blind, physically debilitated, and senile. Apparently his general faculties for sensing heat and pain were impaired as well as his ability to communicate. On this occasion, he was being assisted out of the tub when he became violent and started kicking the attendant. The patient accidentally turned on the hot water and, before he could be taken out of the tub, suffered first-, second-, and third-degree burns on the buttocks and feet.

The court held that evidence established that the injuries had been caused by the negligence of hospital authorities in permitting scalding water to stand in the hot water pipe leading directly into the bathtub. The injured patient received a jury award of $10,000.

Kopa v. U.S., 236 F.Supp. 189 (Hawaii 1964).

Sometimes burns occur through the use of various types of equipment in the hospital.

A nurse was aware of the result of applying too much current and continued diathermy treatment despite the patient's complaint of a burning sensation. She had pretended to turn the current down but instead had switched it up.

The nurse was held liable for the burns the patient was given by the diathermy machine.

   Wood v. Miller, 158 Ore. 444, 76 P.2d 963 (1938).

The previous case, although one of the older court cases directly involving negligence by a nurse, remains an excellent example of an important principle that nurses should always be aware of—what the patient says should be listened to carefully.

Action was brought against a surgeon when an electric cautery machine burned a patient during a hemorrhoidectomy. The machine had been used four times earlier that same day. The first two times the surgeon attempted to use the machine during the hemorrhoidectomy, it did not deliver sufficient heat to cauterize the vessels, and the surgeon requested the circulating nurse to check it. Thereafter, the machine worked satisfactorily, and the operation was completed. After the operation, it was discovered that the patient was burned where she had come in contact with the electrode. The case was settled before trial as to the hospital and the nurse.

The court held the surgeon not liable, stating that where opportunities for prevention of injury to a patient depend on the care with which the equipment is monitored and with the selection and training of personnel to operate it, it is proper to place the burden of defective equipment and negligent personnel on the hospital.

   May v. Broun, 492 P.2d 776 (Oregon 1972).

A patient suffered leg burns during the removal of a mole. The court held that there was sufficient evidence to go to the jury relative to the liability of both the nurse and the surgeon. There was evidence that the electrode was improperly placed against the body of the patient when the doctor was not present. However, there was also evidence that the nurse asked the surgeon to check the placement and that he did so. There was evidence that the nurse was aware that other patients in same the hospital who were having moles removed had been burned by the same type of electrosurgical machine when there was insufficient contact between the patient's body and the contact plate of the machine.

   Monk v. Doctors Hospital, 403 F.2d 580 (D.C.Cir. 1968).

Cases involving equipment frequently impose liability on both the physician and the nurse. There is a joint duty and responsibility on the part of all professionals to evaluate the equipment that is being used for patient care. Equipment with obvious defects should not be used for patient care.

There are a number of cases from various states on the issue of the patient who is not capable of smoking safely and who therefore receives a burn.

A 65-year-old man suffered from chronic brain syndrome and diabetes. His children advised the nurses that he often burned himself while smoking and should not be left alone with a cigarette. He was restrained in a chair, left alone, and found in flames.

The hospital was held liable for his death because the nurses, based on the warnings, should have foreseen the risk of fire.

Kent v. County of Hudson, 245 A.2d 747 (N.J. 1968).

Failure to observe the patient properly has imposed liability on the nurse and the hospital in most cases. Precautions should be taken and documented on the patient's medical record in the event that an injury occurs and a claim is filed.

MEDICATION ERRORS

The most potentially hazardous therapeutic activity that a nurse engages in is the administration of medications. As with other areas of medicine, the complexity of this topic has increased tremendously over the years.

Courts have established that the duty of the nurse in handling drugs is to use such care that no harm comes to the patient who has been entrusted to his or her care.

Today many hospitals use a system for dispensing medications called the unit dose system. In this system, the nurse is no longer required to prepare the medications. The medications arrive from the pharmacy individually packaged for each patient with the proper medication prepared as a unit dose. This safeguard reduces the chance for nursing error in the preparation of the medication. However, in hospitals that have the unit dose system, there are some stock items that are kept on the unit, the preparation of which is done by the nurse as the medications are given. The unit dose system does not remove the nurse's responsibility for checking to make sure the medication that was sent from pharmacy is both the proper medication and the correct dose for the particular patient.

PROCEDURAL SAFEGUARDS

A cardinal safety rule, known to all nurses, is the necessity for reading all drug labels three times—once before taking the medication off the shelf, once while pouring it, and once again after replacing it. This procedure is meant to ensure safety in drug administration. The court discussed this standard in the following case:

A hospitalized patient was to be given milk of magnesia and Cascara as a laxative. Instead she received pHisoHex; the two bottles were stored in the same area. The patient attempted to prove that the hospital was negligent in not carrying out proper procedures for storing medications.

Evidence established that the procedure requires that the label of the medication be read three times. Therefore, the nurse who breached this duty was held liable, as well as the hospital.

Habuda v. Trustees of Rex Hospital, Inc., 164 S.E. 2d 17 (N.C.1968).

The duty of the nurse to read medication labels is so clear that it is unlikely that the physician who administers a medication handed to him by a nurse will be held liable if the evidence establishes that the physician is relying on the nurse's fulfillment of her duty.

A nurse was held liable when she neglected to read the label on a medication bottle and supplied the physician with formalin rather than Novocain.

The physician was held not liable because evidence established that it was a customary practice for the doctor to accept instruments and medications for use in the operating room without looking at them.

Hallinan v. Prindle, 17 Cal.App.2d 656, 62 P.2d 1075 (1937).

While the previous case is one of the older nursing malpractice cases, it is still applicable in most jurisdictions.

DELAY IN ADMINISTERING MEDICATION

Failure to administer drugs on time may result in an allegation of liability against a nurse.

A 14-month-old infant was brought by her mother, on each of four consecutive days. She was finally admitted; and intravenous medication was ordered that was not given until two hours later. The child's condition worsened and she died the next day.

The court entered a judgment in favor of the defendant.

Gasbarra v. St. James Hospital, 406 N.E.2d 544 (Illinois 1979)

The patient, a geologist, suffered an elbow injury and was operated upon for cervical spondylosis. Following surgery the patient became disoriented and suffered hallucinations. A psychiatrist was consulted who ordered 100 milligrams of Mellaril to be administered immediately. The drug was not administered until two hours later. Approximately four hours later, the patient jumped out of a window. He is permanently paralyzed and a quadriplegic.

The lower court allowed a judgment against the patient but this was overturned on appeal.

Farrow v. Health Service Corp., 604 P.2d 474 (Utah 1979)

UNFAMILIARITY WITH DRUGS

As well as being held liable for procedural errors in the administration of drugs, nurses have been found negligent for a lack of familiarity with drugs that they have administered.

A physician wrote a medication order specifying when the drug was to be administered. The nurse asked the intern to inject the medication. He did, and the patient's heart stopped. Evidence indicated that the drug was unusual and potent, requiring the specialized skill and knowledge of an anesthesiologist for proper administration, as was noted on the medication label.

The nurse was found negligent for failing to read the literature that would have given the necessary precautions.

Campbell v. Preston, 379 S.W.2d 557 (Mo.S.Ct.1964)

The subject of therapeutic equivalents is becoming widely used in most hospitals; therefore, when a medication is ordered, a generic equivalent may be dispensed by the pharmacy. This causes some difficulty for those who have to administer the medication, particularly nurses, who may be unfamiliar with the medication that is dispensed even though they may be familiar with the therapeutic equivalent that is normally used. If the nurse is unsure of the medication that is being used, the nurse has an obligation to question the medication by either referring to the hospital's formulary, the Physician's Desk Reference, or the pharmacy to make sure that the patient's medication is the proper medication for filling the order, as is shown later in *Norton v. Argonaut Insurance Co.*

ROUTE OF ADMINISTRATION

Errors may result when a nurse fails to determine the correct mode of administration of a drug.

A nurse failed to read all the entries in the patient's chart and missed the change of medication from injectable to oral. The patient told the nurse that she was making an error, but the nurse insisted on administering the medication after reassuring the patient that she had checked the doctor's orders. The nurse was held liable for negligence.
Larrimore v. Homeopathic Hospital, 54 Del. 449, 181 A.2d 573 (1963).

As this case indicates, failing to listen to the patient may lead to an error. Most patients are aware of their medications and alert to changes.

The error of administering an oral dose intramuscularly, as illustrated in the preceding case, is always a potentially hazardous error, since the oral dose of a drug, which must be absorbed through the gastrointestinal tract and into the blood stream, must be much higher than the intramuscular dose in order for a therapeutic level to be achieved. An oral dose administered as an injection may be fatal.

Failure by a nurse to read carefully orders relating to drugs has resulted in a number of legal actions against nurses as well as a number of seriously injured patients.

A patient admitted to the hospital for a hernia repair received two drugs intravenously rather than intramuscularly, as ordered. A grand mal seizure occurred immediately. The court held that the jury should be permitted to determine if the nurse who administered the medications was negligent.
Moore v. Guthrie Hospital, 403 F.2d 366 (4th Circ.W.Va.1968)

The manner in which a medication is administered accounts for some cases in which a nurse is held liable.

Proper standards of care for pediatric patients require the attendance of two people (a nurse and one person to assist) when an injection is being administered to a child. It is clearly foreseeable that a child might move suddenly during the injection.

An 11-month-old child suffered permanent crippling after receiving an injection of Imferon in the buttocks. Evidence established that the standard procedure was to inject into the upper outer quadrant of buttocks using the Z-track method of injection to avoid the sciatic nerve.

Because the student nurse who gave the injection injured the sciatic nerve, the child suffered permanent crippling, and the nurse was held liable.

Honeywell v. Rogers, 251 F.Supp. 841 (1966).

In this case, one issue was whether an assistant should have been present. A second issue was the method used for injection. Again, the question of foreseeability is raised in regard to what the nurse should anticipate when administering an injection to a child.

FAILURE TO QUESTION ORDERS

Nurses will be held negligent for administering a drug when in doubt about the order. Failure of a nurse to call the physician and clarify a questionable or unclear order often imposes liability.

The assistant director of nursing services of a hospital was covering a pediatric unit temporarily while the charge nurse was busy with an emergency. She questioned an order written by a physician for Lanoxin to be administered to a 3-month-old infant. The physician, who was not the physician ordering the drug, misunderstood her question. He thought she was referring to an oral dosage of medication rather than an injection. She administered the amount ordered, which was an overdose as an injection, and the child died. The nurse, the physician who ordered the medication, and the hospital were all liable for negligence.

Norton v. Argonaut Insurance Co., 144 So.2d 249 (La.1962).

A related subject involves investigational/experimental drugs that may be ordered by a physician. Each hospital should have a procedure for approving the use of such drugs. This should include a consent from the patient to the use of the investigational/experimental drug. Since the nurse dispenses many of these medications, the nurse may be the final check point to make sure that the hospital's procedure relative to investigational/experimental drugs has been followed.

NEGLIGENCE IN PATIENT EDUCATION

An interesting new malpractice issue concerns nurses' liability for instructions given or not given to patients about medications. Physicians may be held liable when they fail to warn patients about side effects of drugs, as this case shows.

A passenger on a bus brought an action against the physician who had prescribed a drug for the bus driver. The bus driver fell asleep, and the passenger was injured when a collision occurred. Evidence was presented that the standard of care in administering this drug includes warning patients of possible side effects.

The court held that the physician, in failing to warn the bus driver of the drug's possible side effects of drowsiness, could be held liable.
    Kaiser v. Suburban Transp. Systems, 398 P.2d 14 (Wash.1965)

It will be interesting to observe whether the principle of health teaching regarding medications will be applied to impose liability on nurses. Health teaching is consistently recognized as a professional duty belonging to the nursing profession.

The patient was admitted for treatment of ulcers, and the physician ordered a 24-hour urinalysis test. The patient, instead of voiding into the urinal, voided into the mouth of the collection jug, which contained hydrochloric acid. Immediately the acid reacted, causing severe and painful burning of the patient's penis, permanent scaring and impotence.

The patient alleged that the nurse did not properly advise on how to safely save the urine.

Judgment was entered in favor of the hospital.
    Chamberlain v. Deaconess Hospital, Inc., 324 N.E.2d 172 (Indiana 1975)

As nurses become legally accountable in more situations, it is likely that negligence in the areas of discharge instruction and health teaching will result in increased liability.

FAILURE TO OBSERVE

In Chapter 3, the theory that nurses have certain unique duties based on their professional status was introduced. Of critical importance is the process by which the nurse assesses the patient and formulates a nursing diagnosis to meet the patient's needs. The initial step of this process involves observation of the patient.

The term *nursing diagnosis* has been incorporated into many state Nurse Practice Acts in recognition of the nursing profession's unique obligation to make judgments while caring for the patient, judgments that are analogous to those of a physician. For example, the nurse who believes the patient is having a coronary occlusion, based on an assessment of subjective and objective signs and symptoms, must notify the patient's physician. Courts, however, have not extended the concept of nursing diagnosis to increase the liability of the nurse by suggesting that a medical diagnosis should also be made.

A patient came into the emergency room with intense abdominal pain and vomiting. A physician was called on the phone by the emergency room nurses. Based on their information, the physician prescribed medication and sent the patient home. The next day the patient's appendix ruptured, and he developed peritonitis. The patient sued the hospital and nurses claiming that the nurses should have made the medical diagnosis of appendicitis even though the physician had not.

The court held that the nurses were not negligent, since the plaintiff had failed to provide evidence that the nurses violated acceptable nursing standards in failing to diagnose medically the patient's appendicitis.

Vasey v. Burch, 262 S.E.2d 865 (North Carolina 1980)

An expectant mother came to the emergency room during the first trimester and said that she had rubella. Her child was born subsequently with permanent physical and mental retardation, cataracts, and heart malfunction.

The nurses were not liable for the defects of the child, since the physician had seen the patient and had told her to leave the hospital. The court stated that the hospital did not breach any duty to mother or daughter since the nurse and attendants exercised ordinary care in performing the only duty they owed to the mother, that is, to admit her and call a physician.

Dumer v. St. Michael Hospital, 233 N.W.2d 372 (Wisc.1975)

In the previous case, the court determined that the nurses were not responsible for making a medical diagnosis.

Any failure to analyze the patient in these professional terms may be considered a breach of duty on the part of the nurse. Failure to observe or monitor the patient properly is an example of this type of breach of duty.

A 6-year-old child was struck by a car while riding his bicycle. He sustained a fractured leg and required traction. Five days later his leg had to be amputated.

The hospital records contained an order by the physician to watch the condition of the patient's toes. There was no evidence in the record that the child's foot was observed during a 7-hour period. At the time of the next observation, his condition had become irreversible.

Collins v. Westlake Community Hospital, 57 Ill.2d 388, 312 N.E.2d 614 (1974).

The patient was undergoing treatment for a leg fracture. The physician provided instructions for the nurse to perform certain tests on an hourly basis to monitor for the development of compartment syndrome.

The tests were not performed for over 4 hours and the patient suffered loss of leg muscle tissue.

The court held the evidence was sufficient to show a connection between the nurse's negligence and the patient's injury.

Jarvis v. St. Charles Medical Center, 713 P.2d 620 (Oregon 1986)

The patient was admitted with a diagnosis of possible pulmonary embolus and placed on heparin therapy. At 5 AM the next morning, a medical technician took a blood sample from the patient. Immediately after the sample was taken, the patient began to experience pain above and below the elbow.

The nurse was told about the patient's condition but did not call the physician until 11:50 A.M. When the physician arrived at noon, he found a large hematoma on the patient's arm. He wrapped and elevated the arm, then reduced the heparin dose by one-half.

The patient suffered nerve damage and a permanent impairment.

The court ruled that the medical technician did not properly understand the extra precautions needed when taking blood from a heparinized patient. The nurse was liable for failing to recognize and respond to the signs of hemorrhaging.

Belmon v. St. Frances Cabrini Hospital, 427 So.2d 541 (La.1983)

There are a significant number of obstetric malpractice cases involving the nurse's failure to observe and monitor the pregnant patient.

A mother entered the hospital for the birth of her thirteenth child. Her first 12 children had been born vaginally and without complications or impairment. She was prepped for delivery and examined. About an hour later, an intravenous drip of Pitocin was begun. The mother testified that during the next 2 hours no one monitored her contractions by placing a hand on her abdomen. Her hospital chart did not reflect any monitoring. About an hour and a half after the Pitocin was started, the mother experienced a sharp pain in her abdomen. The child's oxygen supply was compromised, resulting in cerebral palsy. The jury awarded $350,000 to the child.

Long v. Johnson, 381 N.E.2d 93 (Ind. 1978).

A woman was about to have her second child. Her husband and mother were in the labor room with her. The husband repeatedly asked the nurse to call the physician, but the nurse refused and said that the patient was dilated only 7 centimeters. The husband told the nurse that the birth of their first child occurred soon after his wife was dilated eight centimeters. The nurse said she was in charge and would do what was necessary. After about 10 minutes the patient screamed that she was going to have the baby.

Evidence indicated that the nurse delivered the baby and asked a physician, who was walking down the hall, to suture lacerations which had resulted from the birth. The patient experienced pain, discomfort, and a reduction in sexual activity.

The court decided that the jury had reviewed sufficient evidence to find that the nurse had been negligent in her duties and that the hospital was liable for her negligence.

Hiatt v. Grace, 523 P.2d 320 (Kan.1974)

FAILURE TO INTERVENE APPROPRIATELY

Malpractice cases tend to focus on the administration of physical care to the patient. If an error occurs during a technical procedure, the patient may be aware of the error. Nursing malpractice cases include examples of every procedure that a nurse may perform for a patient.

Subsequent to the patient's hysterectomy, it was necessary for her to be catheterized on a number of occasions. The catheterization leading to the lawsuit was the twelfth performed on the patient.

She testified that she experienced unusual pain and advised the nurse. Another patient testified that she observed blood in the patient's urinary bag. The chart did not document unusual pain or a blood-filled bag.

Following discharge the patient had an inability to void and susceptibility to infection.

The court found for the defendant.

Schmidt v. Intermountain Health Care Inc., 635 P.2d 99 (Utah 1981).

Sometimes the breach of duty occurs because a nurse fails to perform a procedure according to proper standards of care.

A nurse was held liable for failing to observe that a patient, who was overweight, required a longer-than-average needle to receive an injection. Dramamine was ordered hypodermically. The injection was administered subcutaneously rather than intramuscularly. The patient incurred a fat necrosis and had an additional 45-day hospital stay.

The nurse was held liable for failing to use good judgment and provide a longer needle.

Barnes v. St. Francis Hospital and School of Nursing, Inc., 211 Kan.315, 507 P.2d 288, (1973).

A patient was admitted to the hospital for varicose vein repair. Preoperatively, he was given an enema. He testified that four attempts were made by a nurse to insert the tube, and each time he felt a cutting or tearing sensation in his rectum. As a result, he suffered a perirectal abscess and fistula that necessitated surgical repair. The court stated that it is a matter of common knowledge among lay people that giving an enema is not ordinarily harmful unless negligently done. Since an expert witness was not needed, the case was sent back for trial on the issue of the nurse's negligence.

Davis v. Memorial Hospital, 26 Cal.Rptr.633, 376 P.2d 561, (Calif.1962)

GENERAL PROCEDURES

Professionals tend to think of malpractice cases as involving sophisticated and complex aspects of health care. In fact, many malpractice cases involve the most common and frequent procedures, as illustrated by the following cases.

A minor male patient was hospitalized for a degenerative bone disease and placed in traction. The patient sustained a fracture that allegedly was caused by the manner in which the nurse pulled the sheets while changing the bed.

The jury was unable to reach a verdict for either side. Evidence was presented that indicated the leg may have been fractured prior to the change of bed linen.

Truluck v. Municipal Hosp. Bd. of City of Lakeland, 162 S.2d 549 (Fla. 1964)

A patient had her tonsils removed. Her physician ordered an ice collar to be applied to the patient's throat and instructed the nurse to change it from side to side every 2 hours.

The following day the physician noted that the patient could not close her right eye nor move the right side of her face.

Medical evidence indicated that the patient's injury was permanent and most likely resulted from the ice collar being left in place too long.

The jury awarded $30,000.

Daugherty v. North Kansas City Memorial Hospital, 570 S.W.2d 795 (Kansas 1978)

The patient had an elective laminectomy. An atrial catheter had been put in place prior to surgery as a preventive measure for air emboli. The catheter was left in place and the patient's vital signs were normal when she was transferred to the postoperative area.

No neurological exam was performed, vital signs were not taken, the patient's chart was not reviewed, and nurses were unaware of the atrial catheter. Nurses assumed the device was an IV. Later that day the patient's vital signs dropped significantly; no physician was notified.

The patient began vomiting and experiencing pain. The physician was not notified. The patient experienced a cardiac arrest. The physician who responded did not realize the device was a heart catheter. He injected all medications directly into the heart. The patient was brain dead and remained in this state for two months. During this time, negligent care of a balloon cushion on the cuff of a tracheostomy tube resulted in the woman's bleeding to death when the cuff worked its way through the back of the trachea and damaged an artery.

The patient's estate received $400,000 in damages.

Sanchez v. Bay General Hospital, 172 Cal.Rptr.342 (California 1981)

A 6-year-old girl was admitted to the hospital for eye surgery. In order to prevent her from touching her eye dressings, the nurse taped restraining boards to the child's arms. The child suffered an injury to one of her arms.

The court held that the jury was permitted to consider whether or not the injury was the result of a nurse applying the board too tightly.

Moore v. Halifax Hospital, Dist., 202 So.2d 568 (Fla. 1967)

The patient sometimes has difficulty proving that the nurses were negligent or deviated from a proper standard of care.

The patient had urinary problems that resulted from paraplegia and underwent extensive surgery. Postoperatively, he developed decubitus ulcers and, as a result, had to have his leg amputated. The nurses testified that pads and doughnut rolls were used to help prevent this problem.

The court held that the patient had failed to prove negligence. According to the evidence, a deviation from proper procedures had not occurred.

Glenn v. Kerlin, 305 So.2d 611, (La.1975)

The nurse's failure to call a formal cardiac arrest team for assistance was recently the subject of litigation.

The patient had thyroid surgery. Postoperatively the nurse detected signs of respiratory difficulty and responded immediately by summoning aid from physicians who were present and bringing a crash cart to the patient's bedside.

The patient alleged that the nurse had breached a reasonable standard of care by failing to invoke the "Dr. Quickstep" procedure.

The jury found no negligence; no additional benefit would result from a "Dr. Quickstep" call over the hospital's public address system.

Battles v. Aderhold, 430 So.2d 307 (La.1983).

A recent case illustrates the proof that is required when a particular procedure is not clearly within the province of nursing.

The patient, who was 9-months pregnant, was examined in her doctor's office and sent to the hospital. The nurses were busy with a complicated delivery when she arrived. Evidence was presented that some hospitals in the vicinity require a vaginal examination by a nurse on the arrival of a pregnant patient for delivery. The evidence did not clearly show that this was generally true and also whether this was necessary when the patient had been examined by the doctor immediately before entering the hospital.

The court said that whether or not the failure to examine by the nurses was negligent would be determined in the light of all the surrounding circumstances. The patient was not permitted to recover damages for the death of her stillborn baby.

Nelson v. Peterson, 542 P.2d 1075 (Utah 1975).

One procedure that is well recognized as the responsibility of the nurse is counting instruments and sponges during surgery.

Sometimes the patient attempts to extend the liability of the nurse to situations involving instrument counts in surgery. In fact, the foreign object cases are among those most frequently brought against nurses.

A patient underwent a radical mastectomy for removal of a malignant tumor. A Kelly clamp was left in the patient, undiscovered for 3 weeks. As a result, she suffered permanent injury to the nerves in her left shoulder area, which caused a limitation of motion. About 18 months later, the patient died of cancer. Her husband contended that the hospital, through its nurses, had a duty to count all surgical instruments used.

The court found that sponge and needle counts fell within the duty of nursing but that the evidence indicated that instrument counts were the surgeon's responsibility.

Mossey v. Mueller, 218 N.W. 2d 514, 63 Wis.2d 715 (1974).

If the procedure is one that is clearly within the duty of the nurse and the nurse completely fails to perform, it is much easier to prove breach of duty. The following case illustrates this concept. In addition, it illustrates a concept that will be explored in Chapter 10. The basic premise is that if a procedure, treatment, or nursing action is not charted, it is not considered to have been done.

A patient had a vagotomy; inadequate postoperative care resulted in serious brain damage. On the day of surgery, a nurse stuffed tissues into the incision when it was bleeding. Also, the physician ordered that the patient's temperature be taken every 15 minutes for 1 hour and every hour for 10 hours. The patient's temperature was recorded only four times during this time period.

The court felt that this was an accurate reflection of how poorly the order had been carried out. The patient developed a massive infection resulting in brain damage. The jury awarded the injured patient $800,000.

Robert v. Chodoff, 393 A.2d 853, (Pa. Super. 1978).

However, while timely observation of the patient is important, it is unreasonable to expect the nurse to be in constant attendance on the patient.

The patient had abdominal surgery and postoperatively had a binder applied.

The nurse, when changing the binder, decided that a clean one was needed. The patient felt a tickle in his throat and called the nurse back. She did not hear him and returned with a fresh binder in 4 to 5 minutes. While the nurse was gone the patient coughed, and the wound ruptured. Immediate surgery was required.

The court felt that the plaintiff did not meet the burden of proving that the binder would have contained the coughing or that the presence of the nurse

would have prevented the patient from coughing or would have prevented the
wound from opening once the coughing started.

Stone v. Sisters of Charity of House of Providence, 469 P.2d 229 (Wash. 1970)

FAILURE TO NOTIFY PHYSICIAN

A nurse may fail to notify the physician after making a patient observation, especially if the nurse does not realize that the observation is
significant. If a reasonable nurse would have realized the significance
of the observation, this failure is a breach of duty and will result in
liability.

If the nurse fails to notify the physician of a significant fact, she or he
may be held liable. This lack of communication will be observed in
many malpractice cases involving nursing and stands as one of the
most critical omissions by nurses.

An emergency room nurse failed to communicate to the physician that the
mother of two pediatric patients had told her of finding a tick on one of the
children. As a result, the physician was unable to diagnose the children's
elevated temperature as a symptom of Rocky Mountain spotted fever, and one
child died. The physician had asked the parents about ticks but was told
nothing.

The trial court dismissed the hospital, but on appeal, the court found that
the hospital could be held liable for the nurse's failure to communicate.

Ramsey v. Physicians Memorial Hospital, 373 A.2d 26 (Md.App.1977)

The significance of information obtained during an interview with
the patient and the need to communicate that information was also
illustrated in the following situation.

A 2-year-old patient's father told a nurse's aide that his son had possibly
ingested some aspirin hours previously. To other health care providers he
indicated only that the child had been nervous, unable to sleep and had
vomited.

The physician diagnosed croup and sent the child home. The next morning
the child had difficulty breathing. He was dead on arrival at the hospital.

The cause of death was salicylate poisoning.

The court found no negligence on the part of the defendants and believed the physician's testimony that he had specifically asked the father if any medication was given to the child and the father had responded negatively.

Johnson v. St. Paul Insurance Co., 219 So.2d 524 (La.1969)

A woman who was 7 months pregnant came to the hospital emergency room for admission. She was examined by a nurse who determined that the patient was having contractions. The nurse then telephoned the physician assigned to emergency room duty and gave him the information. The nurse and physician both testified that he had said to have the patient call her own family physician and see what he wanted her to do. The patient, however, testified that the nurse had told her to go and see her own doctor.

The court ruled that the jury should be given the opportunity to determine whose testimony was correct.

Childs v. Greenville Hospital Authority, 479 S.W.2d 399 (Texas 1972).

An emergency room nurse who refuses to call the physician to attend a patient may be liable if her failure to call results in injury to the patient.

A man called the hospital to ask if a doctor was available in the emergency room. He was assured that one was. On the patient's arrival, the nurse attempted to call the patient's physician who was out of town. The patient's wife testified that she then asked the nurse to call any available doctor. Her husband was in pain and vomiting. She said that the nurse refused to call another physician. The nurse testified that she had offered to call but that the patient stated he would wait until his own doctor returned. The jury believed the testimony of the wife and, further, that the nurse's failure to obtain medical attention for the patient was the cause of his death.

Carr v. St. Paul Fire and Marine Insurance Co., 384 F.Supp.821 (1974).

Many examples of failure to notify involve emergency department cases. However, this issue also arises with inpatient care.

A young man was admitted following an automobile accident. He was not seen by any physician from the time he left the emergency room on Saturday evening, May 15, 1971, until Monday morning, May 17, 1971.

The nurses notes indicated that he was seen by the nurses every 2 hours. The nurses were unable to reach the attending physician but did call the ER physician to report that the patient had back pain and had not been seen by a physician. The ER physician prescribed a sedative but did not see the patient.

On Sunday evening the nurses noted that the patient did not appear able to move his lower extremities.

According to hospital policy, if a patient was in need of a doctor, it was the duty of the floor nurse to call the admitting physician. If the admitting physician could not be located, it was the nurse's duty to call the physician covering for him, and if he could not be found, it was the nurse's duty to call the staff physician who was on call for that week. There is no evidence that the floor nurse attempted to contact any of these physicians except the attending physician.

Expert witnesses for the defense testified that plaintiff's paralysis occurred at the time of the accident. The jury found for the defense.

Sendejar v. Alice Physicians & Surgeons Hosp., Inc., 555 S.W.2d 884, (Texas 1977).

The experienced nurse will listen carefully to the patient who is requesting that a physician be notified about a change in the patient's own condition.

The patient had gall bladder surgery. The day before discharge. the patient's physician removed the T-tube.

Shortly after the physician left, the patient began to experience severe pain and inability to void. During the next ten hours the patient repeatedly asked for a doctor, was apprehensive of death, and requested a priest. The nurse had attempted to call the doctor one time but was unable to reach him and made no further effort to secure medical attention during the next 10 hours. The patient complained to the nurses some 13 times about his condition.

The patient's condition was now critical, and further hospitalization was necessary.

The court believed the hospital was liable for an inadequate effort in attempting to secure medical care for the patient.

Karrigan v. Nazareth Convent & Academy, Inc., 510 P.2d 190 (Kansas 1973).

VERBAL ORDERS

Another area of communication that presents liability problems for nursing is that of verbal orders.

Nurses frequently express concern regarding problems encountered with verbal orders. The concern is well justified, since most nurses have, at one time or other, encountered problems with these kinds of orders.

Verbal orders should be distinguished from telephone orders. Verbal orders are those given by a physician to a nurse when he or she is physically in the nurse's presence. The classic scene is the busy physician calling back over his or her shoulder an order for pain medication as he or she leaves the nurses' station. This is another area where miscommunication plays an important role in malpractice cases. If the nurse fails to hear correctly the order given, the potential for patient injury has occurred. It is extremely difficult to defend this situation in the courtroom. The jury may find it hard to understand why the physician did not take the time to write the order thereby ensuring that an accurate order was transmitted. Although there is nothing illegal about a verbal order per se, it does increase the probability of an error occurring. Every effort should be made to have verbal orders written by the physician before he or she leaves the nursing unit.

Most institutions have policies regarding the nurse's responsibility for verbal orders. These policies are often written to comply with state regulations. Many institutions require that verbal orders be countersigned by the physician within 24 hours. This signature authenticates the order. In most cases, the order will already have been implemented. Some institutions specify who may receive a verbal order. Often only registered nurses are permitted to take a verbal or telephone order.

Telephone orders are more easily justified, particularly if they involve emergencies. Many times a telephone order is needed at night for pain medication. Hospital nurses and physicians should strive to anticipate the possible need for such orders and to have the order put in writing when the physician is present.

In an emergency it is easier to understand the need for a telephone order. Therefore this is easier to defend from a legal standpoint as well. Telephone orders should be countersigned within 24 hours.

Nurses should take some elementary precautions when taking a telephone order. Misinterpretation of instructions is a common cause of error. This can be eliminated to some extent if the recipient of the order always repeats it to the physician. It should be clearly established what the order is and which patient is involved. The nurse should never assume that he or she and the physician are speaking about the same patient.

Often errors occur when patients with the same or similar names are admitted to the hospital at the same time. Clarification of the patient's identity is absolutely vital. Litigated errors range from those involving the wrong test or procedure performed on the patient, incorrect medications administered to the wrong patient, to surgical procedures performed on the wrong patient.

ORDERS NOT TO RESUSCITATE

Most verbal orders are written by the nurse and are subsequently countersigned by the physician according to hospital policy and state law. The only order that is given as a verbal order but often does not appear on the patient's medical record is the order not to resuscitate a particular patient.

Historically this problem has developed, in large part, because nurses have failed to assert their authority and refuse to accept this type of order. Nurses must recognize that it is clearly a medical responsibility to initiate this order. It must be a written order. Otherwise the nurse stands in legal jeopardy by failing to call for resuscitation on any patient. Without a written order, the nurse must respond as if no order exists. If no written order existed and the nurse failed to initiate resuscitation, she or he would be, in effect, making a medical decision. This would be tantamount to practicing medicine without a license. The commonly accepted practice of writing this order on the nursing care plan, which is not signed by the physician and which is subsequently destroyed, offers no legal protection for the nurse or the institution. The possibility exists that an action may be brought based on failure to respond to the emergency.

To protect the nursing staff personnel from the allegation of practicing medicine without a license, many hospitals have initiated policies requiring that the "no-code" order be written on the patient's chart. If this is not done, the nurse will automatically initiate the resuscitation.

In 1974 the American Medical Association proposed that decisions not to resuscitate be formally entered in the patient's progress notes. The fact that nurses continuously and currently question what should be done with an unwritten order not to resuscitate is a reflection of situations where the above recommendation has not been followed. Physicians who continue to insist that the order not to resuscitate or that the no-code order is not to be written are posing a hazard to patient care and exposing the nursing staff and themselves to potential liability. Verbal orders, unwritten orders to respond slowly, and notations on the patient's care plan, which are subsequently destroyed, are poor methods for directing the care of a patient.

For the legal protection of the medical staff, the physician should consult with members of the family and, if possible, with the patient as well before issuing a no-code order. This discussion should be documented in the patient's medical record before the writing of the order. The written order is the minimum requirement to protect the nurse from possible civil and criminal liability. The hospital should have a written policy relative to no-code orders, and it should be followed.

NURSES' RESPONSIBILITY FOR CARE PROVIDED BY OTHERS

A critical aspect of practice for the nurse relates to nursing responsibility for care provided by others. Included in this are judgments related to the ability of other health care professionals to perform their tasks in an acceptable manner. Since the nurse is often in the best position to observe the care rendered by others, it falls to the nursing profession to ensure that patients receive adequate and safe care.

One of the most sensitive issues in nursing is the nurse's responsibility when another nurse or a physician is rendering improper care.

Nurses often question what their legal duty is when such a situation occurs. Courts have recently offered some guidelines for the nursing profession in this area.

A man fell from a ladder at work and was taken to the hospital. He sustained severe fractures of his arm and subsequently had an amputation. Several nurses testified at trial that his injured arm was swollen, black, very edematous with foul-smelling drainage. He had a high temperature and was delirious. The attending physician was called but did not come. The nurse did not call another physician or the departmental chairman as she should have according to hospital policy.

The hospital and nurses were held liable for failing to provide medical treatment for the patient.

Utter v. United Hospital Center, 236 S.E.2d 313 (W.Va.1977).

If the nurse fails to identify a situation in which reasonable standards of care have been violated, the nurse may be liable as well as the other health care providers.

A patient suffered injuries to her throat, vocal cords, and voice box when the attending physician left an endotracheal tube in her throat for 5 days. Several hospital nurses testified that generally endotracheal tubes are left in place for no more than 3 days.

Neither the nurse nor the inhalation therapists at the hospital reported the deviation in treatment to their supervisors or to the treating physician.

Affirming the jury verdict, the court held that if a nurse or other hospital

employee fails to question a physician's orders when they are not in accord with standard medical practice and the omission results in injury to the patient, the hospital will be liable for the negligence of its employees.

Poor Sisters of St. Francis v. Catron, 435 N.E.2d 305 (Indiana 1982)

Following the birth of her child, the patient began to bleed. The nurse told the physician three times that the patient was bleeding excessively. The physician instructed the nurse to keep watching the patient.

Some time later the nurse checked the patient and found that she was bleeding. She did not call the physician because, in her opinion, he would not have come anyway.

Finally the physician was notified, but the patient died shortly after his arrival from a hemorrhage due to laceration of the cervix.

The appellate court ordered a new trial and stated that the evidence was sufficient to support a finding that the nurse who knew the mother was bleeding excessively was negligent in failing to report to her superior the circumstances of the mother's peril so that prompt and adequate measures could be taken to safeguard her life.

Goff v. Doctor's General Hospital, 333 P.2d 29 (Calif.1958).

In the previous case, the court pointed out that the nurses involved had sufficient time to report the facts and circumstances of the patient's peril to a superior in the hospital corporation for the purpose of taking prompt and adequate measures to safeguard the patient's life.

A difficult problem facing many nurses is the physician who fails to respond to a patient's complaint or responds only in a perfunctory manner. If the lack of response results in poor care for the patient, what can the nurse do? Legally, it is clear that courts will impose a duty on the nurse to advise hospital administrative officers when the patient's care is jeopardized.

A woman was admitted to the hospital for surgical correction of a hammertoe deformity. After surgery the tips of her toes were left exposed to facilitate postoperative care.

When she complained of severe pain, the nurses called this to the attention of the doctor. In response he ordered an x-ray but found nothing. After discharge, however, infection developed at the site of incision. When antibiotics failed to control the infection, the surgeon decided to debride the area. The procedure resulted in loss of tissue and additional bone from both toes.

The court found the nurses had satisfied their duty by informing the physician of the patient's complaint. However, the court added that failure of an attending physician to act on information from nurses regarding a patient's

complaint would warrant the nurses' advising hospital administrative officers
of the physician's refusal to act.

Brown v. St. John's Hospital, 367 N.E.2d 155 (1977).

SUMMARY

Once the standard of care has been established and a legal duty demonstrated on the part of the nurse, the injured party must prove that this duty has been breached.

Lawsuits in which nurses are named as defendants include injuries from falls, burns, and medication errors. Specific types of errors may be failure to follow proper procedures, failure to observe and intervene appropriately, and failure to communicate. Communication problems also occur when verbal orders are frequently given. A particularly troublesome problem for nurses is the verbal order not to resuscitate a patient. Nurses sometimes breach their duty to patients by failing to recognize that their responsibility includes monitoring the care provided by other health care providers. Nurses have both an ethical and a legal duty to ensure that patients receive quality care.

CHAPTER 5

CAUSATION

Often the injured party in a negligence suit has no difficulty proving that a duty has existed and that a breach of duty has occurred. But proving causation, the third criterion of negligence, can be difficult. *Causation* means that the injury must have been actually caused by the breach of duty. Legally, this concept of frequently divided into two subconcepts—*cause in fact* and *proximate cause*.

CAUSE IN FACT

Cause in fact means that the cause of the damage was the breach of duty. If it were not for the breach of duty, the injury would not have occurred. For example, in a surgical case in which a sponge is left in the patient's abdomen and the patient suffers subsequent abdominal damage, it may be easy to prove that the sponge was the cause of the damage that occurred.

The patient had a cesarean section. After the incision was closed one sponge was missing. X-ray films were taken, but the hospital failed to have them properly reviewed. The patient was sent home and 3 days later returned with symptoms. She also needed a third procedure to treat an abscess that had localized where the sponge had lodged.

The jury awarded the patient $36,000.

Kirshnan v. Garza, 570 S.W.2d 578 (Texas 1978).

PROXIMATE CAUSE

Proximate cause refers to legal cause; that is, what the courts will consider as a basis for liability. Proximate cause is much more difficult to understand and to prove. It encompasses the concept of foreseeability discussed previously (see Chapter 4). The basic question underlying proximate cause is a policy determination. How far does the liability of the defendant extend for the consequences following the negligent activity? The following famous case studied by law students throughout the country will serve as an illustration.

Mrs. Palsfrag was injured when some scales at the end of a train platform fell on her. The scales fell because a package of fireworks belonging to a passenger was dislodged from his arms when the railroad's employees attempted to assist the passenger who was hurrying to catch his train. When the package fell on the rails, it exploded, thus causing the scales to fall.

Mrs. Palsfrag won a $6,000 verdict against the railroad. However, on appeal this was overturned. The court felt that there was nothing in the situation to suggest to the most cautious mind that the parcel wrapped in newspaper would spread wreckage through the station. The proximate cause was too remote to be foreseeable.

Palsgraf v. Long Island R. Co., 248 N.Y. 339, 162 N.E.99 (Sup.Ct. of N.Y. 1928).

The New York court felt that the railroad employees in helping the passenger on the train could not have anticipated the harm that came to Mrs. Palsfrag as a result. That is, the element of foreseeability could not be carried to this extreme.

A recent malpractice case illustrates how far the courts have progressed in applying the concept of foreseeability.

A man was injured when his car collided with a serviceman's car. He sued the United States, charging that a government doctor had improperly given the serviceman an excessive supply of Valium and that this negligence caused the accident. The court concluded that the physician's negligence in prescribing the tranquilizer without checking the serviceman's known psychiatric history and condition was a proximate cause of the victim's injuries. A foreseeable consequence of prescribing Valium under such circumstances is that a patient with psychiatric problems will drink and that such a patient, when he has ingested Valium and alcohol, may injure others, as happened here.

Watkins v. U.S., 589 F.2d 214 (5th Cir.1979).

It is quite clear that in the 50-year interim between the *Palsfrag* and *Watkins* cases, courts have expanded the scope of the foreseeability doctrine.

Examples of this type of consideration regarding causation in the medical malpractice area are frequent.

A pedestrian sued the physician of the driver of a car that had injured him. The physician had advised his patient that he could safely drive although the patient had recently had a seizure. The court felt the physician might have been negligent in failing to diagnose and ascertain the cause of the first seizure and in failing to advise the driver of possible consequences.

Freese v. Lemmon, 210 N.W.2d 576 (Iowa 1973).

The *proximate cause* element has elicited some very interesting discussions involving an injury to a person and then subsequent malpractice adding to the injury. The question that arises is whether the initial accident or the subsequent medical care was the cause of the injury.

A 27-year-old seaman injured his eye while using a welding torch aboard a ship. The company that owned the ship was negligent in supervising the procedure. The seaman was hsopitalized for eye surgery. Although the seaman's eye had not been properly prepared for surgery, the ophthalmologist proceeded to operate, tearing the patient's iris and puncturing his lens and then failing to control postoperative bleeding. Each defendant, the company and the physician, paid the portion of damages caused by his own negligent conduct. Since the court felt the proximate cause element was satisfied, liability was imposed.

Penn Tanker Co., v. U.S., 310 F.Supp. 613 (1970).

Proximate cause is sometimes a consideration in accident cases where the injury suffered in the accident is compounded by medical malpractice.

The question of causation was discussed by the court at great length as one aspect of the following nursing malpractice case. Not only must it be shown by evidence that the nurse breached a duty but also that this conduct was a causative factor for the patient's injury.

Twin girls born prematurely were placed in incubators. Oxygen was ordered at 6 liters per minute for 12 hours and 4 liters per minute thereafter. The nurses continued the oxygen at 6 liters, however, and the infants both lost their vision; one became completely blind. At the time, a research study was being conducted at the National Institutes of Health to determine whether a high concentration of oxygen might cause blindness. One issue discussed at the trial was whether the infants might not have sustained the same damage if 4 liters had been used. In other words, was the use of 6 liters really the causative factor?

The trial court had dismissed the complaint against the hospital. The court of appeals sent the case back for a trial. The new trial was not a reported opinion.

Toth v. Community Hospital at Glen Cove, 239 N.E.2d 368 (New York 1968).

A premature infant suffered a cyanotic episode in the hospital nursery on the morning of her birth. The infant was mentally retarded and had cerebral palsy.

The parents alleged that the nurse caring for the infant negligently caused or exacerbated the cyanotic episode and that this episode contributed to the child's injuries.

The court held that evidence failed to establish causation in the negligence case against the nurse.

Lhotka v. Larson, 238 N.W.2d 870 (Minnesota 1976).

When an injured party is relying on an expert witness to prove proximate cause, the expert must be able to state with reasonable medical certainty that, in his or her professional opinion, the injuries complained of most probably resulted from the alleged negligence.

A man began experiencing severe chest pains. His wife called the hospital and was advised to bring him in. She did so, and a physician ordered an EKG. However, due to a faulty electrical outlet, the EKG machine failed to work. The physician directed that another EKG machine be found and then left the hospital. A second machine could not be found, and the patient's wife took him to a physician's office. He died while the EKG was being taken. The court held that the hospital could be held liable only if the hospital's negligence was a substantial factor in the patient's death.

Hamil v. Bashline, 392 A.2d 1280 (Pa.1978).

The issue being argued in the previous case was whether the hospital's negligence had to be the sole cause of death in order for the hospital to be liable.

Expert testimony is not always necessary to prove proximate cause as the following case which involves student nurses illustrates.

The patient was recovering from abdominal surgery. Two student nurses brought a portable x-ray machine into the patient's room, the wheels got tangled with electrical cords and caused the machine to fall on the patient. The patient said that he suffered pain in his arm and abdomen.

The appeals court held that the jury verdict for the patient was supported by the evidence presented without need for an expert witness.

Thomas Carter v. Anderson Memorial Hospital, South Carolina, No. 0360 (1985).

It is difficult to defend the nurse's failure to foresee a particular consequence when the death of a patient occurs *and the nurse's failure to foresee seems unreasonable.* If the failure to foresee is the direct cause of the patient's death, then legal causation will be established.

A 44-year-old woman was admitted to the hospital with abdominal pains. She had major surgery and needed oxygen postoperatively. She was temporarily disconnected from her oxygen supply while being moved from one room to an adjacent room. Unfortunately, after her bed was moved, it was discovered that the oxygen hookup could not be made, because the design of the outlet was different. By the time an oxygen supply was obtained, the patient had stopped breathing. Efforts to resuscitate were unsuccessful.

The court held the hospital negligent for failing to provide the patient with an adequate oxygen supply. Hospital personnel had failed to foresee that the consequence of an inadequate oxygen supply would be serious injury to the patient.

Bellaire v. Campbell, 510 S.W.2d 94 (Texas 1974).

A patient became a paraplegic following a femoral arteriogram. The jury found both the hospital employees and physicians did not meet their duty; however, the jury felt that their failure to meet their duty was not the cause of the disability.

Failure to take blood pressure and pulse as often as ordered, though below the standard of care, did not contribute to the cause of his paralysis. The physician's liability related to lack of an informed consent.

Scaria v. St. Paul Fire and Marine Insurance Co., 227 N.W.2d 647 (Wisc.1974).

Policies and procedures, as discussed in a previous chapter must be written in order to provide consistent, quality care to patients. Complying with these policies may be evidence of proper standards of care. Noncompliance with either a written standard or a commonly understood standard, such as handwashing, will result in liability if the effect of noncompliance is an injury to a patient and causation can be proven.

While the nurse may have acted contrary to hospital or customary policy or may have failed to follow a physician's order, this does not necessarily establish a causal connection.

The patient had a resection of the colon and a large incision in his lower abdomen. Eight days later while on the commode, his incision separated and an evisceration occurred. The patient alleged that the physician was negligent in suturing and the hospital nurses were negligent for failing to keep a binder around the abdomen.

The court held that causation was not established.
Jamison v. Debenham, 21 Cal.Rptr. 848 (1962).

The patient had a colon resection which subsequently separated and required re-operation.

As a result of erroneous instructions given by the Hospital's night charge nurse, the dietary department sent trays of solid food for all three of the patient's meals. The patient protested the food and requested that his physician be called. The nurse, who had been sent by a registry at the patient's request, stated that she did not want to bother the doctor and assured him that the food would not have been sent to his room if it was not all right for him to eat.

A number of possible causative factors were placed into evidence. The patient failed to prove that giving him solid food contrary to doctor's orders was a cause in fact of the opening in the mesentery.
Lenger v. Physician's General Hospital, Inc., 455 S.W.2d 730 (Texas 1970).

The hospital's duty to foresee must also be established by the evidence if the issue involves hospital liability.

The patient's treating physician had ordered the patient to be transferred from a ward to a private or semiprivate room. The patient was struck by a chair thrown at him by a mental patient who shared the same room.

The court held that the possible breach by the hospital of its duty to carry out the physician's order was not the proximate cause of the patient's injuries since the hospital could not have foreseen the assault as a result of the breach.
Burns v. Forsyth County Hospital Authority 344 S.E.2d 839 (N.C.App. 1986).

The following case further illustrates the importance of causation.

A patient was hospitalized for acute urinary retention. He had a catheter inserted, and an order was left by the physician to measure the urinary output. The patient alleged that the hospital was negligent in failing to sufficiently record his urinary output.

The court held that the patient had the burden of proving that the hospital failed to comply with standards of proper care. In this case no evidence existed that causation would have been established as to subsequent injuries even if failure to measure the urine adequately was proven. Therefore, no hospital liability resulted.
Ybarra v. Cross, 317 N.E.2d 621 (Illinois 1974).

INFECTIONS

In the nursing malpractice realm, many of the cases in which causation is difficult to establish involve infections. A patient who is admitted to a hospital and subsequently develops a serious infection may believe that a negligent act was the cause of his infection. But this must be proven, and often this is difficult. The fact that an infection occurs after surgery does not necessarily mean that hospital personnel were negligent.

A patient developed an acute infection at the site of her incision resulting in further hospitalization.

The jury awarded $1000 against the physician defendant but held that the hospital was not liable. There was no evidence to support the allegation that the infection occurred because of the nurses' failure to observe a proper standard of care.

Brown v. St. John's Hospital, 367 N.E.2d 155 (Illinois 1977).

The patient may be able to prove that proper aseptic technique was not practiced.

In an action against an infirmary and a physician to recover damages for the death of a young girl who died from lockjaw following an appendectomy, evidence as to the unclean condition of the floor, improper sterilization of instruments, insufficient heating of the patient's room, and improper care of her wound after surgery were admissible to show causation.

Woodlawn Infirmary v. Byers, 216 Ala. 210, 112 So. 831 (1927).

The previous case decided in 1927 is applicable in law today and has been used as a precedent in similar cases.

If the hospital does not take adequate measures to protect against cross contamination between patients, causation can be proven more easily.

A patient contracted a staphylococcal infection while in the hospital. He was able to prove that his roommate had had a similar infection and that the hospital personnel did not protect against cross contamination by washing their hands between caring for the two patients.

The jury returned a verdict for $67,839.97

Helman v. Sacred Heart Hospital, 62 Wash.2d 136, 381 P.2d 605 (1963).

A nurse erroneously gave a lactating mother the wrong infant to nurse. The infant had impetigo, which was subsequently diagnosed in the woman's own child, who died a few days later. An award of $6,000 was made.
   Criss v. Argehes Hospital Association of Los Angeles 13 Cal.App.2d 142, 56 P.2d 1274 (1936).

Although the previous case was decided in 1936, the court would apply the same principles of proper identification today.

Even if negligence on the part of hospital employees cannot be proven in any other way, failure to isolate an infected patient, either from other patients or employees, can constitute negligence. Causation may be shown by the simple fact that isolation did not occur, as in these cases.

A baby girl born prematurely at a U.S. Naval hospital developed osteomyelitis in the hips as a result of a staphyloccal infection she acquired in the hospital. The baby's parents recovered damages for the injuries and deformity the osteomyelitis produced in their child. One nurse in the nursery had had a positive nose culture for staphylococcus. Evidence indicated that she had not undergone a physical examination when reporting for duty at this hospital, although she had had an examination shortly before leaving her previous post of duty.
   Kapushinsky v. U.S. 248 F.Supp. 732 (South Carolina 1966).

A baby died from tuberculosis after being cared for in the hospital nursery by a nurse with the disease. The nurse had a cough, but neither she nor her fellow workers had reported it. The court held that it had been negligent of the hospital to allow the nurse to work.
   Taajc v. St. Olaf's Hospital, 271 N.W. 109 (Minn.1937).

This principle requires hospitals to monitor the health of their own employees.

Many hospitals now employ specialized nurses trained to handle infection control problems and to ensure that proper procedures are followed. The infection control nurse is part of an infection control team that may include a physician and a committee; the team reviews policies and procedures within the institution to ensure compliance with proper standards.

Noncompliance with infection control policies and procedures may result in liability for the institution and its employees. However, evidence must indicate that noncompliance is a causative factor in the injury.

One of the first skills taught to all health care providers is that of proper handwashing. If this basic procedure is not followed, liability may result.

A patient experienced a *Staphylococcus aureus* infection at the site of an intravenous cannula in her right arm. The patient alleged that the hospital nurses did not wash their hands in her room before inserting the intravenous cannula, that they did not properly disinfect her skin, and that the intravenous cannula had been unsterile.

Medical experts testified that there was no way to sterilize skin completely and that in a certain number of cases, infections will occur despite the best possible technique and without any negligence. The hospital and nurses were not held liable.

Sommers v. Sisters of Charity of Providence, 561 P.2d 603 (Ore.1977).

The staff nurse has a duty to communicate with the institution and physician regarding all patients with infections. It is his or her duty to keep the infection control nurse informed as to possible cases of infection.

A hospitalized patient became infected with a contagious disease from exposure to a hospitalized roommate. He was permitted to sue the physician for failure to provide notice to the hospital so that precautions could be taken.

Gill v. Hartford Accident and Indemnity Company, 337 S.2d 420 (FLa.1976).

A patient suffered an infection following cataract removal resulting in removal of his right eye.

Testimony at the trial indicated that the nurse had failed to call the intern or physician when the patient began to experience pain and that the infection was possibly caused by one of three instruments used in the eye operation.

The court held that sufficient evidence existed for the jury to find the hospital guilty of negligence, which was the proximate cause of the patient's injuries.

Yeates v. Harms, 401 P.2d 659 (Kansas 1965).

These cases emphasize again that a deficiency in communication is often the cause of a malpractice claim.

When an infection results from use of a nonsterile hypodermic needle for an injection, or improper procedures causation is more easily proven, since the infection usually occurs at the site of the injury.

The patient testified that a nurse entered her room and gave her an injection without preparing her skin with an alcohol sponge. The patient further testified that her thigh began to hurt immediately. A few days later, an abscess had formed. The nurse was found negligent for not properly cleaning the skin according to the usual standard of care.

Kalmus v. Cedars of Lebanon Hospital, 132 Cal.App.2d 243, 281 P.2d 872 (1955).

A 76-year-old patient, following implant of a hip prosthesis, developed an infection after the surgical wound was opened during the therapy session.

The wound was exposed to unsterilized bath water and was covered with an unsterilized towel.

The jury awarded the patient $75,000.

St. Paul Fire and Marine Insurance Co. v. Prothro, 590 S.W.2d 35 (Ark. 1979).

Sometimes expert testimony is needed to prove the element of causation in an infection case.

The patient received an injection while hospitalized and stated that her arm became swollen the next day at the site of the injection. About 1 month later, she developed an infection.

The court felt that in view of the patient's having been in and out of the hospital during the 1-month period, there could have been other factors causing the infection. Mere occurrence of an infection following an injection is not enough evidence to prove negligence in the administration of the injection particularly when a lapse of time has occurred before the development of symptoms.

Rohdy v. James Decker Memorial Hospital 170 N.W.2d 67 (Mich.1969).

Expert testimony is unnecessary in an infection case when the circumstances indicate that the exercise of common knowledge and experience of reasonable persons would allow them to make an assessment and evaluation of professional conduct.

A patient with psoriasis was admitted to the hospital for a liver biopsy. The physician later notified the patient that the needle used at the biopsy might have been used on another patient who had infectious hepatitis. The patient was then required to undergo a painful series of gamma globulin injections.

These injections necessitated the discontinuance of other therapy for her psoriasis and that condition worsened.

The patient was awarded $16,000. The court held that where sterile and nonsterile needles were stored in the same cabinet, expert testimony was not essential to show negligence.

Suburban Hospital v. Hadary, 322 A.2d 258, (Maryland 1974).

Situations not requiring expert testimony could fall under the doctrine of res ipsa loquitur.

AIDS

The appearance of acquired immune deficiency syndrome has raised a number of legal, ethical, and moral dilemmas in society. As an infectious disease, AIDS cases will face the same difficulty with legal causation issues that have been described previously. An AIDS patient alleging that the disease was contracted in the health care setting through blood transfusions or contact with health care providers who are AIDS carriers will have to prove that a failure to follow a reasonable standard of care has caused his or her disease. The elimination of possible sexual contacts or intravenous drug use that may have been the causal factor could prove to be quite difficult. While it is likely that a great deal of litigation will occur in regard to various AIDS issues, the issues of legal culpability may be difficult to resolve in favor of the claimant.

RES IPSA LOQUITUR

Because causation is the most difficult element of negligence to prove, courts have sometimes resorted to the theory of res ipsa loquitur to satisfy the need of the injured party who is unable to prove negligence or determine which of several named defendants was the actual person responsible for the injury.

The three conditions for the application of res ipsa loquitur are: (1) the injury would ordinarily not occur unless someone were negligent; (2) the instrumentality causing the injury was within the exclusive control of the defendant; and (3) the incident was not due to any voluntary action on the part of the plaintiff.

When the court applies the three conditions of res ipsa loquitur, a presumption of negligence is raised if no other explanation exists. In fact, the literal translation of res ipsa loquitur is "the thing speaks for itself." Usually in a negligence case, negligence is not presumed. Rather, it is presumed that ordinary care has been used, and the person charging negligence must prove otherwise. The doctrine of res ipsa loquitur allows proof of negligence by circumstantial evidence when direct evidence of the cause of injury is primarily within the knowledge of the defendant.

The doctrine of res ipsa loquitur stems from an old English case as follows.

A passerby in the street was hurt when a barrel of flour fell from a second floor warehouse window. The injured party was unable to prove which of the employees inside the building had actually allowed the flour to fall. Res ipsa loquitur was applied to hold the employer liable.

Byrne v. Broadle, 1863 2H. & C. 722, 159 Eng.Rep. 299.

These conditions were applied by the court to the first malpractice case involving the doctrine of res ipsa loquitur in 1944.

A man who had had an appendectomy testified that before surgery, he had never had pain in or injury to his right arm and shoulder, but when he awakened from surgery he felt a sharp pain and subsequently could not lift his arm at all. The plaintiff sued all those involved—his attending physician, his surgeon, the anesthestist, three nurses, and the owner of the hospital.

The court held that the plaintiff was obviously unable to prove which of the defendants was negligent but that negligence had obviously occurred and the doctrine of res ipsa loquitur could be applied. Therefore, all defendants were held equally liable.

Ybarra v. Spangard, 146 P.2d 982 (Calif.1944) aff'd 154 P.2d 687.

The court decided to allow the doctrine res ipsa loquitur to be applied largely because the plaintiff was unconscious at the time of the incident. Therefore, it was impossible, without the effective testimony of those present, for the patient to prove who was at fault.

If the three conditions for res ipsa loquitur are met, the injured party can recover damages, and the defendants as a group can then determine among themselves who was negligent and should actually pay the judgment.

If an injured party was unconscious at the time of the injury as in a surgical case, it is obviously extremely difficult for the plaintiff to prove what actually occurred.

A rongeur broke off while a surgeon was manipulating it in a patient's spinal column during a surgical procedure.

The court held that where an unconscious or helpless plaintiff suffers an admitted mishap unrelated to the scope of surgery and *res ipsa loquitur* applies, the burden of proof shifts to all those who owed the patient a duty of care or a duty not to furnish a defective instrument.

Anderson v. Somberg, 67 N.J. 291, 338 A.2d 1, cert. denied, 423 U.S. 929 (1975).

If the injury is such that it was probably the result of negligence and the defendants are probably the persons responsible, the doctrine may be involved, as in this case.

A healthy 6-year-old boy was admitted to the hospital for corrective eye surgery. While in the operating room, he suffered cardiac arrest and brain damage, resulting in his becoming a spastic quadraplegic, blind, and mute. Testimony in the case indicated the following: 90 percent of deaths resulting from cardiac arrest during surgery occur because of faulty intubation; if the open-heart massage had been performed within 3 minutes of the heart's stopping, brain damage would not have occurred; an elevated temperature and apprehension increase the risk of complication; the child was very agitated before surgery and had an elevated temperature; the preoperative record of the patient's temperature had been altered to reflect a normal temperature. The court felt that all this evidence would permit the doctrine of *res ipsa loquitur* to be applied. Damages of $4 million were awarded.

Quintal v. Laurel Grove Hospital, 397 P.2d 161, 41 Cal.Rptr. 577 (1965).

Although the circumstances under which a patient has sustained an injury have, in some cases, warranted the application of res ipsa loquitur to actions in which nurses were defendants, these cases have also involved other defendants.

When a woman died after a hysterectomy and a large number of violations of proper standards of care by the hospital employees including nurses who cared for her during her stay in the hospital were later discovered, the court allowed the application of *res ipsa loquitur.*

Cline v. Lund, 31 Cal.App.3d 755, 107 Cal.Rptr. 629 (1973).

The rationale for res ipsa loquitur has been extended over the years to apply to situations in which injury occurs to a portion of the patient's body outside the field of treatment.

In an action against a nurse and the hospital, the plaintiff alleged that she had developed gangrenous sores as a result of straps being too tightly applied during surgery.

The court held that the evidence presented an issue for the jury as to whether the defendants were guilty of negligence that proximately contributed to the injury.

Palmer v. Clarksdale Hospital, 213 Miss. 601, 57 So.2d 473 (1952).

A patient suffered paralysis in her foot following hip surgery. Evidence indicates two possible causes of the nerve damage, both of which resulted from negligence of hospital employees. The elastic bandage may have been wrapped too tightly, or the traction device may not have been monitored properly so that the weight of the patient's leg itself could have caused the paralysis. The court felt that the jury should be allowed to decide this case using the doctrine of *res ipsa loquitur.*

Adams v. Leidholdt, 563 P.2d 15, (Colo.App.1977).

Res ipsa loquitur has also been applied in situations in which the patient has been heavily sedated but is not unconscious.

When a patient admitted to the hospital in a diabetic coma with severe pneumonia regained consciousness, she found that she had burns on her body from an unknown cause. She was allowed to recover damages under *res ipsa loquitur* when evidence was presented that she did not have any burns on arrival at the hospital. The hospital argued that it was unlikely the burns could have been caused by any treatment the physician had ordered, but the court ruled in the patient's favor.

West Coast Hospital v. Webb, 52 So.2d 803 (Fla.1951).

Res ipsa loquitur may be applied when hospital equipment is an element in the incident.

When a nurse pulled the patient's bed away from the wall and the bed leg collapsed, *res ipsa loquitur* was applied to allow the plaintiff to recover damages. There was no evidence as to the cause of collapse of the bed leg. The court held that *res ipsa loquitur* would be permissible to raise an inference of negligence.

Mapp v. Cedars of Lebanon Hospital, 249 So.2d 521 (Fla.App.1971).

Res ipsa loquitur applies normally when a layperson is considered capable of determining from common experience that a certain event would not have occurred unless someone were negligent. This is a very important legal principle, since it can eliminate the need for expert testimony on the issue of causation.

Some courts exhibit reluctance to apply the doctrine of res ipsa loquitur and, therefore, do not eliminate the need for expert testimony in all situations as illustrated by the following case.

A 75-year-old patient claimed injury during administration of a soap-suds enema given while she was hospitalized. The patient said that the nurse was in a hurry, and, as the liquid began to flow into her rectum, she felt as if she were being pinched. A large hemotoma developed and had to be removed surgically.

The patient asked that res ipsa loquitur be applied. The court felt that expert testimony was necessary and that res ipsa loquitur was not applicable.

Kelly v. Hartford Casualty Insurance Co., 271 N.W.2d 676 (Wisc.Sup.Ct.1978).

Some courts believe that res ipsa loquitur should not be applied to cases involving health care providers because of the fact that, generally, the occurrence of an unfortunate event is not sufficient to authorize an inference of negligence. Rather, these courts believe breach of duty and causation must be specifically proven by expert testimony.

A 22-year-old woman exhibited signs of toxemia during pregnancy and had a cesarean section. The mother recovered, but during the next few days, the baby began to show signs of jaundice. It was determined that she had obstructive jaundice, and surgery became necessary. The patient was connected to a Bird respirator in the recovery room. A short time later one of the nurses noticed that she no longer heard the sound of the respirator in operation. Thereupon, she administered heart massage and another nurse called for a physician. The nurse accidentally called the emergency room rather than the cardiac arrest team.

The court felt that expert testimony was necessary to prove negligence.

Hill v. Hospital Authority of Clarke County, 137 Ga.App. 623, 224 S.E.2d 739 (1976).

A patient was admitted for bypass surgery and placed in a surgical intensive care unit. A few days later he was moved to a secondary cardiac surgical care facility. He died two days later of a pulmonary embolism.

His wife filed suit alleging that placement of a seriously ill cardiac patient in a general hospital room lacking proper facilities for cardiac monitoring was contrary to accepted medical practice for treatment of cardiac patients.

The court held for the defense because the patient was unable to provide an expert indicating that lack of postoperative monitoring caused the patient's death.

Devine v. Queen's Medical Center, 574 P.2d 1352 (Hawaii 1978).

If all the facts concerning an injury are known and testified to by witnesses at the trial, then the conditions for application of res ipsa loquitur are not met.

INJECTIONS

An injection administered incorrectly to a patient may result in a case being initiated against nursing staff and the hospital. These cases are typical examples where the res ipsa loquitur theory is applicable.

Nurse educators are well aware of the need to teach beginning nursing students the proper method of administering injections. There are few nurses who do not remember their first injection and the anxiety they experienced in using a needle.

The typical injection case dealing with causation involves a sciatic nerve injury resulting in foot drop.

When a sciatic nerve injury occurred to a patient after he received an injection, res ipsa loquitur was applied to allow the patient to recover damages from the hospital and the nurse.

Edgar v. Paris Hospital, Inc., 57 Ill.2d 298, 312 N.E.2d 259 (1974).

When there is direct evidence of the precise cause of an injury involving an injection, res ipsa loquitur will not be applied. Res ipsa loquitur is used as an inference of negligence. It shifts the burden of proof to the defendant to show that no negligence occurred. If evidence exists showing why the injury occurred, then the theory of res ipsa loquitur is not needed.

A 4-year-old boy received an injection of penicillin in a physician's office. He immediately complained of pain in his left leg and foot. The child later suffered gangrene and subsequent amputation of part of his foot. It was alleged that the physician failed to provide proper follow-up care once the injury became apparent.

On the issue of the negligent administration on the injection, the court held that res ipsa loquitur inappropriate since evidence indicated exactly how the injury had occurred.

DeLaughter v. Womack, 164 So.2d 762 (Miss.1964).

A 7-year-old child was admitted to the hospital for drainage of an abscessed appendix. The physician wrote an order for an antibiotic to be administered by injection. The nurse administered the injection and damaged the sciatic nerve. The child permanently lose the normal use of her right foot.

While the court held the nurse to be negligent, on the theory of specific negligence, it did not allow the application of *res ipsa loquitur* because there was no uncertainty as to the cause of the injury.

Bernardi v. Community Hospital Association, 443 P.2d 708 (Colorado 1968).

Some courts refuse to applx *res ipsa loquitur* to injection cases because of the belief that expert testimony must be given to show some variance from a recognized standard of care that produced the injury.

A patient had a gastric resection. Immediately after receiving a postoperative injection, she experienced a burning sensation at the site of the injection. The court held that undesirable and unforeseen reactions could occur from a number of causes other than negligence. Therefore, *res ipsa loquitur* was inapplicable to hold the nurse liable.

Bialer v. St. Mary's Hospital, 427 P.2d 957 (Nevada 1967).

Two recent malpractice cases held that the jury should be permitted to decide whether professional negligence had, in fact, occurred.

The patient was admitted for delivery of her baby. She was given three injections. Subsequently she experienced an infection at the site of the injection and gangrene.

At the conclusion of the presentation of the patient's case, the defendants moved for a dismissal that was granted by the judge.

On appeal, the court ruled that the case should be decided by the jury. This decision was based largely on a nurse expert witness who testified as to causation and standard of care.

Tripp v. Humana, Inc., 474 So.2d 88 (Alabama 1985).

The patient underwent a surgical procedure. Following the procedure, a nurse employed by the hospital administered an injection to the patient about 3 or 4 inches above her knee. She suffered an injury to a nerve in her thigh.

The appeals court held that the jury should determine if negligence had occurred.

Holbrooks v. Duke University, Inc., 305 S.E.2d 69 (N.C.App. 1983).

In a few states where the doctrine of res ipsa loquitur cannot be applied in medical malpractice cases, the court may allow a statutory presumption of negligence.

The patient received an injection of Vistaril into the deltoid muscle. She alleged that the drug should have been administered into her hip.

The appeals court held the trial court erred by refusing to instruct the jury regarding the statutory presumption of negligence.

Little v. Arbuckle Memorial Hospital Board of Control, 665 P.2d 1227 (Okla. App. 1983).

SUMMARY

Once a breach of duty is established, the plaintiff must prove causation. The concept of causation means that the injury must have been caused by the breach of duty; otherwise the injury would not have occurred. Proximate cause is a policy determination by the courts as to how far liability should extend, the key factor being foreseeability. Infection cases present an example of the difficulty in proving causation. Because of this difficulty in proof, courts have permitted the theory of res ipsa loquitur to be applied. This shifts the burden to the defendant to show that negligence did not take place.

CHAPTER **6**

DAMAGES

For the plaintiff to recover damages in a malpractice action, actual damages must have occurred to the injured party. The basic purpose of awarding damages in a negligence action is compensatory rather than punitive. The goal is to restore the injured party to his or her original position in so far as this is possible. In most cases it is impossible to restore the patients to their original physical condition. Therefore financial damages are awarded. Punishment of the defendant is not the aim of the damage award.

GENERAL DAMAGES

The injured party may recover for damages that are inherent in the injury itself. These damages are known as general damages. General damages include pain and suffering (past, present, and future) and any disfigurement or disability.

Although expert testimony may be helpful in establishing the award for pain and suffering, it is not necessary. In the absence of any explicit evidence showing pain, the jury may infer such pain, if the injury is such that the jury in its common experience knows it to be normally accompanied by pain.

A patient had a prescription incorrectly filled at a hospital pharmacy. For a 26-day period the patient took an antibiotic (Prostaphlin) rather than the prescribed cardiac medication (Pronestyl). The patient had visited a physician complaining of angina, extreme fatigue, and arrhythmia.

The patient stated that his heart palpations continued during the time he was taking the wrong drug. However, there was no evidence that the patient had sustained any physical injury to the heart as a result of the improperly filled prescription.

The court stated that mental anguish was grounds for financial recovery by the patient.

McLean v. U.S. 613 F.2d 603. (Florida 1980).

A minor has been permitted to recover damages for pain and suffering even though she could not remember the illness.

Shortly after a child's birth and discharge from the hospital, she developed symptoms of a gastrointestinal disorder that caused her recurrent distress throughout the entire first year of her life. At various times she suffered projectile vomiting, severe diarrhea, dehydration, cramps, and shock. At times the dehydration was severe enough to require the introduction of intravenous feeding devices. When she was 5 months old, the attending physician concluded that her condition had so deteriorated as to jeopardize her life.

Laboratory tests of her stools at that time indicated the presence of the bacteria Salmonella, and her physician decided that the Samonella infection was the primary cause of her symptoms. Following treatment for salmonellosis, she gradually improved. Ultimately, she recovered completely and suffered no permanent disability.

The court held that even though the child (who was now 6 years old) was healthy, happy, and could not even remember her illness or pain, she was permitted to recover damages against both the doctor and the hospital. The court pointed out that infants can feel pain and discomfort even if they do not know the source of it.

Copelouto v. Kaiser Foundation Hospitals, 7 Cal.App.3d 889, 500 P.2d 880, 103 Cal.Rptr. 856 (1972).

SPECIAL DAMAGES

In addition, the injured party may recover damages for all losses and expenses incurred as a result of the injury. These expenses include medical bills and lost wages (past, present, and future).

EMOTIONAL DAMAGES

Emotional damages are also compensable but generally only when the allegation of emotional harm occurs in conjunction with other apparent physical harm to the injured party. Anxiety is usually a compensable element of recovery of damages if attached to a claim for actual injury.

A pregnant woman noted vaginal bleeding and called her physician. He advised her to take aspirin and a shot of whiskey. A few days later she visited his office because of cramps and continued bleeding. Her physician diagnosed a bladder infection and prescribed medication accordingly.

A week later the bleeding had become quite heavy and cramps and pain had increased. She went to the hospital where the physician examined her, reaffirmed his diagnosis, and advised her to go home.

Two days later she became violently ill, suffered convulsions, and continued to bleed. A short while later the child was born. No anesthesia was administered, no episiotomy performed, and no member of the physician's group was present at birth.

The baby weighed 3 pounds 6 ounces. The baby girl was cyanotic and suffered central nervous system difficulties.

The court held that the mother could recover damages from her emotional upset caused by anxiety over possible harm to her child even though the child recovered and had no permanent injury.

Friel v. Vineland Obstetrical and Gynecological Professional Association, 400 A.2d 147 (N.J. Super.Ct. 1979).

Recently courts have considered cases for recovery based on the concept of wrongful birth. A recovery for mental and emotional damages in these cases is usually permitted.

A child was born with Down's syndrome to a 38-year-old woman. The husband and wife asserted that if the physician had recommended amniocentesis, which would have revealed the fetal problem in this high-risk group, they would have opted for abortion.

The court allowed the suit for mental and emotional damage but not for expenses in rearing the child. The justices concluded that "one of the most deeply held beliefs of our society is that life—whether experienced with or without a major physical handicap—is more precious than non-life." There is no injury suffered by being brought into existence.

Berman v. Allan, N.J.Super.Ct., June 26, 1979.

In some states the civil action of outrage is compensable. This occurs where no physical injury is present but some deliberate, inexcusable behavior occurred that would be expected to cause emotional suffering.

A premature infant was transferred soon after birth to a larger hospital. Two days later the baby died. A hospital employee phoned the mother to report the

death. The parents then attempted to confirm the death and claim the body but could not recover the body for three weeks.

The court held that the long delay was not deliberate nor had the body been mishandled. Therefore, outrage had not been proven.

> Muniz v. United Hospital Medical Center-Presbyterian Hospital. 370 A.2d 76 (N.J.Super.Ct. 1976).

A woman gave birth prematurely to a stillborn child. Six weeks later she returned to the hospital to question the burial of the infant. A laboratory employee handed the mother a gallon container with the shrivelled body of her baby floating in formaldehyde. After this experience, the patient suffered nightmares, insomnia, and depression. Eventually she needed psychiatric treatment.

She was awarded $175,000.

> Johnson v. Woman's Hospital, 527 S.W.2d 133 (Tenn.App.1975).

The courts have yet to define fully the parameters of liability for emotional anguish where no physical harm has occurred. Since emotional harm is subjective by definition, it is sometimes difficult to evaluate the degree of emotional harm suffered.

For a plaintiff to recover damages based on the tort of outrage, he or she must be an immediate family member of the person and emotional distress must be inflicted intentionally or recklessly. In addition, the defendant's conduct must be outrageous and severe, and such conduct must have resulted in severe emotional distress to the plaintiff.

A husband filed a claim based on outrage arising out of his wife's death.

He claimed that the hospital and his wife's physician's were reckless and that it was outrageous in that plaintiff was required to witness the terrifying agony and explicit pain and suffering of his wife while she proceeded to die in front of his eyes. He alleged that he was helpless because of his inability to secure any medical treatment for his wife and that such conduct caused him severe mental anguish resulting in physical symptoms such as insomnia and headache.

The appeals court held that the plaintiff had a cause of action for outrage that was sufficient to present to a jury.

> Grimsby v. Samson, 530 P.2d 291 (Wash.1975).

A pharmacist was found liable for the mental anguish of a woman who witnessed her child's adverse reaction to a medication overdose that resulted after the pharmacist increased the dosage on a prescription. Because the pharmacist assumed that the prescription was for an adult and that the physician had mistakenly written the dosage as 1 milligram, the pharmacist rewrote the prescription to read 10 milligrams. In fact, the prescription was for a 4-month-old child, who suffered a severe reaction to the medication and was rushed to the hospital. The child survived with no apparent permanent injury, but a jury awarded the mother damages for the mental anguish she experienced.

The Arkansas Supreme Court upheld the award, ruling that there is a right to recover when intentional or willful misconduct results in mental anguish even when there are no physical consequences. In this case, as the court pointed out, the pharmacist received the prescription from a woman who was holding a baby, did not ask the patient's age, and did not contact the prescribing physician. The court therefore concluded that the jury had substantial evidence to conclude that the misconduct was willful rather than negligent.

Lou v. Smith, 685 S.W.2d 809 (Ark. 1985)

The cases dealing with recovery of damages based on mental anguish in the malpractice realm are based on previous case law precedent dealing with mental anguish in the area of general negligence.

A mother whose child was struck by the defendant's vehicle while she observed the accident suffered a severe emotional disturbance.

The court allowed recovery for mental anguish based on the mother's proximity to the scene of the accident and the nature of the mother-child relationship.

Dillon v. Legg, 441 P.2d 912, 69 Cal.Rptr. 72,68 Cal.2d 728 (1968).

The following year California courts extended this rule to apply for recovery of emotional damages to a mother who did not witness the accident but came to the scene shortly after.

The issue of spouses and relatives being permitted to recover for witnessing the suffering of a relative has recently been addressed in a New York case.

A patient's husband and daughter-in-law were in the patient's room when she received a transfusion of the wrong type of blood.

The patient subsequently died, and the husband filed a claim for medical malpractice. An additional claim from the daughter-in-law listed mental anguish from witnessing the event.

The court ruled that the daughter-in-law was a participant in the transfusion because she assisted her mother-in-law during the hospitalization. Because she played an active role, the court pointed out that she may have suffered mental trauma.

Lafferty v. Manhasset Medical Center Hospital, 425 N.Y.S.2d 244 (New York Sup.Ct.1980).

Other jurisdictions have also allowed recovery of damages for emotional distress in the general negligence area.

A funeral director misled the plaintiff regarding the funeral of his father and stepmother who were killed in a car accident. The funeral director told the plaintiff that it was necessary to have sealed caskets because of the odor and condition of the bodies.

This was a false statement and caused the plaintiff severe emotional distress. Shortly thereafter, he experienced a myocardial infarction. The plaintiff requested $80,000 in damages. The appeals court held that a sufficient basis for the suit existed.

Meyer v. Nottger. 241 N.W.2d 911 (Iowa 1976).

While this rationale for recovery has thus far been accepted in only a minority of jursidictions, it is clear that in many medical malpractice cases emotional distress could be an alleged element of damages.

Where conduct exceeds that which a reasonable person could be expected to endure and serious emotional injury results, there is societal interest in allowing recovery of damages, both to compensate the victim and to delineate the boundaries of permissible activity.

Sometimes the cases have involved patients with the diagnosis of cancer who were misdiagnosed and did not actually have cancer as they subsequently discovered.

The claim that a cancer phobia occurred because a physician had acted negligently did not result in an award of damages in the following case.

A patient developed cancer phobia after an intern negligently inserted a catheter. The catheter broke leaving two pieces in the patient's body that could not be found. The patient believed that the portions of the catheter remaining would cause cancer to develop in the future.

The appeals court held that even though ihe negligent action caused the phobia, to allow the patient to recover damages would place too unreasonable a burden on health care providers. The trial court had awarded the patient $45,000 for pain, suffering, and disability.

Howard v. Mt. Sinai Hospital, Inc., 219 N.W.2d 576 (Wisc.1974).

A misdiagnosis may be accepted as a basis for a claim of emotional distress.

A woman went to her health maintenance organization for a routine physical examination. A staff physician examined her and told her incorrectly that she had syphilis. She was advised to tell her husband of the diagnosis and was administered massive doses of penicillin. Her husband underwent a blood test establishing that he did not have syphilis. The diagnosis resulted in a divorce.

The husband sued asking damages for mental suffering and medical expenses incurred for counseling in an effort to save the marriage.

The court ruled that the husband could bring a claim for the negligent infliction of serious emotional distress.

Molien v. Kaiser Foundation Hospitals, 616 P.2d 813 (Calif.1980).

In a mistaken identity case the hospital is not liable as long as its conduct is reasonable.

A man who was found unconscious at the scene of a car accident was rushed to a hospital in serious condition. The police assumed that the patient, who possessed no personal identification, was the owner of the car, and transmitted that name to the hospital. Officials then telephoned the parents in the early morning hours and informed them of their son's condition. Seven hours later, hospital personnel discovered that the patient had been misidentified. The parents sued the hospital for negligently causing them to suffer severe emotional distress, and a jury awarded them five hundred dollars.

The South Carolina Supreme Court, however, overturned the award, finding that the hospital was not guilty of negligent infliction of emotional distress. There is no indication that the hospital staff made the misidentification, the court explained. While struggling to save the patient's life, hospital personnel relied on the police identification. Further, the parents did not suffer physical injury, the court concluded, and would not have been entitled to compensation even if the hospital had been negligent.

Dooley v. Richland Memorial Hospital, 322 S.E.2d 669 (S.C. 1984).

PUNITIVE OR EXEMPLARY DAMAGES

A claim of malicious, willful, or wanton misconduct may result in the imposition of punitive damages. If malice or intent to do harm is proven, punitive damages will result in a much larger award for the jury. The purpose of punitive damages is to deter an unacceptable type of activity in the future both for the actual defendants and society at large.

It should be noted that punitive damages may not be covered under a liability insurance policy.

Punitive or exemplary damages are not too common in the average malpractice case. However, their frequency is increasing.

SUMMARY

The fourth condition that must be proven for the injured party to recover damages in a malpractice action is damages. Patients may be unhappy and express dissatisfaction with their hospital care, but if they have not been damaged, there will be no recovery of damages.

Compensatory damage include all expenses incurred as result of the injury such as medical bills and lost wages, pain and suffering, and an award for any disfigurement or disability. In selected cases, patients may also recover damages for emotional harm. If punitive or exemplary damages are awarded, the patient's financial recovery will be much larger than the amount of harm suffered would indicate.

CHAPTER 7

DEFENSES

After the injured party has proven the four essential elements of malpractice, the defendant has his or her "day in court" and the opportunity to defend the case. Although proof has been offered on all four essential elements, duty, breach of duty, causation, and damages, there are certain defenses that will negate these elements.

In any negligence action that would include malpractice, there are two basic types of defenses that are available. One is a defense of law; the other is defense of fact. These defenses will be discussed in this chapter.

An example of a defense of law is the Statute of Limitations, which provides that the patient is barred from bringing his or her claim because of a state statute that precludes claims that are stale or too old. This concept will be discussed later in this chapter.

Defense of fact may be asserted, for example, stating that, factually, the care provided by the health care provider was not below the standard of care, or that even though the standard of care may have been breached, it was not the cause of the injury to the patient. In this area, a very useful tool that the defense counsel uses in preparing for the defense is that of alternative hypotheses. What this means, simply, is that even though the patient may indeed have a serious injury, that injury could have been caused by several alternate hypotheses, only one of which may be the one asserted by the patient and his or her attorney. Therefore, by giving all the alternative hypotheses, the assertions by the patient could be doubted, and it could be shown that there were many other circumstances that could have led to the same injury.

For example, in a general negligence action, such as a car accident, the defendant may be able to prove that the plaintiff was also negligent. In some jurisdictions, this will completely bar the plaintiff's right to recover damages. This is called *contributory negligence*. An example of this is a case where the defendant was traveling over the speed limit but

111

was able to prove that the plaintiff went through a red light at the intersection where the crash occured. Since the plaintiff was also negligent, he or she may not be able to recover damages. The modern view, called *comparative negligence*, would not bar the plaintiff's recovery completely, but would lessen the award for damages based on the percentage of negligence for which the injured party was responsible.

CONTRIBUTORY NEGLIGENCE

Contributory negligence is not as successful a defense in the medical malpractice area as it is in the general negligence area. This is accounted for, at least in part, by the discrepancy between the status of the patient and the status of the health care practitioner. Because of the plaintiff's illness and the decreased knowledge of the hospital environment as well as the implications of his or her own symptoms, it is often difficult to argue that the patient was in a position to contribute to his or her injury. The health care practitioner, on the other hand, is assumed to be both knowledgeable and experienced in caring for patients.

A patient had surgery on his hand. The surgeon made a mistake and injured a nerve but did not tell the patient why he was in intense pain. He did advise the patient to go to another hospital, but the patient refused.

The court held the surgeon liable and pointed out that as a layman with a disastrous experience with hospitalization, it was reasonable for the patient to fear further treatment.

Johnson v. U.S., 271 F.Supp. 205 (Ark.1967).

The same principle is applied to hospital liability. Courts are reluctant to prevent the hospitalized patient's right to recover damages by allowing the defense of contributory negligence.

A patient was admitted to the hospital with pneumonitis and placed in a private room. He was acutely ill, suffering from a fever, blurred vision, and a lack of coordination. On the day of the incident, he was observed by some construction workers standing on the balcony and calling for a ladder. The workers alerted the hospital. The physician then requested that the patient be watched closely and placed in a posey belt and cloth wristlets. Since the hospital was understaffed, the nurse called the patient's wife and asked her to

send someone to sit with her husband. The patient's wife agreed but said it would take 10 minutes. The charge nurse replied that she could not possibly have the patient watched for 10 minutes. When the relative arrived, the patient had fallen from his window and was injured.

The court held the patient was too disoriented to have contributed to his own negligence, and the hospital was held liable.

Horton v. Niagara Falls Memorial Center, 380 N.Y.S.2d 116 (1976).

In the following case, contributory negligence was a successful defense, but it is important to note that the injured party attempting to claim damages was a physician.

A physician became ill at his office. He asked his partner to give him an injection. Following the injection he felt worse, lay on his office floor, and vomited into the wastebasket. His condition worsened, and his partner offered to examine him more carefully. He refused and would not allow his wife to be called. When he finally arrived home, his wife took him to the hospital and a stroke was diagnosed. After his partner left to practice elsewhere, the physician sued him for negligent misdiagnosis.

The court dismissed the claim and stated that the entire episode was the fault of the sick physician himself and noted that it was perfectly possible for a physician to commit malpractice on himself.

Nimmer v. Purtell, 230 N.W.2d 258 (Wisc.1975).

While the hospital is often held liable for injuries occurring to patients because of falls or burns, the defense of contributory negligence may remove the liability if the facts are clear that the patient was negligent.

A patient died of burns from a flash fire in an oxygen tent. Her daughter alleged that the patient had been allowed to wear silk nightgowns in the tent, and that the fire was the result of a spark caused by static electricity. Testimony from nursing personnel indicated that the patient was wearing a cotton hospital gown and that a book of matches was found inside the oxygen tent after the fire.

Since the patient was alert, the court held she was responsible for her own injuries.

Evans v. Newark-Wayne Community Hospital, 316 N.Y.S.2d 447 (N.Y.1970).

A nurse came into the patient's room. The patient told her that there was water on the floor of her bathroom, and the nurse went to get a mop. The patient, meanwhile, went into the bathroom and fell, sustaining a back injury.

The court said that the cause of the patient's accident was her own failure to use due care for her safety under known conditions.

Goodeaux v. St. Martin Hospital, Inc., 333 So.2d 717 (La.1976).

A patient was admitted for treatment of a back problem. Because of constant pain, she received a number of sedative drugs. She was a heavy cigarette smoker and smoked about two packs of cigarettes per day if she could obtain them. The nurse on duty, when she learned of this, told the head nurse that she thought the patient should not be allowed to smoke unless a nurse or visitor, such as her husband, was present to see that she did not fall asleep while smoking. Accordingly, her cigarettes and lighter were taken away, and she was told they would be kept at the nurses' station on her floor. The patient was instructed to call the nurse when she wanted a cigarette. This resulted in 15 to 20 calls a day.

The patient allegedly purchased cigarettes from the volunteer cart. She inadvertently dropped a match before it was extinguished and was burned.

The court held the hospital was not liable, since the patient was conscious of the correct procedure and capable of appreciating the danger to which she was exposing herself.

Seymour v. Victory Memorial Hospital, 376 N.E.2d 754 (Ill.1978).

It also must be evident that the patient is capable of comprehending instructions and is sound mentally. The patient who is confused or disoriented cannot be contributorily negligent.

A 65-year-old patient who was senile was admitted to the hospital. His family told the nurses that he had had previous cigarette fires. The nurses asked members of the family to stay with him while he smoked. The nurses took away his cigarettes and issued orders that he was not allowed to smoke unless an attendant was with him. Some time later, a nurse found the patient on fire. He died of his burns.

The hospital and nurses were held liable. The court held that the evidence was insufficient for the jury on the allegation of the patient's contributory negligence.

Kent v. County of Hudson, 245 A.2d 747, (N.J.1968).

In the previous case, the patient's mental status prohibited the defense of contributory negligence from being successfully applied.

A gynecologic patient was confused with another surgical patient and mistakenly had an incision made for thyroid surgery before the problem was discovered.

The court rejected the argument that the patient was contributorily negligent and awarded $100,000 in damages.

The court felt that the patient's response to another patient's name, when she was awaiting surgery and was at best in a confused state of mind, could not be considered negligent. The court noted that the hospital had a system of checking identification bracelets designed to avoid such mistakes.

Southeastern Kentucky Baptist Hospital, Inc. v. Bruce, 539 S.W.2d 286 (Kentucky 1976).

Documentation in the nurses' notes indicating a patient's ability to comprehend instructions and the fact that such instructions were given is invaluable to the defense of these malpractice cases.

The age of the patient alone, as illustrated in the following two cases, may not necessarily account for whether contributory negligence can be used as a successful defense.

A 73-year-old patient was told not to get out of bed. Her physician ordered a vaporizer placed in her room, and hospital personnel placed it next to her bed. She got out of bed contrary to instructions and burned herself.

The court held that because of her age and infirmities there could be no contributory negligence.

Clark v. Piedmont Hospital, 162 S.E.2d 468 (Ga., 1968).

A 72-year-old man was hospitalized for treatment of arthritis. He was neither senile nor sedated. He was instructed not to get out of bed without assistance, and the siderails were put up. However, he climbed over the rails, fell, and broke his hip. He died immediately after surgery was performed.

The court held that he was contributorily negligent.

Jenkins v. Bogalusa Community Medical Center, 340 So.2d 1065 (La.1976).

The hospital is not an insurer of the patient's safety. The hospital is not designed to protect the patient against reasonably anticipated risks if the patient is mentally capable and aware of his or her surroundings.

The same issue may be considered in a case involving a minor. Whether contributory negligence is a successful defense may depend on the age and intellectual development of the child.

Sometimes the parents' contributory negligence is a defense to an action against a physician when a child is involved.

An 8-year-old girl broke her arm. The physician set it improperly, and an infection resulted. She was given corrective orthopedic exercises but failed to exercise. Her arm was permanently crippled.

> The court held that she was incapable of contributory negligence but the jury should be permitted to determine if the parents were contributorily negligent and, if so, whether recovery of damages should be barred.
> Flynn v. Stearns, 145 A.2d 33 (N.J.1958).

A more recent case illustrates this point and sheds an interesting light on one court's interpretation of the role of the nurse's aide.

> A 2-year-old child ingested a large amount of aspirin without his parents' knowledge. Some time later he began vomiting. The child's parents took him to the emergency room. They told the nurse's aide that they suspected aspirin ingestion but did not tell this to the physician despite the fact that the aide had told them to do so. The child died of aspirin poisoning.
> The court held that the nurse's aide was not negligent in failing to inform the attending physician. The parents were not contributorily negligent, since they had given the information to the nurse's aide. However, the court held they had no right to recover because no negligence had occurred.
> Johnson v. St. Paul Mercury Insurance Co., 219 So.2d 524 (La.1969).

The contributory negligence defense is difficult to apply in a malpractice action since the patient, who is ill and may be in great pain, cannot be relied on to exercise judgment in a normal manner.

However, when a visitor is injured on hospital premises, the considerations are different.

> A woman's husband was a patient at a hospital. She went to a restroom located adjacent to the waiting room. She said the restroom was dirty and there was not enough tissue. She took off her shoes and attempted to stand on the seat of the commode. She fell and injured herself. About an hour later she returned to the restroom and again tried to use the same seat in the same manner.
> The jury awarded her $13,000 for her lower back sprain, but on appeal the court dismissed the charge and stated that her injuries resulted from using the commode seat in a manner in which it was neither designed nor intended to be used.
> St. Mary's Hospital, Inc. v. Bynum, 573 S.W.2d 914 (1978).

Any examples of noncompliant behavior should be documented. This includes the patient who is not following instructions and the patient who tampers with his or her traction or biomedical equipment.

COMPARATIVE NEGLIGENCE

Because of the harsh effect of contributory negligence, that is, barring the patient from the ability to recover any damages even for minute negligence on his or her part, the courts and the legislatures of many states have adopted the concept of comparative negligence. Under this concept, the negligence of the patient is weighed and balanced with that of the health care provider; a nurse, physician, or hospital. Even if the patient were negligent, the patient would not be barred from recovering for the damages; however, the amount of damages received would be offset by the percentage of negligence attributable to the patient. For example, if a patient were able to establish that he or she received damages in the amount of $100,000 and it could be shown that the health care providers—the nurses, physicians, and hospital—were 60 percent negligent and the patient 40 percent negligent, the patient could still recover damages. However, instead of receiving the full $100,000, the patient would receive 60 percent of the damages. Therefore, the patient would receive $60,000. There are four formulas used by the various states to determine the percentage of negligence of the patient. The common factor in all these is that the patient would not be barred from recovering damages because of his or her own negligence.

ASSUMPTION OF RISK

A more unlikely defense in a medical malpractice case is the assumption of the risk. This doctrine means that the patient understands the possibility of all risks and knowingly consents.

This defense is difficult to apply because it is often impossible to prove that the patient has been fully informed. This doctrine is related in that respect to the doctrine of informed consent.

Hospital patients may be held to assume the risk of failure to take reasonable care of themselves if the danger is obvious.

A patient was injured when she crawled out over the foot of the hospital bed after allegedly waiting 30 to 40 minutes for assistance to the bathroom. She fell and injured her hip.

The court held that the patient had been warned of the danger and, therefore, had assumed the risk.

Munson v. Bishop Clarkson Memorial Hospital, 186 N.W.2d 492 (Neb.1971).

A patient was hospitalized with a heart condition. Siderails had been placed on his bed. He attempted to crawl out of bed over the footboard and was injured.

The court held that the hospital was not liable for the injuries the patient received when he fell since there was no reason to anticipate he would attempt to climb out of bed over the footboard.

Hellerstein v. General Rose Memorial Hospital, 478 P.2d 713 (Colo.1970).

A patient had his ears washed out at his physician's office on those occasions when they became plugged with wax. He came to the office, and told a nurse that he wanted his ears washed out. He was told that both physicians were at the hospital and that his ears could not be treated until one of the physician's could examine him and order such a procedure. He insisted that the nurse do it without requiring him to wait for the physician's return, and she reluctantly agreed. During the washing process, both eardrums were ruptured.

The court held that the patient had assumed the risk.

Brockman v. Harpole, 444 P.2d 25 (Ore.1968).

In many jurisdictions the nurse's judgment in carrying out the above procedure despite the patient's insistence would have superceded the defense of assumption of risk. As with the doctrine of contributory negligence, it is clear that courts view the patient in an unequal position to the health care provider.

A 73-year-old ambulatory patient who attempted to go to the bathroom during the night without calling for assistance in violation of specific orders from her physician fell and was seriously injured.

The court held that the patient assumed the risk of falling and that there was nothing unusual about the patient's condition to require the use of siderails.

DeBlanc v. Southern Baptist Hospital, 207 So.2d 868 (La.1968).

STATUTE OF LIMITATIONS

A defense that could bar the injured patient's presentation of a malpractice case is the statute of limitations. The statute of limitations is the limited number of years during which the injured party can pursue a claim.

Statutes of limitation are set by the legislature of each state. In general there are two types of legislative enactments. The state legislature may decide that an injured party who has a negligence claim may bring the claim within a specified number of years (usually 2) from the date the incident occurred or from the date of discovery of the incident. The latter statute usually gives the injured party a longer time period in which to pursue the claim. Many states shortened the statute of limitations during the malpractice crisis of the mid-1970s.

The classic situation that illustrates this concept is the patient who has a foreign object remaining in place following surgery. It may be a number of years before the discovery of this problem particularly if the patient has no immediate physiologic effects.

In discussing these types of cases, some courts distinguish between the "traumatic injury" cases and the "disease" cases. In the traumatic injury cases, the injury is usually such that the patient knows or should know that someone may be legally responsible. Therefore, the time period for bringing the claim should be applied more strictly. In nearly all states, the statute of limitations for a minor is longer than for an adult. In some states, it may be up to age 18 or 2 years after attaining age 18.

If the injured patient knows that causation and damages exist in his or her situation but does not know that a breach of duty has occurred, courts might allow his or her recovery of damages even though the statute of limitations has run.

A Korean War veteran was treated for osteomyelitis with neomycin after which he suffered a hearing loss. He knew that the hearing loss was related to the use of the drug, but it was not until 2 years later when another ear specialist told him that this drug should not have been used for his treatment that he became aware of the breach of duty.

The court held that the statute of limitations did not begin to run until 2 years from the visit to the second specialist. The plaintiff received $320,536.
Kubrick v. U.S., 581 F.2d 1092 (1978).

Because of the unusual factors associated with the discovery of harm caused by medical malpractice, courts tend to apply the statute of limitations very broadly to allow the injured party an opportunity to be heard in court. If the injured party can prove that he did not know nor should have known that treatment was improper, the courts will allow the claim to be brought. This test is usually applied on a subjective basis. This means that whether or not it was reasonable for this particular patient to be unaware of the negligence must be considered.

In one case where the injured party was a registered nurse and had reviewed her medical records soon after treatment, the court allowed the statute to bar the patient's right to recover damages.

A nurse suffered a ruptured uterus and lacerated bladder during the course of the cesarean delivery of her child. Subsequently, she developed a kidney infection. The court pointed out that 9 years had passed since the incident, and the patient had been in possession of her records but failed to examine them for 3 years. Therefore, the claim was barred.

Sanders v. U.S., 551 F.2d 458 (1977).

A patient's failure to take his physician's advice may result in the statute of limitations beginning to run.

A man was injured when a window pane fell on him, and fragments of shattered glass penetrated his neck. A clinic physician treated his wounds. Two years later he returned to the doctor complaining of pain. The physician made an appointment for the patient with a specialist, but he failed to keep it and consulted a chiropractor instead.

The court held that the statute began to run when the patient failed to take his doctor's advice, and his claim brought 3 years from that time was now barred.

Snyder v. Tell City Clinic, 391 N.E.2d 623 (Ind.1979).

Where fraudulent concealment serves to prevent the patient from discovering an act of negligence, the statute of limitations will not serve as a bar to the claim. Mere silence may be construed as fraudulent concealment. Although the physician is usually found negligent for failure to disclose information, the hospital may be held liable as well.

A 32-year-old woman noticed a lump in her right breast. When malignancy was discovered, a radical mastectomy was performed. Radiation therapy was then begun. The patient suffered severe complications from this treatment and subsequently needed reconstructive surgery.

Six years later, she discovered that the radiation treatment was the cause of her problem.

The court held that the statute of limitations did not begin to run until the patient knew or had reason to know that the treatment was negligently administered.

Lopez v. Swyer, 279 A.2d 116 (N.J.1971).

GOOD SAMARITAN STATUTE

Another type of legislative enactment that serves as a defense to malpractice claims is the good samaritan statute. These statutes have been enacted to protect health care providers from civil liability that may be incurred in stopping to render aid at the scene of an accident. The intent of the laws is to encourage those with health care expertise to render care at the scene of an accident without fear of reprisal.

These statutes are not designed to apply to the hospital care given to a patient. Although the laws differ from state to state, most jurisdictions specifically identify the nurse as a professional who is covered by the scope of the statutes.

Some statutes provide that the health care professional may still be sued by an injured victim for gross negligence. This would encompass an activity on the part of the nurse that would be clearly outside the realm of usual nursing care, for example, a nurse who performs a tracheotomy negligently on a patient when she has had no training or experience with this procedure. The good samaritan acts are meant to provide liability protection for the usual acts encompassed by the standards of the profession. Most states' statutes require that the health care provider should not charge the patient if he or she wants to be protected by the statute.

Although health care providers fear liability for rendering aid in an emergency, such liability has not been imposed in any jurisdiction of the United States.

CHARITABLE IMMUNITY

Historically, the doctrine of charitable immunity provided a strong defense for the institution.

Hospitals were once considered charitable institutions since a large number of patients were treated without payment for these services. With the advent of health insurance policies and other third party reimbursement programs such as Medicare, hospitals no longer provide as much charitable care. Hospitals function more as business institutions.

The abolition of charitable immunity in most jurisdictions reflects the belief that the hospital, by charging and receiving money for what it offers, also must assume the obligations incurred in running the business. One of these obligations is to exercise a proper degree of care for its patients. Requiring hospitals to respond in damages for the carelessness of employees ensures the installation of safety methods and the enforcement of strict supervision over hospital personnel. Since hospitals can purchase insurance, it is appropriate for patients to receive compensation.

SOVEREIGN IMMUNITY

The concept of governmental immunity, sovereign immunity, was established to prevent the government from being sued for negligence. This principle, as many of our legal principles, derives from the evolution of our legal system from that of England. The basis of sovereign immunity is the idea that the King can do no wrong and that the ability to sue the King or the government was inconsistent with their sovereignty. Therefore, historically, in the United States, the government and the governments of the various states were immune from tort liability.

Today, however, the federal government can be sued under a congressional act entitled the *Federal Tort Claims Act*, which allows the government to be sued. The states as well have begun to overturn the doctrine of sovereign immunity, and many states are no longer immune from tort liability. One of the main reasons for the abolition of this governmental/sovereign immunity was that the states were able to buy insurance to indemnify themselves from the loss under tort; therefore, there was no reason an injured person could not be compensated for his or her injuries from the state. It should be noted, however, that sovereign immunity still does exist in certain states.

While the patient was working on a pig farm, a crate slipped onto his hand and cut and crushed a finger. He was rushed to a hospital for emergency treatment by a doctor and a nurse under the direction of the doctor. The nurse administered a tetanus booster injection. He then came under the care of his family doctor. About a week later, the patient died of tetanus.

His widow filed a complaint against the two doctors and the nurse with the Administrator for Arbitration Panels for Health Care. The nurse contended that there was no cause of action against her because she was a state employee acting within the scope of her employment and therefore immune. The Administrator found that the nurse was a "low employee" of the state as opposed to a "high public official" and was therefore entitled to conditional immunity for "ordinary negligence when acting within the scope of her employment." The widow appealed.

The appellate court noted that, since this cause of action arose, the state law on sovereign and official immunity had undergone "extensive scrutiny and revision."

The appellate court, therefore, remanded the case to the Administrator to determine whether the nurse met the criteria for immunity.

DuBree v. Commonwealth, 481 Pa. 540, 393, A.2d 293 (1978).

The application of sovereign immunity to malpractice is narrow. Even when completely effective, it only applies to governmental entities—federal hospitals, state hospitals, and municipal hospitals owned by the government. Because of the large number of federal, state, and city/county hospitals, including state university hospitals, the doctrine has had an impact on the ability of injured patients to sue many health care providers in this country.

SUMMARY

After the injured party has proven the four essential elements of malpractice, the defendant has an opportunity to defend the case. The defenses that are frequently applied in general negligence cases, such as contributory negligence and assumption of the risk, are not often applied to malpractice cases.

A third defense, the statute of limitations, may prevent the injured patient from recovering damages if a long period of time has elapsed since the injury and if the patient knew that the injury was caused by negligence.

A fourth defense, the good samaritan statute, applies to emergency care rendered by a health care provider outside the hospital.

Charitable immunity was historically a defense that prevented any recovery of damage against the hospital. This defense is no longer accepted in most jurisdictions.

CHAPTER **8**

INFORMED CONSENT

The theory of informed consent as a basis for liability in a medical malpractice action is an important new development. This theory contends that an adult of sound mind has the right to decide when treatment is necessary and advisable.

Before any procedure can be performed on a competent adult, the patient must consent to being touched. Otherwise, a battery or unconsented touching has been committed (see Chapter 9).

A 23-year-old patient died as a result of undergoing extraction of teeth under general anesthesia.

The court stated that consent by the patient to a surgical operation is a prerequisite when the patient is able to be mentally and physically consulted about his or her condition. Absence of such a consent in these circumstances constitutes assault and battery.

The case was returned for a new jury trial based on the issue of whether or not an informed consent was obtained.

Saura v. Shea, 390 A.2d 259 (Pa.Super.1978).

This is the basic principle of all consents—the patient's right to consent to being touched.

The classic legal statement of this principle was articulated by Justice Cardozo in 1914: "Every human being of adult years and sound mind has a right to determine what shall be done with his own body."

Schloendorff v. Society of New York Hospital, 211 N.Y. 125, 129, 105 N.E.92.93 (1914).

INFORMED AND EDUCATED CONSENT

In recent years, the law has advanced; not only must the patient consent to being touched, but also the patient must be allowed to make a knowledgeable choice as to which of several alternatives might be pursued or whether any treatment is necessary at all. This is the basis of an informed consent. The first case discussing this principle at length occurred in 1960.

A malpractice action was brought against a hospital and a physician for burns suffered by a patient as a result of excessive cobalt therapy.

The court held the physician liable for failure to warn of the risks of radiation therapy.

Natanson v. Kline, 350 P.2d 1093 (Kansas 1960).

The nurse's role in the informed consent legal area should be one of minimal involvement as will be discussed later in the chapter.

Since 1960 courts have heard many cases based on the theory of lack of informed consent.

A woman's stomach was perforated during performance of a gastroscopy. She had signed a general consent form authorizing any medical procedures that the attending physician found advisable.

The court held that because the patient was not advised of consequences and alternatives, an informed consent was not obtained.

Cooper v. Roberts, 220 Pa.Super. 260, 286 A.2d 647 (1971).

Before the patient undergoes a procedure, information must be given about it. This information must include diagnosis, material (significant) risks, complications, and alternatives to treatment including the effect of no treatment.

The issue of information related to alternatives including non-treatment has been litigated with various results.

An infant born 4 weeks prematurely in October 1980, was treated, with consent of the parents, for hydrocephalus. Following successful surgery, the infant left the hospital and has been institutionalized with severe neurological defects.

The physician did not inform the parents that they had the option of non-treatment which would have resulted in death.

The court ruled that death was not a legally-sanctioned alternative.
Renee Iafelice et al v. Saul M. Lucks et al, Superior Court of New Jersey, Hudson
County, No. L-013685, (August 6, 1985).

**A child fractured his arm in a snowmobile accident. The orthopedic surgeon
recommended immediate surgery.**
The parents testified that the physician said the child would lose the use of
the arm unless surgery was performed within 2 hours and did not inform them
that alternative treatment would have been to immobilize the arm and allow
the child to be transferred to his home.
The jury found for the defendant, the physician, but the appellate court sent
the case back for retrial.
Marino v. Ballestas, 749 F.2d 162 (3rd Cir. 1984).

In surgical cases, the choice of anesthesia, the use of blood, and
tissue disposition may be important aspects of the informed consent. It
must be presented in such a manner that it can be understood by the
patient. This information should be conveyed by a physician, prefera-
bly by the physician who will be performing the procedure.

Some decisions have discussed the patient's right to choose which
surgeon performs the operative procedure.

**The patient, a nurse, requested that a specific member in a group practice
perform her surgery. On the day of surgery when the physician was absent,
the patient demanded that the procedure be delayed. Her request was not
honored.**
The Court held the gynecologist liable even though the surgery was not
performed negligently.
Pugsley v. Privitte, 263 S.E.2d 69 (Va.1980).

**After performing lymph node surgery, a physician discovered that a surgical
sponge was left in the man's lower abdomen. Although he notified the patient
of the problem and advised immediate removal of the sponge, the patient
refused to permit the physician to perform the surgery. He requested a second
surgeon who said he would operate only if the first physician were present.
The patient agreed to the presence, but refused to allow the first physician's
participation.**
The first physician's name appeared as the Chief Surgeon on the medical
record. He was held liable for fraud.
Johnson v. McMurray, 461 So.2d 775 (Ala.1984).

In the area of informed consent, there is great legal debate over what is a material risk and to whom the risk should be material. The concept is that only those risks that are material to the patient need to be disclosed. There are two tests being used today, the objective test and the subjective test. The subjective test means that the patient involved in this claim will be asked whether this risk was material to him or her and if the patient would not have had the procedure had someone disclosed the particular risk. This is obviously a subjective test, and since this particular patient is suing the health care provider, it would be a rare instance in which this particular patient would say that the information was not material and that it made no difference in his or her decision. Obviously, it is almost impossible for a health care provider to win a suit when the subjective test is used.

Most states today use the objective test, which asks whether the risk would be material to a reasonable person similarly situated. Would a reasonable person, in similar circumstances, consider this risk material to such a degree that he or she would refuse to have the procedure or the operation, knowing the risk. This seems fairer; it takes away the subjectivity of the particular patient and evaluates it in a more objective view, that of a reasonable patient.

A man had a medical history revealing past coronary problems. At the age of 37, he had his first heart attack. For the following 10 years he continued to have problems. It was suggested that he would be a candidate for a cardiac surgery procedure. If the procedure was unsuccessful, a mechanical heart substitute would be implanted until a human heart donor could be found. The patient died shortly after the mechanical heart was implanted.

The court held the surgeon was not liable for lack of an informed consent. Evidence indicated that in making a determination of what to tell a patient about surgery, the physician must decide what details to give depending on the emotional condition of the patient.

Kaup v. Cooley, 349 F.Supp.827 (Texas 1972).

Courts have also determined that a physician is not required to give a patient a detailed medical explanation which in all probability the patient would not understand.

A patient became paralyzed as a result of an aortogram. There was considerable dispute in the testimony as to what the patient was told. The patient stated that he was told that in "one of a thousand cases there will be a possibility of some complications, but that's not important." The following

morning he asked the physician to explain the complications. The physician replied that there was a possibility of a clot forming at the site of the injection. The patient asked "What will happen if a clot is formed?" The physician replied, "It can be easily removed." The patient asked "Is that all?" to which the physician replied "That's all."

According to the physician's version, he informed the patient that the risk of the procedure was less than that of an appendectomy and that the most common problems would be pain in the groin, that he could have a problem bleeding, primarily into the skin near the puncture site, possibly developing into a hematoma or blood clot, that possibly a clot could develop in the vessel at the puncture site or an embolism could go peripherally into his leg, but that these complications could be handled surgically. He also told the patient that the chances of a complication were less than one in a thousand. The physician did not recall being asked "Is that all?" with respect to the enumerated risks, but admitted the possibility.

The physician testified that he was aware of other risks about which he did not inform the patient, including the possibility of plaque traveling into a vein in the leg, a punctured artery, a pseudoaneurysm, a punctured aorta, an asthmalike condition, and paralysis or loss of a limb.

The physician stated that although he did not mention the possibility of death, he assumed the patient realized that one of the conceivable risks of an appendectomy is death, and that since he had compared the risk of the aortogram to those of an appendectomy, the patient should have been aware that death was an "outside risk" of the aortogram.

The patient denied being informed that the risks were comparable to those involved in an appendectomy and claimed that he relied on the physicians disclosure. He said that if he had been apprised of all the possible complications he never would have consented to the procedure because he felt he could successfully control his high blood pressure, he did not want to jeopardize his new job, and he would have wanted to consult his brother, a physician, before undergoing the procedure.

The court held the physician could be held liable for lack of an informed consent based on what the *reasonable* patient would want to know.

Scaria v. St. Paul Fire and Marine Insurance Co., 227 N.W.2d 647 (Wisconsin 1975).

In the previous case, the court also stated that a physician should not be required to discuss risks which are apparent or known to the patient or extremely remote possibilities which might falsely alarm the patient.

A California decision discussed the duty of the physician to inform the patient of the risks of not having a test that the patient has refused.

A general practitioner who saw the patient on a routine basis requested that she have a Pap Test, but she refused.

About six months later she was seen by a second physician who diagnosed advanced carcinoma of the cervix. She died six months later at the age of thirty.

Her children contended that their mother's refusal was based on cost and that she had not been informed of the necessity of the test.

The California Supreme Court held that the physician was under an affirmative duty to disclose the risks of refusal.

Truman v. Thomas, 27 Cal.3d 285 (1982).

The landmark decision, described below, states the modern view on informed consent, thus eliminating the need for expert testimony. This makes it easier in many situations for the plaintiff to pursue this type of action (lack of informed consent) rather than one based on negligence. The physician must disclose as much information as the average, reasonable person, in the same set of circumstances as the patient, needs to accept or refuse the surgery or procedure. This is the objective test discussed earlier.

A 19-year-old patient was paralyzed after a laminectomy.

The court rejected the physician's claim that it was not a common practice to disclose this risk and upheld the patient's right to sue.

The court stated that the patient's right of self-determination shapes the boundaries of the physician's duty.

Canterbury v. Spence, 464 F.2d 772 (1972) cert. den. 409 U.S. 1064, 34 L. Ed 2d 518.

Although the modern view eliminates the need for the testimony of a medical expert, some courts still find this necessary in an informed consent case.

A man who had been experiencing chest pains was advised by his physician that coronary bypass surgery should be performed. The physician warned him that he might not survive the operation but did not describe a risk of damage to the central nervous system that did occur.

The court held that an expert's testimony regarding practice in the medical community of warning the patient of the dangers of particular surgery was permitted. The expert's opinion resulted in the case being dismissed.

Ficklin v. MacFarlane, 550 P.2d 1295 (Utah 1976).

The physician may be able to justify nondisclosure if an emergency exists or if the physician believes disclosure would be detrimental to the patient's emotional well-being.

A 64-year-old woman complained of abdominal pain, vomiting and weight loss. She subsequently developed severe thrombophlebitis. Her son consented to surgery required to prevent the blood clots from breaking loose. However gangrene developed and the leg had to be amputated. The physician did not secure consent from the patient or her son.

The court held for the physician because the patient's condition was a life threatening emergency, the patient was incompetent to consent for herself, a person authorized to consent was not readily available, and any delay in treatment may have been harmful to the patient.

Stafford v. Louisiana State University, 448 So.2d 852 (La. Ct. App. 1984).

The patient was a dentist suffering from hypertension. His physicians were afraid that disclosure of possible side effects from use of the medium in performing a thoracic aortogram to diagnose an aneurysm might have an adverse effect on the patient. After the procedure, the patient was paralyzed from the waist down and had no control of his bowel or bladder.

The court held there was no liability for lack of informed consent and that the physician may, in some instances, limit his or her explanation. Since the patient was a dentist, it would be expected that he would have some knowledge of the dangers of such a procedure.

Nishi v. Hartwell, 473 P.2d 116 (Hawaii 1970).

This exception must be applied strictly or the result would be an erosion of the rule. However, in these two previous situations, an explanation should have been given to the available family members.

An exception to the need for specific consent may occur under the extension doctrine. Under this theory the physician has the right to extend the scope of the consented procedure if an unexpected life threatening situation is encountered. An example would be abdominal surgery performed for removal of the gallbladder during which an abdominal aneurysm, previously undetected, was discovered. However it is clear that the courts will allow this expansion only if an emergency exists.

The surgeon performed exploratory surgery and discovered endometriosis. The woman's reproductive organs were so severely damaged that she was sterile. The physician removed all of her reproductive organs.

The court held that the removal did not involve a life threatening situation and therefore, the physician could be liable for damages.

Pizzalotto v. Wilson, 437 S.2d 859 (La.1983).

Damages in an informed consent case differ from the usual awards in a malpractice case. Since the basis of an informed consent is the patient's right of self-determination and the invasion of such a right is not readily measureable in monetary terms, the award may be larger than the actual physical and monetary damage permitted in the usual malpractice case.

The patient was told that a biopsy of his parotid gland needed to be done. This procedure would require a 1-inch incision in his neck.

Instead, the parotid gland was removed. The patient had a permanent 8-inch scar and a concavity in his neck. Subsequently, plastic surgery was required to remove the scar tissue.

The patient was awarded $50,000 in damages based on the inadequacy of the consent.

Defulvio v. Holst, 414 A.2d 1087 (Pa.Super.1979).

In some states, injured patients have attempted to expand the doctrine to apply to the administration of therapeutic drugs. The issue is whether the physician has a duty to explain to the patient the possible side effects of medications. In at least one state the court has ruled that this should not be an informed consent issue, but rather the case should be based on malpractice.

The physician prescribed Butazolidin and the patient had a severe reaction.

The court held that traditional medical malpractice actions were adequate for compensating patients for the injurious consequences of therapeutic drug treatment.

Boyer v. Smith, 497 A.2d 646 (Pa.Super.1985).

WHO OBTAINS CONSENT—THE NURSE'S ROLE

Nurses should understand that the responsibility for informed consent rests with the physician who is going to perform the procedure. This is a principle that is misunderstood by many health care practitioners. However, courts have consistently held the physician rather than the nurses or hospital liable for failure to obtain an informed consent.

In many medical malpractice cases, courts have imposed joint liability on the hospital and the physician. However, current case law is clear that in the area of informed consent, courts recognize clearly that it is the responsibility of the physician to obtain an informed consent.

A woman was admitted to the hospital for bilateral cataract extraction and signed a consent for surgery in the admitting office. Subsequent to the surgery, she became blind. At trial, she stated that the surgeon had failed to warn of risks involved, and the hospital had failed to obtain an informed consent.

   The court held that the hospital had no duty to obtain an informed consent. The clerk in the admitting office was only performing an administrative function to implement the consultation between the patient and physician. A layperson would not be competent to describe the procedure or discuss the possible consequences.

   Cooper v. Curry, 589 P.2d 201 (New Mexico 1978).

The patient died of a pulmonary embolism three days after undergoing vein stripping surgery.

   The trial court directed a verdict for the hospital that was affirmed.

   The court stated that the duty to obtain the patient's consent was that of the attending physician, not the hospital, and therefore the hospital had no affirmative obligation to question the patient as to whether the risks had been explained to him, particularly where the patient had read and executed a consent form.

   Ackerman v. Lerwick, 676 S.W.2d 318 (Mo. App. 1984).

The nurse's role in obtaining an informed consent is being clearly delineated by the courts. No longer should the physician hand to the nurse a blank consent form and ask her to have the patient sign it. If this is done, the physician is clearly assuming a liability risk that could be indefensible in a court action. This would be viewed as an abrogation of the duty to practice medicine according to a proper standard of care. Since the nurse, as a hospital employee, cannot act as an appropriate substitute for the physician in this realm, the hospital should not be held liable for the lack of an informed consent. Only the physician bears this direct responsibility. The documentation of the consent process through the use of a printed form, should not be confused with the actual explanation given to the patient and the informed consent itself.

A 35-year-old mother was experiencing abnormal vaginal bleeding. Her physician, after appropriate diagnostic tests, advised a radium implant. She developed a large vaginal-rectal fistula. Her testimony indicated that she had not been told of alternative procedures such as a hysterectomy and had received no information regarding possible complications of radium.

The physician was held liable.
Pegram v. Sisco, 406 F.Supp. 776 (D.Ark.1976).

A woman with complaints of vaginal bleeding and pain on intercourse consulted a physician. The surgeon performed a vaginal hysterectomy.

After her discharge from the hospital, she continued to have problems from a fistula that was allowing urine to leak from the bladder into the vagina. She underwent two more operations to correct this condition.

Her claim against the surgeon, who died before the case came to trial, was settled for $4,500.

She also sued the hospital claiming that the hospital had a duty to explain to her the risks and possible complications of the hysterectomy and possible alternative methods of treatment. Although she signed a printed hospital consent form, she said she did not read all of it, and nobody explained it to her.

The court held that the hospital had no duty to inform a patient of surgical risks.
Roberson v. Menorah Medical Center, 588 S.W.2d 134 (Mo.1978).

Sometimes nurses question whether residents rather than attending physicians can obtain the patients consent to surgery. If the operative procedure is totally the responsibility of the resident then the resident becomes, in fact, the "attending" physician. However, in the majority of operative cases, the resident is assisting an attending physician. If the hospital allows residents, by policy, to obtain patients' surgical consents in these cases, the liability for lack of an appropriate informed consent remains that of the attending physician.

The patient alleged that at the time the consent was signed she had a detailed discussion with the resident who informed her as to the risks and advantages of surgery but did not advise her of a number of significant risks.

The resident did not in any way participate in the surgery.

The court held that the hospital resident's failure to obtain proper consent from the patient imposed no liability on either hospital or resident, but it may on the attending.
Hill v. Seward, 470 N.Y.2d 971 (Sup.1983).

The hospital may be able to facilitate the consent process by providing a policy and form that is complete and provides legal protection for the physician. Some hospitals have eliminated the formal consent form and have suggested that physicians document their explanation in the progress notes. Others have gone to very specific forms that differ for every procedure. These forms describe the specific risks involved with a particular procedure, for example, a cholecystectomy or open heart surgery. Specific forms may also be used for invasive procedures such as intravenous pyelograms and angiograms. In order to comply with certain accreditation standard and insurance regulations, a consent covering required information must be in the chart before the procedure is performed.

Although it is clear that the nurse has no direct responsibility for explaining the procedure to the patient, it will undoubtedly continue to be part of the nurse's role to clarify what the physician has said and to answer the patient's questions. This is in keeping with the important role of the nurse as a health care educator. The presence of a nurse in the patient's room during the explanation of this procedure is vital to an understanding of what communication the patient has already received and of how assistance can be provided to support and clarify this explanation. However, specific informed consent questions should be referred back to the physician.

Legally, since a nurse is with the patient on a 24-hour basis, it is the nurse's responsibility to notify the physician of any change in the patient's condition that might cause a delay in surgery. The physician must also be notified of any change in the patient's decision to have surgery or of a lack of understanding on the part of the patient in regard to what the procedure may involve, if this is communicated by the patient.

If a competent adult patient has a right to determine if he or she wants to have the procedure, then the patient should have an absolute right to revoke the consent at any time before the procedure.

Two hours before the patient was scheduled for surgery to eliminate pain, he informed a nurse that he did not wish to go through with the surgery. The nurse called the operating room but was unable to speak to the physician; she documented the circumstances on the patient's chart.

Shortly after, the physician ordered medications administered in preparation for surgery. The patient did not object then or throughout surgery, during which he was awake.

The patient later brought suit claiming that his silence was not implied consent because he was heavily sedated.

The court noted that the patient was awake and smoking a cigarette following surgery and that he responded clearly to questions about the location of pain during surgery. The court concluded that consent had been present.

Busalacchi v. Vogel 429 So.2d 217 (La. App. 1983).

The hospital and its nurses may be held liable for lack of informed consent if they knew or should have known that there had not been adequate disclosure.

A 14-year-old boy died following surgery for correction of scoliosis. The surgery was not the generally accepted medical treatment for scoliosis; it was a procedure used in this country only by this particular surgeon who had used it for 5 years. During those 5 years in at least five of the 35 instances in which the procedure was used, there had been unexpected and untoward results.

Approximately 1 year before this operation, one of the defendant physician's patients had suffered an immediate paralysis when one of the screws inserted into her spinal column severed her spinal cord. As a result, the hospital where that operation had been performed withdrew permission for the defendant physician's use of its facilities for this type of procedure.

The court held that since no immediate emergency existed, the defendant physician was obligated to make a disclosure to the parents of his patient that the procedure he proposed was novel and unorthodox and that there were risks incident to or possible with its use.

In addition, because the hospital knew the nature of the proposed operation, the history of its use by the defendant physician and the fact that it had not been recognized by the medical profession in the community or in the country, as an accepted method for correcting scoliosis, the hospital was obligated to ascertain that the physician had made such a disclosure.

Fiorentino v. Wagner, 19 N.Y.2d 407, 227 N.E.2d 296 (1967) rev. g. 26 App.Div.2d 693, 272 N.Y.S.2d 557 (1966).

The hospital nurse, in some institutions, does have the responsibility to remind the physician that the consent should be signed, dated, and witnessed a reasonable time before the procedure is done. Many authorities agree that a patient who consents before hospitalization may be better informed because of a less coercive environment than a patient who consents after admission. The patient should not be sedated at the time of the explanation. The nurse may serve as a witness to the patient's signature.

The patient was admitted to the hospital for an arteriogram. Two nurses presented him with a consent form and obtained his signature. They then signed as witnesses. They did not explain the procedure to the patient and did not know whether it had been explained.

The patient signed a consent form for a bilateral carotid arteriogram; the physician performed a vertebral arteriogram during which the patient experienced paralysis of all extremities which was permanent.

The hospital was not held liable. The physician was liable for $2,000,000. The court held that the nurses' obtaining of the patient's signature did not impose liability upon the hospital.

Trapp v. Cayson, 471 So.2d 375 (Miss. 1985).

The nurse should witness only the fact that the patient signed the form, not that the explanation was given and understood by the patient. It is the physician's duty to determine whether the patient understood the explanation. The nurse may provide additional information to the patient or clarify and respond to questions after the initial explanation has been given by the physician. It is preferable for the defense of the physician in an informed consent case to have a member of the patient's family witness the explanation and sign the form as a witness.

WHO GIVES CONSENT

Questions are often presented, and many times need to be answered by nurses, as to who should provide consent in various situations.

There is no doubt that an adult who is competent should always consent to his or her own procedures, except in an emergency, when consent is implied. But even in emergencies, there may be a duty of disclosure to the family. With a minor, the parents' consent must be obtained before treatment if time permits. This rule may be relaxed if the minor is capable of appreciating the nature, extent, and probable consequences of the procedure, and the parents are unavailable.

The woman had undergone major surgery and was unconscious. As her daughter, who had been visiting, left her mother's room, she caught her finger in the door. The 17-year-old was taken to the emergency room for treatment. A resident surgeon repaired her finger. The injured minor's parents were divorced, and her father resided 200 miles away. The daughter was viewed as intelligent and capable and raised no objection to the surgical repair.

A claim was filed by her mother based on a lack of informed consent. The suit was unsuccessful.

The court held that generally consent of a parent to treatment of a minor child is necessary; exceptions can be made when an emergency exists, when the child is emancipated, when parents are so remote as to make it impracticable to obtain timely consent, and when the child is close to maturity and knowingly gives an informed consent. One of the basic considerations is whether the proposed operation is for the benefit of the child and performed to save either life or limb. Sufficiency of the minor's consent depends on an ability to understand and comprehend the nature of the procedure, the risks involved, and the probability of attaining the desired result in the light of circumstances.

Younts v. St. Francis Hospital and School of Nursing, Inc., 205 Kan. 292, 469 P.2d 330 (1970).

In some instances, with a mature minor, it would be appropriate for the physician to get the minor's consent as well as the parents if possible.

An emancipated minor may also give valid consent. The definition of emancipation varies from state to state but usually requires the minor to have a home separate from his or her parents and to be responsible for his or her own financial situation. An example might be a married minor who is employed and living with spouse. State laws may also permit a minor to consent to such treatment as examination for veneral disease, for drug or alcohol dependency, and for pregnancy.

In the area of experimental drugs, the federal government has set forth strict guidelines dealing with consent and what the patient needs to be told in order to make such a consent informed. Concerns that need to be further addressed include those of the minor who is subjected to treatment by an experimental drug. A debatable issue is whether the parents can consent for such experimental treatment of their child. This issue becomes especially crucial if the drug does not provide any therapeutic effect to the child but is used only for experimental purposes.

If the patient is mentally incompetent, consent must be obtained from the person legally authorized to give consent for the patient. The hospital may look to state statutes for determination of the person and order of kinship.

The informed consent doctrine has been expanded in recent court decision.

An informed consent case was permitted on behalf of an infant against a physician for prenatal injuries arising out of the failure to advise its mother of the risks and alternatives of obstetric care.

Hughson v. St. Francis Hospital of Port Jervis, 459 N.Y.S.2d 814 (App. Div. 1983).

Hospitals have made an unsuccessful attempt to limit their liability through the use of release forms.

The patient was treated in a dental clinic. Following removal of a tooth, her jaw was fractured.

She had previously signed a form waiving her right to sue for negligence. The court held the form was invalid and stated that health care professionals cannot avoid liability for their actions by forcing patients to sign releases before treatment.
Porubiansky v. Emory University, 275 S.E.2d 163 (Ga. App. 1980).

In addition to expansion of the doctrine through judicial precident, various legislatures have enacted consent legislation both general and specific.

In Massachusetts hospitals are now required to inform maternity patients, prior to admission, of various annual birth statistics within the facility, such as the annual rate of cesarean sections and annual percentage of deliveries involving inductions, epidurals, and general anesthesia (S.B. No. 2186 [1985 New Laws] effective March 31, 1986).

PATIENT'S RIGHTS

The patient's rights movement, which is exemplified by the document known as "The Patient's Bill of Rights," published by the American Hospital Association (AHA) in 1972, embodies the concept of informed consent.

The patient has the right to receive from his physician information necessary to give informed consent prior to the start of any procedure and/or treatment. Except in emergencies, such information for informed consent should include but not necessarily be limited to the specific procedure and/or treatment, the medically significant risks involved, and the probable duration of incapacitation. Where medically significant alternatives for care and treatment exist, or when the patient requests information concerning medical alternatives, the patient has the right to such information. The patient also has the right to know the name of the person responsible for the procedure and/or treatment.

It must be remembered that this document was a response to the need felt by health care consumers to become participants in health care, rather than the quiet recipient.

The role of the physician is moving away from the traditional paternal model and toward the model of physician as advisor to the patient who is a consumer-participant.

Many states today have implemented Patient Bill of Rights Acts.

In one case the hospital's "Pregnant Patient's Bill of Rights" was used by the patient as evidence.

The patient was overdue for the delivery of her child. The physician indicated that the best course of action would be a cesarean section.

She was admitted to the hospital and Pitocin was administered by a different physician, which resulted in a vaginal delivery and a brain damaged child.

The Court held that the patient had not been given the opportunity to consent to the Pitocin and therefore the hospital had violated its own policy.
Kohoutek v. Hafner, 366 N.W.2d 633 (Minn.1985).

CONTRACTUAL BASIS FOR INFORMED CONSENT

A second basis for liability that is sometimes asserted in an informed consent case is based on the allegation that a contract has been breached. The two cases where this is asserted most frequently in the informed consent area are plastic surgery and sterilization.

An example is the case where the doctor guaranteed the patient that after plastic surgery, she would be as beautiful as a movie star. Unfortunately, the surgery was not a success, and the person was obviously not as beautiful as a movie star. The physician did not fulfill his warranty and he breached his contract; therefore, the patient should be able to seek damages against him.

The other example is sterilization procedures. If a doctor guaranteed/warranteed that a woman would not be able to have children after she had the procedure for sterilization and she becomes pregnant or has had another child, then the doctor has not kept his promise and has broken his contract; the patient should be able to sue under contract theory as opposed to under negligence theory.

These actions are being brought under contract law as opposed to negligence law. There are several advantages to this; one is the statute of limitations in most states is considerably longer for contracts than it is for negligence. Also, the burden of proof that is necessary for the plaintiff under negligence, expert testimony and expert witnesses, is not necessary if a contractual basis for liability can be established.

SUMMARY

The theory of informed consent is based on the fact that an adult of sound mind has the right to decide when treatment is necessary and advisable.

The documentation of an informed consent is vital in the proof of a malpractice case. The informed consent should be part of an educational process in which the patient becomes a participant in health care. The information given to the patient should include all material risks, complications, and alternatives to treatment. In some jurisdictions, expert testimony is unnecessary in an informed consent case.

In states where informed consent cases have been initiated, courts have consistently recognized that it is the physician's responsibility to obtain an informed consent. It is not the nurse's duty to provide the initial explanation to the patient. Even though it is not the responsibility of the nurse to obtain the patient's signature on the consent form, it is the practice in many hospitals. The hospital may assist in this procedure by providing a form for the physician's use. The nurse may play a supplementary role in answering questions that the patient may have once the procedure is explained by the physician.

An adult of sound mind should consent to his or her own treatment or procedure. Parents should consent for the treatment of a minor. In an emergency, minors may be permitted to give their own consent, or consent may be implied for patients of all ages. If the patient cannot consent, the legal representative or next of kin may give consent.

The Patient's Bill of Rights sponsored by the AHA or state legislatures supports the need for an informed consent.

CHAPTER 9

INTENTIONAL TORTS

Although the majority of lawsuits brought against nurses are based on negligence, a significant number involve another area of law known as *intentional torts*.

As discussed in a previous chapter, a tort is a civil wrong punishable by damages and monetary compensation rather than imprisonment. Negligence is a major category of tort law. The intentional tort is a second major category. Some of the intentional torts for which nurses may be held liable will be discussed in this chapter. These are assault and battery, defamation of character, breach of confidentiality, invasion of privacy, misrepresentation or fraud, and false imprisonment.

The intentional torts involve actions that may not be covered financially by standard malpractice or liability insurance policies. The intentional torts do not require proof of the four elements of malpractice and physical harm is not required. The amount of monetary compensation awarded is based upon a subjective judgment of how significant an infringement of civil rights has occurred.

ASSAULT AND BATTERY

Assault is the unjustifiable attempt to touch another person or the threat of doing so. Battery is the actual carrying out of threatened physical contact.

Assault and battery are sometimes alleged rather than negligence as a basis for a legal action. This charge eliminates the need for expert testimony. Negligence does not have to be proven in an assault and battery claim. Any unlawful or unconsented touching of a person provides the basis for a valid claim.

One element of the assault and battery case that must be proven is the absence of consent.

A patient consented to have teeth extracted by an oral surgeon. The patient was told that 11 teeth would be removed. Just before surgery after pre-operative medication was administered, the surgeon allegedly told the patient that an additional 16 teeth should be removed. The patient had no recollection of this conversation.

The patient had no ill effect from the removal of all the teeth but brought a battery action for the "unconsented" removal.

The court held that the patient has the right to withdraw this consent until the operation is begun.

Bailey v. Belinfante, 218 S.E.2d 289 (Georgia 1975).

An actionable battery includes the performance of an operation by a surgeon without the patient's consent.

The adult patient who is alert and oriented has the right to refuse any aspect of his treatment. As a recent case indicates the patient also has a right to specify which physician should perform a surgical procedure.

A patient was a 44-year-old registered nurse who underwent an exploratory laparotomy and removal of her ovaries. During the surgery, the ureter connected to her only functioning kidney was injured, and the patient suffered severe postoperative complications. The patient filed suit, charging negligence and battery.

The jury found the gynecologist had not been negligent in performing the surgery and entered a verdict in his favor on the negligence count.

However, on the battery allegation, the patient testified that she had wanted another surgeon present during surgery. She testified that she had made this clear to the gynecologist and had confirmed with the surgeon's office personnel that the other surgeon would be available. On the morning of surgery, the patient asked where the surgeon was and stated she did not want to be put to sleep until he arrived. The operation was performed in the absence of the requested surgeon. The jury found the patient had revoked her consent to surgery and entered a verdict against the gynecologist based on the battery claim for $75,000.

Pugsley v. Privette, 263 S.E.2d 69 (Va.1980).

A nurse who has an adult, competent patient held down to administer an injection or forces the administration of an oral medication has committed an intentional tort.

A patient was taken to a mental hospital. She was dirty and unresponsive to questions. She was then involuntarily committed to the hospital. She was a practicing Christian Scientist and refused medications as well as other treatment.

The court held that compulsory medication could be given over the religious objection of the patient only if she has been harmful to herself or others.

The court allowed her to recover for assault and battery, since she had never been found mentally ill or incompetent, nor was her conduct harmful to herself or others.

Winters v. Miller, 446 F.2d 65 (1971).

A patient came to a mental hospital as a voluntary admission. When he attempted to leave, a physician and members of the hospital staff forcibly administered ether and placed a tourniquet around his neck. To do this he was held down on the floor by a physician and six nurses. He died from either an overdose of the ether or the application of the tourniquet.

The jury awarded the deceased patient's mother $15,000.

Bellandi v. Park Sanitarium Association, 6 P.2d 508 (Cal.1931).

Although the previous case was decided many years ago, it is a useful example of a patient being subjected to forced treatment. The amount of damages awarded for such a case today would be significantly more.

The injured party may recover damages if there has been consent to physical contact but the consent has been exceeded. The patient must be able to prove that the scope of the consent did not extend to the act in question.

An assault and battery charge may be a criminal offense and subject the defendant to imprisonment in addition to civil damages. Criminal liability may also extend to a charge of manslaughter.

An elderly patient in a state hospital required help with eating. The defendant, a practical nurse, fed her cubed potatoes. She held the patient's head back by grasping the patient's hair with one hand and feeding her with the other. During the feeding, the nurse occasionally covered the patient's mouth and nose with a towel. Another attendant held the patient's arms. The patient died from aspiration of stomach contents.

The nurse was found guilty of involuntary manslaughter. She was put on probation for a term of 3 years on the condition that she serve 1 year in a county detention facility.

People v. McCaughan, 317 P.2d 974 (Cal.1957).

Before a nurse can be convicted of causing the death of a patient, it must be proven that the alleged action caused the death (see Chapter 5).

A registered nurse was in charge of a state institution for the mentally retarded. She administered paraldehyde to an unruly patient. Unknown to her, it was four times the normal strength. The patient died of pneumonia 5 days later. Medical testimony indicated that if the overdose had been the actual cause of death, the patient would have died within 4 to 6 hours. Without more evidence of the exact cause of death, the conviction could not be sustained. Therefore the nurse was not guilty.

State v. Comstock, 70 S.E.2d 648 (W.Va.1952).

The physician or hospital may be liable for assault if the hospitalized patient assaults someone else and there was knowledge that the patient was dangerous.

A nurse's aide was beaten when she came to the rescue of a patient who was being attacked by another patient. She sued the physician for failing to warn the nursing staff that the man was dangerous and for failing to restrain or segregate him on admission.

The appeals court held that she had a basis for suit against the physician. The case was sent back to the trial court for resolution.

Jones v. Sheck, 210 N.W.2d 808 (Mich.1973).

A patient objected to being placed in a semiprivate room with a roommate she knew had episodes of violent behavior. She was told no other room was available. The roommate tried to strangle her. She sued the hospital on the basis that the institution knew or should have known of the roommate's propensities.

The court held that the defendant must establish that it did not have actual knowledge that the patient's condition was such that an assault and battery might be expected to follow.

Kelly v. Board of Hillcrest Hospital, 529 P.2d 1233 (New Mexico 1974).

The hospital may also be held liable if an employee assaults a patient.

A state hospital patient filed a claim seeking an award for injuries sustained when assaulted by a hospital employee.

Evidence established that the patient was assaulted by the employee. The state hospital administration was aware that the employee had an alcohol problem and continued to employ him after incidents involving alcoholism.

The court held the state liable for punitive damages, and the patient was awarded $5,000.

Hayes v. State, 363 N.Y.S.2d 986 (1975).

More recently, malpractice cases involving physicians have included sexual assault as a basis for claim.

A young single woman consulted the defendant physician for a physical examination. After part of the examination, he suggested they continue the examination at her apartment. After arriving at her apartment, he gave her an injection, and she lost consciousness. When she awakened, he was sexually molesting her, but she pretended to be unconscious. After the appointment, she phoned the police who instructed her to keep her next appointment. When the physician came back again, a closed circuit television had been set up, and the physician's behavior was observed.

This video transmission was made with the full cooperation and consent of the victim and was admissible in court. The defendant physician was convicted of assault and battery and sentenced to 5 years in prison.

Avery v. Maryland, 292 A.2d 728 (Maryland 1972).

DEFAMATION OF CHARACTER

Defamation of character is an intentional tort where one person discusses another in terms that diminish his or her reputation. Written defamation is called *libel;* oral defamation is known as *slander.* Defamation of character may be the basis for an award of civil damages.

A 13-year-old girl had a foot infection. Her family physician advised that she stay at home. On his note to the teacher, he incorrectly stated the girl was pregnant. Her parents tried to obtain the report or have him correct it. He told them to bring it to his office, and he would correct it, but the school refused to release it. Her parents repeatedly called the physician, and finally his office nurse told them to stop bothering him.

On the basis of libel, the jury returned a verdict of $7,000 against the physician.

Vigil v. Rice, 397 P.2d 719 (New Mexico 1964).

Specific financial injury does not have to be proven if the slanderous statement charges a contagious or venereal disease, a crime involving moral turpitude, or a comment that prejudices a person in the profession, trade, or business in which he or she is engaged.

A patient was admitted for treatment of lesions on his lips. Almost immediately, difficulty arose between the patient and his physician. The next day the physician notified the hospital administrator of his decision to terminate the case and discharge the patient. Later the administrator told the patient that hospital regulations required a patient to have an attending physician responsible for the patient's medical care and treatment, and since the patient had no attending physician, it would be necessary to discharge him. Immediately before the discharge, the administrator, in the presence of an assistant, purportedly said to the patient "Do me a favor and see a psychiatrist."

The court denied the patient's request for one million dollars in punitive damages stating that the utterance did not affect the patient in his business capacity; therefore, he was obliged to prove that he was specifically damaged.

Modla v. Parker and Southside Hospital, 495 P.2d 494 (Ariz.1972).

Actual malice may have to be established in certain defamation claims.

A man was treated in a hospital emergency room for various ailments over a 2-year period. His complaints and frequency of hospital visits prompted the hospital attendants to place his name on a list of "problem" patients. The list included the names of persons who were suspected drug abusers or were accident prone.

On one particular hospital visit, the man complained of pain resulting from a fall. He was diagnosed as having a muscle sprain. However, because of the patient's persistent requests for medication, a nurse called the man's doctor the following day and allegedly informed the doctor's secretary that the man was suspected of being a drug abuser and of having added blood to his urine sample. The man sued the hospital, the nurse, and a physician's assistant who also identified the man as a "known drug abuser" for defamation.

The New York Supreme Court said that, since hospital personnel had a duty to communicate their findings to a treating physician and other hospital personnel, their communications were protected by a qualified privilege requiring the man to provide evidence of actual malice. The court found that the man failed to produce evidence sufficient to raise an issue of fact as to actual malice and to overcome the privilege.

Jerome Griffin v. Cortland Memorial Hospital et al., New York Supreme Court, Appellate Division, Third Judicial Department, No. 40511 (December 23, 1981).

Nurses are also named as defendants in defamation suits. All hospital employees must realize that they work in an environment where they are likely to be aware of sensitive information regarding patients. Sometimes patients do not want others to know they are in the hospital or why they have been hospitalized.

A female patient had a condition that raised false-positive results in Wasserman tests. She did not have and had never had syphilis. At a social occasion where the patient was working as a caterer, the nurse told the hostess that the woman was being treated for syphilis. This information destroyed the patient's business.

The appeals court held that the patient had a valid basis for her claim. The case was sent back to the trial court for resolution.

Schessler v. Keck, 271 P.2d 588 (Cal.1954).

An area where the nurse must be extremely cautious is that of comments made about physicians in the hospital.

A head nurse of an emergency room department made several derogatory remarks about some of the hospital's physicians at a committee meeting. These remarks resulted in her being asked to resign.

She resigned and filed an action alleging infringement of her civil rights.

The court, in denying her action, suggested it was not her complaints but rather her tactics in dealing with her complaints that resulted in her job dismissal.

Bach v. Mount Clemens General Hospital, Inc., 448 F.Supp.686 (1978).

Any hasty action or comment may subject the nurse to a defamation action.

A hospital and a nurse were liable for $750 in damages for slandering a hospital orderly, a District of Columbia appellate court ruled.

The orderly was summoned to take a patient's clothing and valuables from the fourth floor of the hospital to a storage room. Two nurses checked the contents when they arrived at the storage room and found that $8.66 was missing. The orderly was paged to report to one of the nurses, who accused him of stealing the patient's money. She asked him to empty his pockets onto the counter. The local police were called, and an officer arrested the orderly. That afternoon the orderly was released from custody at the behest of the hospital.

The orderly later filed suit against the nurses, the hospital security guard, the police officer and the District of Columbia for slander, assault and battery, and false arrest. A trial court directed a verdict in favor of the District and the police officer, granted judgment for the security guard on the slander count, and to the security guard, the nurse and the hospital on false arrest claims. The court entered a final judgment for $750 against the nurse and hospital for slander. Both parties appealed.

Affirming the lower court's decision, the appellate court said that whether the nurse and hospital were liable for slander was a jury question. The jury's $750 verdict was upheld. The other individuals were not liable for assault and battery or false imprisonment. A statement made by the security guard to the police officer was privileged and could not be the basis for a slander claim, the court said.

Smith v. District of Columbia, 399 A.2d 213, D.C. Ct. of App. (Feb. 21, 1979).

Truth is a defense in the ordinary defamation suit. A defamation action may be brought by the nurse if she feels that her reputation has been injured.

A nurse was dismissed by the hospital for unprofessional conduct when she became openly critical of the postoperative treatment given to a patient by the physician. The charges she brought against the physician were dismissed by a hospital grievance committee. Later she was reemployed by the hospital on the condition that she would not discuss hospital business outside the hospital. When the physician discovered this, he called the administrator and said the nurse was unfit to care for patients.

She recovered $5,000 when she sued for defamation.

Farrell v. Kramer, 193 A.2d 580 (Maine 1963).

A male nurse worked in a first aid unit for union employees of the U.S. Postal Service. A union official sent a letter to the postmaster alleging various complaints against the nurse including one that he had "attempted to probe female visitors in debauchery." The letter was posted on a bulletin board accessible to employees. The nurse testified that he was subjected to ridicule by fellow employees because of the letter.

The jury awarded the nurse $10,000 in damages. The court found substantial evidence of malice and no evidence to establish the truth of the statement. Before the letter, the nurse had refused to give the union official an unauthorized prescription.

White v. American Postal Workers Union, 579 S.W.2d 671 (Mo.1979).

Nurses have also sued physicians for defamation.

A physician wrote a letter to a nurse implying that she had illegally substituted medication for a patient. The court ruled that the letter did not constitute defamation because it was not "published." Both the physician and the nurse had a duty to ensure safe medication practices. Therefore, dictating a letter to the secretary was not considered publication.

In the previous case the court pointed out that publication to a third party is a required element in defamation cases.

Farris v. Twedten, 623 S.W.2d 205 (Ark.1981).

The nurse, who had worked in the doctor's office for over a year, mistakenly had a patient take a repeat rubella test. According to the nurse, once she realized her error, she informed the doctor, explaining that she'd made the mistake because the laboratory slip saying "repeat rub" (repeat rubella test), dated 7/25/80, was on the top of the chart. She hadn't looked any further in the chart, so she had missed a later laboratory slip indicating that the repeat test had been done.

The doctor's response was, "That's fine."

Later that day, however, he asked to see the chart. After reviewing it, the doctor contended he'd seen the laboratory slips before in a different order: The latest laboratory slip (dated 8/26/80), showing that the test had been performed, had originally been on the top of the chart. He told the nurse to find out who had rearranged the slips. If she couldn't produce that person, she'd have to confess to having done so herself or be fired.

Because the nurse could not explain the change in order, the doctor fired her the next day. That evening, he called a meeting of his office employees and told them he couldn't work with anyone who was a liar, untrustworthy, and disloyal.

The nurse then filed a suit for defamation of character.

The jury decided that the doctor's statements did meet the legal definition of defamation: false statements made with malice, with the knowledge that they were false or with reckless disregard for the truth. It awarded the nurse $125,000 in damages: $25,000 for the injury to her reputation; $40,000 for mental anguish, embarrassment, and humiliation; and $60,000 for "exemplary damages."

A number of defamation cases have been initiated by physicians. In one case the court pointed out that expressions of opinion are not defamation.

After a hospital refused to renew a physician's contract of employment in its pathology department, the physician was not entitled to recover damages from former colleagues on the theory that they had defamed him by writing letters to the hospital's officers and directors in which they expressed a "vote of no confidence" in him and referred to their "lack of confidence" in his "reporting ability" and his "attitude and performance over the past several years," since, regardless of the possible existence of malice, the letters amounted only to expressions of opinion, did not impute incompetency or unfitness, and did not imply undisclosed defamatory facts. The same ruling was required with respect to a letter in which the hospital's executive director requested that plaintiff return books and keys, and reimburse the hospital for his personal telephone calls, notwithstanding plaintiff's claim that the letter implied that he was a thief.

Gordon v. Lancaster Osteopathic Hospital Ass'n., Inc. (Pa. Super. 1985), 489 A.2d 1364, HC-435, 5620,6220, 6260, 6435.

In at least 45 states, laws have been enacted to provide a qualified privilege for physicians engaged in peer review activities. Qualified privilege protects a physician who, in good faith and without malice, reports his concerns about a peer to the appropriate committees of the hospital or medical staff.

A physician's suit for defamation against a second physician over comments made before an executive committee of a hospital was not barred by the Medical Studies Act, an Illinois appellate court ruled.

The first physician contended that at the committee meeting the second physician (1) expressed his unwillingness to continue to work with the first physician because of his dishonest and unethical practices; (2) stated that the majority of the physicians' colleagues had a very low opinion of the first physician's abilities; (3) advised that he had warned several people of the physician's shoddy practices and that one such practice had prompted his dismissal from another hospital; and (4) cited an example where the first physician's method of delivery had resulted in serious injury to an infant.

In the first physician's complaint against the second physician for compensatory and punitive damages, he claimed that the remarks were made with knowledge of their falsity or with reckless disregard of their truth or falsity. He charged that the second physician neither consulted hospital records or made any investigation to determine the accuracy of the statements. The first physician contended that he had lost patients and was not reappointed to the hospital staff because of the statements. A trial court dismissed the complaint on the ground that the remarks to the committee were absolutely privileged.

Reversing that decision, the appellate court said that the remarks enjoyed only a qualified privilege. The purpose of the Medical Studies Act was to improve the effectiveness of in-hospital peer group review by insuring that those providing information could speak freely. There was no purpose served by allowing one physician to defame another with impunity before a hospital executive committee.

The Act did not bar the physician's suit for defamation, the court concluded.

Matview v. Johnson, 388 N.E.2d 795, Ill. App. Ct. (March 7, 1979); rehearing denied (April 27, 1979).

Other hospital employees have also brought defamation actions. The following case discusses the communication of information in an employee's personnel file to supervisory personnel within a hospital and whether this can be considered defamatory.

A former hospital pharmacist sued the hospital and its executive director to recover damages for libel.

Her annual evaluations included comments that she possessed "poor interpersonal relationships skills" and had a "flagrant disregard for others."

The court ruled in favor of the hospital stating that communication of employee personnel files containing required evaluation material to supervisory personnel within the hospital does not constitute a basis for defamation.

Ellis v. Jewish Hospital, 581 S.W.2d 850 (Missouri 1979).

While a majority of defamation cases deal with the spoken word (slander) there are a minority of cases dealing with the written word (libel).

In a recent case one nurse attempted to bring a lawsuit based on libel because a second nurse had prepared a written report as requested by her supervisor.

Two nurses on duty at a hospital disagreed over the interpretation of a medication order for a patient. The first nurse mistakenly told the second nurse to administer morphine instead of magnesium sulfate. The head nurse directed the second nurse to submit a written report of the incident. A letter of admonishment was placed in the first nurse's official file.

The first nurse brought an action for defamation, alleging that the second nurse had published information in an official report that contained a libelous statement. The second nurse contended that her statements were absolutely privileged because they were made at the direction of her superior and required by duty.

The court found that the written report was absolutely privileged and could not be the basis for a cause of action in libel.

Malone v. Longo, 463 F.Supp.139 (D.D.,N.Y.,January 8, 1979).

Fourteen-year-old Ruby Edwards was brought to the outpatient clinic of the University of Chicago Hospitals and Clinics for treatment of pain on her left side. She visited the outpatient clinic twice, on February 17 and 22, 1983. A number of diagnostic tests were performed during these visits, including a pregnancy test and a pap smear.

The plaintiff's mother signed the "Group Hospital Insurance Report" which authorized the hospital to send the bill for medical services rendered directly to the plaintiff's insurer, the Health Insurance Administration, Inc. The form contained a line designated "Final Diagnosis from Records" which was not filled in at the time the plaintiff's mother signed the authorization.

Approximately one month later, the plaintiff's mother received from her health insurance company a copy of "Group Hospital Insurance Report" which she had signed on her daughter's first visit to the clinic. The hospital had filled in the "Final Diagnosis from Records" with the words "R/O atopic pregnancy." Forwarded to the plaintiff's mother at the same time was a statement of the tests performed and their cost. On this form, a box entitled "Certificate of Illness" had been filled in with the words "atopic pregnancy." The court noted that both entries were apparently misspellings of "ectopic pregnancy" which refers to the development of a fertilized ovum outside of the uterine cavity.

Ms. Edwards' mother met with an employee in the hospital's finance department after receiving these documents from her health insurer. The employee told the patient's mother that a diagnosis of a specific illness had to be filled in on the form or her health insurance company would not make payment to the hospital. The employee told the patient's mother that this was the reason for the diagnosis appearing in the "Certificate of Illness" box on the form. After being informed of the patient's real reason for visiting the clinic, the employee allegedly crossed out the phrase "atopic pregnancy" and replaced it with "Constant pain L. Side and Kidney Infection."

The following month the hospital sent the plaintiff's health insurance company a new set of claim forms, again seeking payment for the medical services rendered. In these forms, the diagnosis in the "Certificate of Illness" category had been changed to "Initial GYNE Visit." Similarly, the "Final Diagnosis from Records" slot was changed from "R/O atopic pregnancy" to "GYN Exam." The plaintiff's mother had not signed this group hospital insurance report form.

Six months later, the patient's mother filed this libel action which claimed that the hospital had maliciously libeled her daughter by sending a diagnosis of "atopic pregnancy" to their health insurance company. The trial court dismissed all the plaintiff's claims.

The appellate court agreed. It found that the hospital was acting under a qualified privilege when it communicated the allegedly defamatory information to the insurance company. The court noted that this diagnosis was published in usual insurance company claim forms and that these forms were prepared in the normal course of business by people who had no personal knowledge of the plaintiff. The persons preparing these forms also shared the plaintiff's interest in having the plaintiff's health insurance company pay the hospital for the plaintiff's medical bills. These factors led the court to conclude that the hospital had acted in good faith and was therefore protected by a qualified privilege.

The court further held that this information was communicated in a proper manner and on a proper occasion by the hospital and that it was sent only to persons authorized to receive it. Thus, the court said, the diagnosis was privileged, even if erroneous.

Edwards v. Univ. of Chicago Hosp. 484 N.E.2d 1100 (Ill.1985).

The issue of supplying references for employees may subject an employer to a charge of defamation.

A nurse anesthetist was given notice of termination of her employment with an anesthesia service. On an application for employment at a hospital, she indicated that an inquiry could be made of her employer at any time.

When the hospital inquired, the previous employer said that the nurse lacked professional competence. Her application was denied.

She then brought an action for slander against her former employer.

The court concluded that the nurse's former employer was not liable.

Gengler v. Philps, 589 P.2d 1056 (N.M. Ct. of App., November 28, 1978); cert. denied 588 P.2d 554 (N.M. Sup. Ct., January 4, 1979).

In the previous case, the court pointed out that public policy necessitates disclosure of an employee's prior services when an inquiry is made with the consent of the employee.

The limits on criticism rendered by physicians about their hospitals have been evaluated in recent cases.

A physician criticized the quality of care at his hospital which was a public hospital. As a result of his public comments his privileges were suspended. The court ruled that his privileges should be reinstated with the following words: " . . . it must be remembered that the exercise of the First Amendment right of freedom of speech cannot be conditioned, indeed within the context of the factual circumstances of this case, on whether the utterances are good for the community or will likely result in an adverse image to the facility and its personnel. The thrust of (the hospital's) arguments appears to be that Dr. Smith was obligated to some degree of personal loyalty to the hospital and medical staff which renders obsolete the public's right to know; that this loyalty is vital to the proper functioning of the medical facility and a failure to adhere to this code of conduct justifies the revocation of (his) staff privileges. . . . Where, as here, comments on matters of public concern that are substantially true, such a concept is overshadowed by the force and effect of the First Amendment. Moreover, the hospital and medical staff had the privilege, and as a matter of fact did so, to rebut Dr. Smith's criticism by stating the facts, as they perceived them publicly."

Finally, the Court held that Dr. Smith's privileges were terminated in retaliation for his public criticism of the hospital, which was protected by the

First Amendment right to free speech. The hospital failed to prove other reasons for its action, and this was crucial.

DISCLOSURE OF CONFIDENTIAL INFORMATION

Disclosure of confidential information may subject the nurse to liability. This occurs when a patient's problem is inappropriately discussed with any third party.

Nurses carry a particularly heavy burden of responsibility because they share many personal and intimate details about patients during the time they provide care. This information is volunteered by patients based on trust that a nurse or doctor will not violate a confidence.

Sometimes the unauthorized disclosure involves the release of medical records to unauthorized individuals.

A patient was admitted to a hospital's comprehensive care unit for treatment of an alcohol–related illness. One of her physicians sent a health insurance form to the office of the patient's husband, addressed to one of the husband's coworkers. The document listed the patient's diagnosis as acute and chronic alcoholism detoxification. The coworker was not an authorized individual for the receipt of insurance payment request forms.

In the subsequent suit the court determined that the hospital could not be sued because the physicians were not employees. However, the physicians and the Comprehensive Care Corporation could be held responsible for an unauthorized disclosure even though it was accidental.

Prince v. St. Francis–St. George Hospital, 484 N.E.2d 265 (Ohio A.App. 1985).

An insurance company persuaded a physician to divulge confidential information about a patient that was gained through the physician-patient relationship.

The court held that the patient must give permission for the release of the information. The physician who, without authorization, divulges confidential information is liable and must pay damages to the patient.

Hammonds v. Aetna Casualty, 243 F.Supp. 793 (1965).

In the previous case, the court pointed out that the public has a right to rely on the code of ethics established by the medical profession. This code guarantees the confidentiality of the physician-patient relationship. The code of ethics for the nursing profession states that it is the duty of the nurse not to divulge confidential information.

DUTY TO DISCLOSE

Some states have enacted privileged communication laws relating to nurses.

These statutes may shield from disclosure in civil or criminal actions any information the nurse acquires while caring for the patient.

In one such statute, the information may be disclosed (1) if the patient consents; (2) if the information relates to the contemplation of execution of a crime in the future; or (3) relates to the neglect or abuse of a child or vulnerable adult.

(Washington State, S.B. No. 4107 (1985 New Laws).

In some situations, however, there is a duty to disclose imposed by state law. These statutes may require reporting of contagious diseases, such as veneral diseases as well as child abuse.

There is also a requirement to disclose if injury would occur to the patient or others from failure to disclose.

A patient was treated for 2 years before tuberculosis was diagnosed. The physician did not inform him of the diagnosis. The patient's 2-year-old daughter contracted the disease and the father sued for her injuries.

The court held that once the disease was diagnosed, the physician had a duty to inform the patient of its nature and any precautionary steps to be taken to prevent other members of the patient's family from contracting it.

Hofmann v. Blackman, 241 So.2d 752 (Fla.1970).

This duty extends to situations where the patient is mentally ill and could be dangerous to others.

A university psychiatrist was held liable for failing to warn a murder victim that specific threats had been made against her life by one of his patients. The patient carried out the threat.

The court held that once a physician reasonably determines that a patient poses a serious danger of violence to others, the physician must take action to protect the foreseeable victim of that danger.

Tarasoff v. Regents of the University of California, 551 P.2d 334 (Cal. 1976).

A psychiatric patient murdered a young woman after discussing this potential act with his psychiatrist.

The court held that a duty exists on the part of a psychiatrist or psychotherapist to take whatever steps are reasonably necessary to inform a potential victim of his patient's intentions.

McIntosh v. Milano, 403 A.2d 500, (New Jersey 1979).

It is logical to assume that this duty of disclosure extends to a nurse in situations involving danger to a third party.

Although nurses may be held liable for disclosure, there will be protection if a mistake has been made in good faith.

A woman became ill at her place of employment and went to the company nurse. Her problem was diagnosed as veneral disease and reported to her supervisor. The employee was fired. Subsequently, it was discovered that the diagnosis was incorrect.

The court held that no damages could be recovered, because the nurse had made a mistake in good faith and had a legal duty to report.
Cochran v. Sears Roebuck and Co., 34 S.E.2d 296 (Ga.1945).

The patient's bill of rights emphasizes the right of the patient to expect confidentiality in the health care relationship. As patients become more knowledgeable in this area, it can be expected that litigation will increase based on allegations of improper disclosure. Requests for information and copies of medical records by third parties should also be handled carefully to preserve the confidentiality of the information.

The nurse must exercise professional judgment, in balancing the duty to disclose against the right to confidentiality.

Many hospitals have established confidentiality policies. A suggested policy with procedure is described below:

Purpose

The Nursing Department has the responsibility to continually safeguard the patient's right to privacy as guaranteed by the Patient's Bill of Rights. All information pertaining to health and personal matters is strictly confidential and privileged.

Policy

The Nursing Department protects the patient's right to have his or her personal affairs and concerns guarded against public scrutiny either by word of mouth or by written information. It must be remembered that the patient's dignity should be protected and the patient's trust should not be violated.

Personnel of the Nursing Department are to refrain from discussing any patient information with any person other than those employees directly concerned with the care of the patient. No patient information should be accessed for any reason other than specific job related activities.

Nursing personnel have a clear moral, legal, and ethical obligation to keep confidential any information relating to a patient's history, illness, and/or hospitalization which comes to their attention during the course of their duties unless specifically authorized by the patient to disclose the information. These provisions apply to all employees, volunteers, and students working within the Department of Nursing.

Procedure

A. Orientees and affiliating students shall be made aware of the Nursing Department's policy about patients right to confidentiality during orientation by the Clinical Program Department.

B. All records or information pertaining to the medical care or personal matters of a patient shall be considered strictly confidential. Such information shall not be removed from the institution.

C. Correspondence about patient cases mailed within the hospital must always be enclosed in a sealed envelope and marked confidential.

D. Any personal or medical information pertaining to a patient should be discussed in areas where these matters can not be overheard. Nursing Department employees, volunteers and students should not discuss such information in public areas (i.e. hallways, elevators, stairwells, cafeteria) within or outside the hospital.

E. Patients should be informed, if appropriate, that if they share information with one staff member which will affect their safety, welfare, or treatment, that information will be communicated to staff members responsible for their care.

F. Computer Confidentiality. All information retrieved from the computer should be relevant to the individual's specific job responsibility and held in confidence. Access to the computer shall be restricted to those who have been given appropriate access codes and passwords. All computers will be turned off when not in use.

G. If a patient chooses to use an alias name, the Nursing Department will respect this right.

H. Information used for teaching purposes, such as orientation, conferences, and educational programs/courses, shall have all identification deleted prior to use.

I. Information obtained from a patient's records in any form will be accorded the same standard of confidentiality as the record itself. Photocopies of patient information may be used in the course of investigation of patient complaints or for other valid hospital purposes only when such information in its specific text is essential to the purpose of the reviewer.

J. Written consent is required from the patient if pictures are to be taken of the patient while in the hospital. Public Relations should be notified. For pictures taken by the press and accompanied by a media story, Public Relations is to be notified, so that additional permission forms are signed.

K. Telephone information regarding a patient's health status should only be given to the immediate family or designated other. An effort should be made to ascertain the identity of the caller. If identity of caller is in question, the call should be forwarded to the nursing service manager.

L. Nursing Department employees, volunteers, and students may not furnish information regarding a patient in response to oral or written inquiries from communications media. Recognizing that the press, radio, and other communications media have a responsibility to disseminate information to the community, the CEO has designated an authorized spokesperson for the media. This spokesperson is usually a member of the Public Relations Department. The admitting department acts for Public Relations as the authorized spokesperson, but may refer to the Nursing Service Manager on duty nights and weekends.

M. Knowledge that confidential information has been disclosed should be reported immediately to the nurse manager of the person divulging such information, whereby appropriate follow up action will be taken.

N. Divulging patient and/or restricted information of any kind constitutes cause for disciplinary action which may include termination.*

The nurses violation of a confidentiality policy may result in termination of employment.

The nurse, who had a Down's Syndrome child, found out that a patient in the hospital's OB-GYN section was carrying a Down's Syndrome child. The nurse acquired the patient's address from another nurse and wrote a letter to the patient pointing out her experience with such a child. The patient's husband complained to the hospital about the fact that the address had been obtained. After being questioned by the hospital, the nurse admitted she sent the letter and was immediately terminated.

The court concluded that the hospital did not prove a violation of its own policy or any other standard amounting to misconduct sufficient to deny unemployment benefits. While the nurse's actions may have shown lack of

*©Lehigh Valley Hosp. Center, Dept. of Nursing, 1986.

discretion and judgment, the court said that they were not actions amounting to misconduct.

Group Health Plan, Inc. v. Louise Lopez, Minnesota Court of Appeals, No. C1-83-1253 (December 14, 1983).

INVASION OF PRIVACY

Disclosure of confidential information is closely related to the concept of invasion of privacy. The leading case based on a cause of action for invasion of privacy against a hospital occurred in 1920.

A maternity patient permitted a film to be made of a cesarean section operation with the understanding that it would be shown in medical societies. It was, however, shown to the public.

On appeal, the patient was granted a new trial because the original trial court had not permitted the introduction of the film into evidence.

Feeney v. Young, 181 N.Y.Supp.481. 191 App.Div. 501 (1920).

Ten years later a patient filed suit to prevent a publication of a photograph.

An infant was born with his heart outside of his body. Surgery was attempted, but the child died.

The hospital permitted a photographer to take a picture of the child, which was given to the press.

The parents sought damages and, in addition, the prevention of further publication.

The court held that the hospital could be held liable for damages. The trial court had originally dismissed the complaint.

Bazemore v. Savannah, 155 S.E.194 (1930).

The patient had cosmetic surgery. Her physician used "before and after" photographs of her face during a television program and subsequent department store presentation on cosmetic surgery.

The jury found that the publicity of the patient's surgery would be highly offensive to a reasonable person.

Vassiliades v. Garfinkel's, Brooks Bros., 492 A.2d 580, D.C. App. (1985).

As the court in the following case points out, the law of privacy addresses the invasion of four distinct interests of the individual. Each of the four different interests, taken as a whole, represent a person's right "to be let alone." These four types of invasion are (1) intrusion on the patient's physical and mental solitude or seclusion; (2) public disclosure of private facts; (3) publicity that places the patient in a false light in the public eye; (4) appropriation for the defendant's benefit or advantage of the patient's name or likeness.

A patient was dying from cancer of the larynx. Many photographs were taken of the patient at the direction of his surgeon.

On the day that he died, evidence indicated that he physically manifested his desire not to be photographed by the physician, but nevertheless the physician photographed the decedent after lifting his head to place a pillow under it.

The court held that the physician could be held liable for invasion of privacy. A new trial was ordered.

Bethiaume v. Pratt, 365 A.2d 792 (Maine 1976).

During the past five years a number of cases involving this type of liability have been pursued against health care providers.

Earl Spring, a senile 78-year old man with a kidney disorder, was in a nursing home. His legal guardians, his wife and son, were embroiled in a prolonged court battle to halt his kidney dialysis treatments. Without the guardians consent, the nursing home staff permitted right-to-life advocates to interview Mr. Spring. The interviewers' published reports aroused interest in the case, and four nurses who worked at the home told other reporters that Mr. Spring had said to them that he did not want to die.

The Superior Court eventually ruled that Spring was too senile to make his own decision and that his family could stop his treatments. Mrs. Spring then sued the nursing home and the four nurses who had spoken to the press for $80 million in damages. She claimed that her husband's right to privacy had been violated.

The attorney for the nursing home maintained that the patient had become a "public figure."

The jury, however, found in favor of Mrs. Spring. She was awarded $2.5 million, a sum later reduced to $100,000 by the Superior Court.

(Unreported opinion cited by Horsley, Jack E.J.P., R.N., September 1983).

In the previous case attention focused on whether the patient was a public figure. Traditionally, in the law those individuals with a public status did not enjoy the same right to privacy as others.

Generally the identity of patients should be protected.

Tissue typing had been performed to determine a woman's suitability as a blood platelet donor for an ill family member, and her name was subsequently placed in the hospital's platelet donor registry. When the facility later established an experimental program involving bone marrow transplants between unrelated persons, the hospital, without the woman's knowledge or consent, transferred her name to the bone marrow transplant registry. Thereafter, a terminally ill leukemia patient, after discovering that this registry included the name of a woman who could prove to be a suitable donor for him, requested that the hospital either (1) make a specific inquiry of the woman in his behalf or (2) disclose her identity to him so he could contact her personally. The hospital refused his request and the patient brought suit, contending that the tissue typing record was not a confidential "patient" record—because the woman was not a "patient" under medical or surgical treatment—but was instead a general hospital record subject to public access.

The state's high court did find that Iowa law grants confidentiality to hospital records concerning "the condition, diagnosis, care of treatment of a patient or former patient, including outpatients." Because a potential donor is a patient within the meaning of the statute, medical records pertaining to a donor cannot be disclosed, the court concluded. It then explained that the relationship between a physician and a donor is identical to that between a physician and a patient, and that potential donors, just as patients in general, have a valuable right to privacy.

A new York Grand Jury subpoenaed records commanding disclosure of all patients treated for knife wounds during a 2-day period.

The court held that the hospital should not disclose the records.

Matter of Grand Jury Investigation of Onondaga County, 450 N.E.2d 678 (NY1983).

The plaintiff gave her daughter up for adoption. When the daughter reached age 21, she attempted to find her mother. She did locate the defendant who had been her mothers attending physician. The physician gave the daughter a letter stating that he could not locate his records, but he remembered giving the daughter DES and that the possible consequences of the medication made it important for the daughter to locate her mother. This information was not true and was made only to help the daughter gain access to confidential information.

Hospital personnel relying on this letter allowed the daughter access to records identifying her mother.

Plaintiff was extremely upset by the unexpected appearance of her daughter and sued the physician for emotional distress. The court held that the plaintiff had a valid cause of action.

Humphers v. First Interstate Board of Oregon, 696 P.2d 527 (1985).

However, in some cases the court does allow disclosure.

The patient's family brought an action alleging that the patient's death was caused by a delay in his examination after he sought treatment at defendant hospital's emergency room.

The hospital was required to produce emergency room records relating to the specific times of treatment for 34 nonparty patients on the night in question.

The court held that this nonmedical information was not privileged since it did not relate to the diagnosis or treatment of the patients, and it was necessary to attempt to prove that overall quality of emergency room care was deficient.

Holiday v. Harrows, Inc., 458, N.Y.S.2d 669 (New York 1983).

In a malpractice action against a hospital, the plaintiff requested medical records of any patients who had developed a bacterial infection or shock after surgery and records revealing whether any patient was hospitalized in the same room as the deceased patient.

The court allowed the discovery of other patients' records. The judge was permitted to examine the records in his chamber.

State ex. rel. Lester E. Cox Medical Center v. Keeb, Mo. Sup. Court, 65440, 65536 (Sept. 1984).

A married woman who was pregnant but not by her husband, advised some hospital personnel that she did not want anyone to know of her presence in the hospital or of the birth.

The patient information operator disclosed the data.

The court allowed no recovery for the patient stating that the details of medical care were not revealed.

Koudsi v. Hennepin County Medical Center, 317 N.W.2d 705 (Minn.1982).

As the patient's right to privacy becomes more firmly established in the law, the previous case may be decided quite differently. The historical custom of releasing the names of patients in the hospital who are not public figures may be revised.

The following unusual case involved a nurse and her husband.

An obstetrical nurse completed her shift, but was obliged to remain on duty because a severe snowstorm had delayed the arrival of nurses coming to work.

The nurse's husband had arrived to pick her up and he decided to wait for her. To give her husband something interesting to do while he was waiting, the nurse asked if her husband could observe a delivery.

The obstetrician had two patients in labor. The husband observed the second patient giving birth; however permission had been obtained only from the first patient.

The jury found in favor of the defendants.

Knight v. Penobscot Bay Medical Center, 420 A.2d 915 (Maine 1980).

The increased use of media has also offered additional exposure when focused upon patient care issues.

A television news documentary was produced about patients in a state mental hospital.

The patient sued alleging that his right to privacy was violated.

The court held in favor of the defendant because the patient's 4-second appearance was too fleeting and incidental to be actionable.

Dilan v. CBS, Inc. 458 N.Y.S.2d 608, N.Y. App. Div. (1983).

Proper authorizations should be obtained from all patients prior to the use of any material that will identify the patient.

The employee's right to privacy may also be invaded.

Prior to his employment via a Veteran's Administration hospital, the employee was a patient in the psychiatric area of the same facility.

He alleged that his hospital supervisor disclosed confidential information from his medical records to other personnel, including the fact that his medical history rendered him mentally unstable.

The court held that the supervisor did not have absolute federal immunity and that the employee should be given the opportunity to prove that the supervisor released privileged and false information.

Collins v. Walters, No. 82 CIV 6014 (S.D.N.Y. July 11, 1983).

MISREPRESENTATION AND FRAUD

If a physician misleads a patient to prevent discovery of a mistake in treatment, an action for deceit or fraud may be brought.

The plaintiff must prove not only that there was a wrongful misstatement but also that it was relied on in making a decision.

As discussed in Chapter 7 regarding the statute of limitations, any fraudulent concealment acts as an exception to the restricted time period. Fraudulent concealment usually applies only if a confidential relationship exists between the injured party and the one against whom the cause of action exists. A confidential relationship is found where a continuous trust is reposed by one person in the skill and integrity of another. Once the relationship exists, there is a duty to speak, and mere silence may constitute fraudulent concealment.

A patient had a node removed from her neck. Following surgery, she told the surgeon that she was experiencing numbness in the right side of her face and neck and that it was difficult and painful for her to raise her right arm.

It was alleged that the physician was aware of the negligent manner in which he had performed the surgery and that as a result of his negligence, the patient had suffered a potentially permanent injury. It was further alleged that he had willfully, falsely, and fraudulently told her that her pain and difficulties were transient and would disappear if she would continue her physiotherapy. The patient was thereby deprived of an opportunity to cure the condition initially caused by the malpractice.

The court held that the patient was permitted to bring a claim and that the claim was not barred by the statute of limitations since it fell under the exception of fraudulent concealment.

Simcuski v. Saeli, 377 N.E.2d 713 (New York 1978).

However, if the patient knew about the problem the statute of limitations (as discussed in Chapter 7) would prohibit the initiation of a claim.

The patient was a registered nurse. Three days after admission for elective surgery she was mistakingly administered a massive overdose of lidocaine by a hospital nurse. She suffered a cardiac arrest but was resuscitated.

Her physician expressed doubt as to the cause of the arrest and told the nurses not to mention it to the patient. Hospital records were altered to delete mention of the overdose.

When the patient specifically asked the physician if an overdose had caused the arrest, he allegedly responded "no one really knew."

Two days later, a second physician did inform the patient that she was administered an overdose of lidocaine that caused a cardiac arrest.

Six months later the physician was suspended from the hospital. Newspaper accounts indicated that the dismissal was the result of her care, and about three years later she was called as a witness to testify against him. A short while later, she initiated a malpractice claim.

The court held that the statute of limitations barred the claim because she knew about the incident at the time.

Sharrow v. Archer, 658 P.2d, 331 (Alaska 1983).

A patient had his spleen removed. Recovery was uneventful. About 6 years later, in the course of an examination by another physician, x-rays revealed the presence of a metal hemostat in the abdomen. The instrument was subsequently removed.

The plaintiff alleged that the x-ray film taken immediately after his surgery disclosed the presence of the hemostat, that the defendant physician and hospital had fraudulently and wrongfully failed to disclose this fact to the plaintiff, and the x-ray was lost or destroyed by the hospital.

The action was dismissed, because the hospital was protected by the doctrine of charitable immunity at the time of the incident.

McCluskey v. Thranow, 142 N.W.2d 787 (Wisconsin 1966).

Most courts have held that when a surgeon knows or has reason to believe that a foreign object was left in the patient's body during an operation, it is the physician's duty to disclose the facts to his patient.

A patient had a section of her lung removed and afterward complained continually of a sharp pain in her chest. She continued to receive treatment from this surgeon until he died 4 years later.

She then visited another surgeon who took x-rays and told her that a metallic object was present in her chest. The surgeon recommended that surgery not be performed, because it did not warrant the risk. The patient continued to have pain in her chest and to be very nervous.

The negligence charged was the failure of the physician to disclose to the patient that a foreign object was left in her body. The patient recovered $70,000.

Tramatula v. Bortone, 288 A.2d 863 (N.J.1972).

Not only the physician but also the hospital may be held liable for failing to disclose negligent acts to an injured party.

A patient underwent surgery twice for prostatic cancer in 1972 and again was subjected to surgery in 1973.

The patient stated that he had repeatedly asked the physician and hospital nursing staff why the third operative procedure was necessary, but no one would answer his question. He did not know until some time later that the retention of a catheter during the second procedure in 1972 necessitated the third surgery in 1973.

The court held that the statute of limitations did not prevent the patient's claim from being brought. The hospital was obligated to divulge all material facts to its patients.

Garcia v. Presbyterian Hospital Center, 593 P.2d 487 (New Mexico 1979).

The damages awarded in a suit based on fraud may be substantial.

A patient had exploratory surgery for cancer. The mass could not be removed. During surgery two hemostats were left in the patient's abdomen.

When told about the hemostats by an x-ray technician a few months after the surgery, the patient became emotionally distraught and remained upset over the situation until his death. The patient died eleven months later as a result of his malignancy. His physical condition was such that additional surgery was impossible.

The appeals court held that the trial court's award of $49,000 was not excessive. The hospital and the surgeon were both liable.

Easter v. Hancock, 346 A.2d 323 (Pa.Super.1975).

FALSE IMPRISONMENT

The tort of false imprisonment results from infringement on a person's freedom of movement. Although most actions for false imprisonment involve psychiatric patients, in some cases medical patients who are not permitted to leave the hospital or are physically restrained for this purpose, clearly have a basis for a claim.

Because the psychiatrist failed to perform an adequate examination, he was liable for damages based on a charge of false imprisonment.

A woman filing for divorce was institutionalized at the request of her husband. She was refused permission for any outside contacts and was treated against her will for 6 days.

She received a jury verdict of $40,000 against the psychiatrist that was upheld on appeal.

Stowers v. Wolodzko, 191 N.W.2d 355 (Mich.1971).

SUMMARY

Nurses may be defendants in actions based on intentional torts as well as those based on negligence.

Examples of intentional torts include assault and battery, defamation of character, disclosure of confidential information, invasion of privacy, misrepresentation and fraud, and false imprisonment. With this classification of civil litigation, the four conditions for negligence do not have to be proven. The amount of damages awarded may be substantial and have no direct relationship to the amount of harm apparently suffered.

Nurses should be particularly concerned with actions involving disclosures of confidential information. These claims also reflect a violation of the ethical relationship a nurse establishes with every patient.

CHAPTER **10**

DISCIPLINARY ACTIONS

PROFESSIONAL INCOMPETENCE

One measure of the professionalism of an occupation is the extent to which the group directs its own development. It is clear that the nursing profession is experiencing a growing sense of professionalism. In the area of professional discipline, nurses have always attempted to establish and enforce standards. This is done primarily through the state licensure boards, which ensure that the profession exhibits a minimal level of competence.

The nurse's first responsibility, the standard for licensure, is clearly to provide quality professional care.

A nurse was licensed in another state and applied for a license in Nebraska. She met the objective statutory standards for licensure; however, the state board of nursing refused to grant the license, because they found the applicant guilty of unprofessional conduct, which was one criterion set by the state. The board found the nurse did not recheck the temperature of a 7-month-old child who was admitted to the hospital with a reported temperature of 105°F and further failed to notify the physician of the child's condition.

The Supreme Court of Nebraska affirmed the board's decision.
Scott v. State ex rel. Board of Nursing, 244 N.W.2d 683 (Neb.1976).

The Pennsylvania State Nursing Board formally reprimanded a nurse who had administered an anesthetic in the absence of a directing physician, which was impermissible.

A state regulation specifically empowered the board to "suspend or revoke" a nurse's license. In this case, the board issued a formal reprimand.

168

The court supported the board's decision and decided that the state board did not exceed its authority in granting the board of licensure this right.

McCarl v. Commonwealth State Board of Nurse Examiners, 396 A.2d 866 (Pa.1979).

The professional practice of nursing is governed in most jurisdictions by the Nurse Practice Act. Since this is a legislative act, courts must interpret the actions complained of according to what the act itself prohibits or permits.

The issue of what constitutes "unprofessional conduct" according to state law has been questioned.

The Idaho Board of Nursing suspended a nurse's license for unprofessional conduct.

The nurse argued that the acts she was accused of did not fall within the statutory definition of "unprofessional conduct." Specifically, these acts consisted of engaging in discussions with a patient regarding alternative methods of treatment for leukemia, such as Laetrile.

Her argument was approved by the Supreme Court of Idaho, which found that no guidelines were provided to forewarn the nurse that interference with the physician-patient relationship constituted unprofessional conduct and could result in suspension or revocation of her license. Therefore, the nurse could not be suspended.

Tuma v. Board of Nursing of the State of Idaho, 593 P.2d 711 (1979).

In the previous cases the court noted that the board of nursing was composed of professional nurses. The court determined that the legislature, in granting licensure authority to the board of nursing, intended the board to use this expertise in making such decisions.

A senior psychiatric aide was charged with misconduct in refusing to obey orders given to her by her superiors.

These charges included failure to observe constantly a suicidal patient, refusal to accompany a patient from the admitting unit to the patient's assigned unit, refusal to attend two meetings, and refusal of an order to wash thermometers.

The aide was dismissed from employment based on these charges. The court held that the dismissal was not an excessive penalty, since the conduct complained of was not an isolated or trivial incident but constituted serious acts with grave risk of harm to patients.

Tilford v. County of Westchester, 415 N.Y.S.2d 437 (1979).

Use of hospital medications for personal use is common grounds for disciplinary action.

A nurse was arrested after she had removed drugs from her place of work and took them to her home.

The Washington Supreme Court held that the action of a nurse in removing controlled substances from the hospital to her home did not amount to *distribution* within the meaning of the Nurse Practice Act since there was no attempt to transfer the drugs to another person. Therefore the nurse's license was not revoked.

Garrison v. Washington State Nursing Board, 550 P.2d 7 (Wash.1976).

A nurse obtained large quantities of a controlled drug by the unauthorized and improper use of her father's physician's Bureau of Narcotic and Dangerous Drug registration number. She injected the drugs in patients as part of a weight reduction program without an order from a licensed physician and without maintaining medical records of "treatments."

The nurse was found guilty of unprofessional conduct, and her license to practice was suspended for 5 years.

Livingston v. Nyquist, 388 N.Y.2d 42 (1976).

A registered nurse was charged with fraud and deceit in violating a state law. She was charged with addiction to drugs, habitual drunkenness and unprofessional conduct.

The nurse admitted to unlawfully taking 200 tablets of Doriden, a controlled substance, in 1969 from a hospital where she was employed and 100 tablets from another hospital in 1973.

The court held that her license was appropriately revoked.

Davin v. New York State Board of Regents, 393 N.Y.S.2d 832 (1977).

Practicing nursing without a license is clearly a basis for disciplinary action in most jurisdictions. One court has stated that the knowledge of a nurse that another person is practicing without a license may lead to a revocation of the license.

A nurse permitted and instructed her daughter to perform as a registered nurse when she knew or had reason to know that her daughter was not licensed to practice in that state.

The state law indicated that a nurse could have disciplinary action taken if he or she engaged in conduct derogatory to the morals or standards of the nursing profession.

The court held that there was substantial evidence to support the nursing board's conclusion that the nurse had acted in derogation of her professional responsibilities.

Ward v. Oregon State Board of Nursing, 510 P.2d 554 (Oregon 1973).

A registered nurse failed to mail in an application for renewal of her license. She continued to practice and was informed that a complaint had been filed with the nursing board concerning her continued practice under a lapsed license. She then requested the appropriate renewal forms. Her license was not renewed.

The court held that her license should be renewed because there was no finding of willful or unprofessional conduct.

Kansas State Board of Nursing v. Burkman, 531 P.2d 122 (Kansas 1975).

Most state laws provide that a nurse be suspended from practice or reprimanded if found guilty of unprofessional conduct.

A nurse should not have been reprimanded for slapping a patient to make him release his grasp on another nurse's arm.

The patient was disoriented. Three nurses were trying to turn him over to change his bed when he grasped the arm of one of the nurses. They asked him to release his grip and tried to pry his fingers from her arm. When that failed, the nurse slapped the back of his hand.

The state board of nurse examiners formally reprimanded her for violating the professional nursing law. On appeal, the court said that the evidence did not support a finding that the nurse violated the nursing law. The court felt that her action was justified.

Leukhardt v. Commonwealth of Pennsylvania State Board of Nurse Examiners, 403 A.2d 645 (Pa. Commonwealth Ct. July 18, 1979).

Violations of the Nurse Practice Act generally include practicing medicine without a license, practicing nursing while under the influence of drugs or alcohol, negligent assignment and employment of unqualified persons, and theft of hospital supplies.

DUE PROCESS

The decisions of the courts to refrain from interfering in determinations involving professional conduct are often reflected in cases involving whether privileges should be granted for physicians applying for membership to hospital medical staffs.

Courts unanimously have indicated a reluctance to overrule the decision of a governing body to refuse the appointment or reappointment of a physician to the hospital medical staff. As long as the due process rights of the physician have been protected according to the by-laws of the institution, courts will usually refrain from becoming involved with the facts.

The due process rights that must be met include a written notice of charges being made or reasons for denial of an appointment, an opportunity for a hearing, a relatively impartial body to conduct the hearing, an opportunity to produce evidence and witnesses, a written notice of the hearing body's recommended decision along with the reasons for the decision, and the opportunity to appeal the decision.

If these due process requirements have been met, courts will be reluctant to overrule the internal decision unless it is proven to be arbitrary or capricious.

This right of the medical staff to due process is granted by the by-laws of the institution. The right to full due process does not extend to the employer-employee relationship of the nurse who is employed by the hospital.

The hospital-employed nurse does not enjoy the due process rights described above.

SUMMARY

As the nursing profession continues to experience a growing sense of professionalism, the need for professional discipline increases. The nursing profession has always been known for its emphasis on self-discipline. The state licensure boards control vigorously the level of competence in the nursing profession. Cases involving discipline for professional incompetence are few compared to the large number of practicing nurses.

Due process rights that are granted to physicians who are members of the medical staff do not extend to nurses who are employees of the institution.

CHAPTER **11**

DOCUMENTATION

PURPOSE OF THE MEDICAL RECORD

The primary purpose of the medical record is to provide continuity of care. With an increasingly mobile society, as well as the age of medical specialization, it is important to ensure that a particular patient has a complete medical record with accurate information. In the average teaching hospital, a large number of hospital personnel will be using the patient's chart during a given hospital admission. Each person is relying on information provided in the chart in making his or her own determinations and professional judgments.

The institution is interested in providing an accurate record for the purposes of assessing the quality of care and for determining if patients are receiving the kind of professional care that the institution would like them to have. The medical record is also used for reimbursement purposes. Utilization review departments continuously review patient records to determine if the hospital and its services are being used appropriately. Patients who no longer need an acute care facility will be "terminated"; that is, their insurance will no longer provide coverage for their hospital stay.

Physicians use the medical record to obtain previous medical history. Physicians also use the record to communicate among themselves as well as with nursing and other ancillary hospital departments during the patient's hospital stay. What is or is not documented assumes critical importance in rendering care to patients.

The patient has a direct interest in his or her medical record (see Chapter 9). Not only does the patient care about the accuracy and reliability of what is in the record, but also the confidentiality of the record is of prime importance to the patient. Patients want to have the information in their record available for their own use. Free access to the record will be discussed later in this chapter. The patient should be

173

aware of what information is being released when the record is sent out. A patient with the following chart entry may hesitate to allow such a release: "Patient discovered he had high blood pressure after his extramarital affair."

The medical record is also used for legal purposes. It will be involved in personal injury cases, disability claims, workmen's compensation, insurance, and medical malpractice cases. In a legal proceeding the medical record administrator will be asked to testify to the authenticity of the record and whether it was prepared in the usual course of business. However, the fact that the medical record is a legal document assumes secondary importance to the use of the medical record as a medical document. The number of records that will be used in legal proceedings are a minority of all medical records that the average health care provider works with on a daily basis. *In general whether particular information should become part of the patient's record depends upon whether the information is significant to the medical care of the patient.*

Documentation on the patient's medical care in a malpractice proceeding is critical to the defense of the alleged claim. The chart may be the health care provider's best friend or worst enemy for what has been documented or omitted respectively. Omissions and alterations, as discussed later in this chapter, are the most frequent problems with charting from the malpractice defense standpoint. *Once a malpractice claim has been initiated against the hospital or a staff member, changes should not be made in the medical record.*

Finally, although we tend to identify the medical record with the hospital setting, the same considerations must be applied to the physician's office record, clinic records, nursing home records, and *any situation where medical care is given and records are kept.*

The proper content of hospital records varies, depending upon applicable state statutes and regulations controlling hospital licensure. Some states require simply the maintenance of accurate, complete, or adequate records; others prescribe broad categories of information to be included; others contain specific requirements about information that must be included. The Joint Commission on Accreditation of Hospitals (JCAH) imposes its own requirements for the content of hospital records, including identification information; evidence of appropriate informed consent or indication of the reason for its absence; medical history; report of physical examination; diagnostic and therapeutic orders; observations of the patient's condition, including progress and nursing notes; reports of all procedures, tests, and their results; and conclusions, including the provisional diagnosis, associated diagnosis, clinical resume, and necropsy reports. It is therefore important that hospitals and agencies have a mechanism to ascertain that its staff comply with all record-keeping requirements. Failure to comply with the requirements can lead to sanction, such as loss of license or accreditation by the licensing or accrediting body, or liability based on negligence.

ROLE OF NURSES' NOTES IN LITIGATION

An important part of the medical record for legal purposes is the area of the record identified as *nurses' notes*. In some institutions, nurses and physicians as well as all other personnel chart their observations in one section that is called *progress notes*. This system of integrated charting is a highly acceptable alternative to the usual method of segregated observations and treatments given to the patient in various sections of the chart. It is much easier to determine what happened to the patient in a 24-hour period when all the charting is grouped together. This is also preferable for legal reasons, since the courts presume that physicians read nurses' notes (and vice versa), and any procedure that will make it easier for that process to occur is commendable. Nurses should become familiar with the hospital policy on charting. Some hospitals use graphic or flow charts to summarize numerical and objective data to facilitate completeness of charting.

Historically, the issue of the role of nurses' notes has come full circle. In the past, emphasis was placed on extensive charting for nurses. Nurses were told to document any care that was given to the patient or any observations made. Some time later nurses were taught to chart only what was significant to the patient—"routine care" was not to be documented. Before too long this was recognized as a mistake.

In a malpractice suit, it is sometimes the absence of routine care that is viewed as negligence. The presumption in the law is that if it was not documented, it was not done. Therefore, the nurse-witness or nurse-defendant may have to testify that the patient was turned and positioned every 2 hours to prevent pneumonia postoperatively as standard nursing practice, even though the documentation does not support this testimony. A common example of this problem are cases involving the nurse's responsibility to take vital signs.

A patient entered Glenwood Hospital on July 21, 1978, for delivery of her second child. The baby was delivered without incident and her doctor left the hospital a short time later. Approximately an hour later, the patient began hemorrhaging severely due to an everted uterus. Two physicians responded to the emergency and attempted unsuccessfully to revert the uterus by manually pushing it back to its original position. An emergency postpartal hysterectomy with the consent of plaintiff's husband was performed. On the day of her anticipated discharge, the wound from the surgery reopened through the several layers of skin and tissue. She was rushed to surgery and a second closure was performed. Three days later she was discharged from the hospital.

Although she had undergone a total hysterectomy (i.e., complete removal of the uterus), she continued to have light monthly bleeding and it was discovered that part of her cervix and some endometrial cells of the uterus had not been removed. She subsequently developed cervicitis (inflammation of the cervix) and underwent surgery for removal of the remainder of the cervix in October, 1981).

She brought suit alleging that the physician was negligent in failing to anticipate poor wound healing, in attempting to perform a surgical procedure beyond his capability, in failing to complete the procedure by removing the cervix, and in removing her fallopian tubes and an ovary without her consent. She further alleged the hospital was negligent in failing to keep adequate records of her condition.

After trial, the jury found the physicians were not negligent in their treatment of plaintiff. They found the hospital negligent, but its negligence was not a cause of the patient's damage. The court stated that while the charts with respect to vital signs were obviously incomplete and poorly kept when measured against hospital regulations, their deficiency played no part in causing the problems suffered by the patient.

Trichel v. Caire, 427 So.2d 1227 (Louisiana 1983).

The patient had extensive abdominal surgery. Postoperatively, the surgeon issued 11 orders including one requiring the checking and recording of the patient's vital signs—including temperature, pulse, respiration, and blood pressure every 15 minutes for 1 hour and then every hour for 10 hours. Despite this order, the patient's temperature was recorded only 4 times during a 24-hour period. During one such time gap the patient's temperature rose from 101.4 degrees F to 105.2 degess F. On the day of surgery, a nurse placed tissue over the incision to stop the bleeding. The patient suffered severe brain damage.

The court held that the hospital failed to render reasonable postoperative care and that this caused an infection leading to fever and brain damage. The patient received an award of $800,000.

Robert v. Chodoff, 393 A.2d 853 (Pa.Super.1978).

The testimony in the previous case included the fact that nurses frequently use a notebook or some other form of notes as they perform patient care and later transfer all of the information to the patient's medical record. The transfer of the information to the patient's record is absolutely necessary in the event that a physician visiting the patient wants to check the patient's condition.

Although the physician in the previous case had ordered a monitoring of vital signs, it is to be expected that where a specific order is not given, it would be within the nurse's responsibility to institute such a procedure. This is in accordance with a judicial system's continuing recognition of the professional expertise of the nurse. An order to contact the physician if vital signs are abnormal should not be necessary. It is within the judgment of the professional nurse to know when to communicate this information.

A 6-year-old child was struck by a car while riding his bicycle. He sustained a fractured leg and required traction. Five days later his leg had to be amputated.

The hospital records contained an order by the physician to watch the condition of the patient's toes. There was no evidence in the record that the child's foot was observed during a 7-hour period. At the time of the next observation, his condition had become irreversible.

Collins v. Westlake Community Hospital, 312 N.E.2d 614 (Ill.1974).

Another case where the nurses' notes played a crucial role discussed the nurses' documentation in regard to a standing order.

Twin girls born prematurely were ordered oxygen at the rate of 6 liters per minute for the first 12 hours and 4 liters per minute thereafter. The infants became blind. Evidence indicated that the nurses did not follow the physician's order to reduce the oxygen, and the pediatrician failed to note the deviation from his order, although he was visiting the infants daily. The nurses' notes contained no specific indication that 4 liters was being administered until 31 days after oxygen therapy began, although there were notations of 10 occasions during the 31-day period that 6 liters were being administered.

The explanation for the absence of notations to that effect was that this was consistent with a standing order, where there was no need for the nurses to make notations other than to note deviations from the therapeutic course established by the physician's order.

Thus, the notations specifying the 6 liters covered those instances when, because of temporary deterioration in the infant's condition, it was deemed necessary, based on medical judgment, to increase the rate of flow. Otherwise, the setting was maintained at 4 liters according to the nurses testimonies.

The complaint against the hospital was originally dismissed by the trial judge, but on appeal the court ordered a new trial.

Toth v. Community Hospital at Glen Cove, 239 N.E.2d 368 (New York 1968).

Unfortunately, there were some inconsistent notations in the record of the previous case. The notation "constant oxygen" was said to refer to the 4-liter rate, but at times it appeared to refer to the use of a 6-liter rate.

If a procedure is initiated on the basis of standing orders, the nurse should document the basis and rationale for its initiation.

A 7-year-old patient in the recovery room appeared to be regaining consciousness normally after an operation to remove his tonsils and adenoids when the patient on the gurney next to him began coughing. The only RN in the recovery room, who happened to be standing between the two beds, gave her attention to the patient having difficulty. As she attended this patient, the 7-year-old boy suffered cardiac and respiratory arrest. The boy's pulse and respiration were eventually restored, but he never regained consciousness and died a few days later.

The child's father brought a lawsuit against the hospital and the surgeon for having caused the child's death through negligence. The defense argued that the child's death had resulted from pre-existing heart disease.

The entries by the RN in the postanesthesia recovery record indicated that at 8:30 AM the child was resting quietly, and at 8:35 AM his vital signs were recorded. The next entry noted that at 8:45 AM the child had no pulse or respiration and a Code 99 alarm had been called. In court, however, the recovery room RN testified that the child's arrest occurred at 8:40 AM.

The trial court returned a verdict in favor of the surgeon, but found the hospital liable for negligence. The hospital appealed the decision.

The Intermediate Court of Appeals of Hawaii rejected the defense's argument because the autopsy revealed no evidence of heart disease. The court found the hospital liable for negligence because it had failed to make certain that recovery room personnel were meeting the standards of care required by law. The hospital was ordered to pay the plaintiff $400,000 in damages.

The court concluded that the RN would have noticed the child's condition earlier if she had monitored him more closely. In addition, the RN's testimony about the time of the cardiac and respiratory arrest conflicted with the entry she had made in the recovery room records. Apparently she had not recorded the event at the time it happened. Therefore, the court determined that she had violated both standards of care listed above.

Yorita v. Okumoto, 643 P.2d 820 (Hawaii App. 1982).

A properly documented record adds to the defensibility of any malpractice claim.

HOW TO DOCUMENT

Nurses' notes are always reviewed by attorneys before litigation is initiated. These notes offer the most detailed observations of the patient. They also document whether the physician's orders were carried out and the results of the treatments.

In general, the notes should reflect factual information—what is seen, felt, and heard; what is being done for the patient; and the patient's response to the action. It is often important to document what the patient has said, not only to aid in care but also for litigation purposes.

If the patient falls and then says "It was my fault; the nurse told me to call, and I did not" or "I fell, but I am not hurt," these words could become vital for the successful defense of a suit for negligence based on an injury from the fall.

If the patient complains of pain, the notes should indicate where the pain is located, its severity, and what it is associated with. If medication is given, the results should be noted.

A complete and honest record is absolutely necessary (see Chapter 9). An alteration in the record can result in an allegation of fraud. The alteration may lead to a case that is impossible to defend because of the damage to the credibility involved.

A 49-year-old nurse in normal physical condition had her gallbladder removed. Two hours into the operation, the surgeon advised the anesthesiologist that he did not feel a pulse. Her heart had been in arrest for about 5 minutes, and the patient suffered permanent brain damage.

Suit was filed against the anesthesiologist for failing to notice the patient's heart was beating weakly and for failing to take remedial measures.

When the records were requested by the attorney, the anesthesiologist went to the record room and began adding to the operation sheet until advised by a clerk that these actions were improper.

The jury awarded a defense verdict. However, the appeals court reversed the verdict and sent the case back for a retrial. The subsequent decision was not reported.

Seaton v. Rosenberg, 573 S.W.2d 333 (Ky.Sup.Ct., October 31, 1978).

The record must reflect everything that has happened to the patient including any unusual events. Although it is necessary to describe any incident, such as the facts of a fall or a burn, it is not necessary nor is it recommended to chart the phrase "incident report filed" (See Chapter 12).

Charting should be on consecutive lines with no spaces in between.

Such spaces might allow an event to be documented after the fact. Each note should have a date and time as well as the name and professional designation of the person making it. There should be continuity in the record. For example, if a patient is inadvertently burned, the following days' notations should describe whether the burn is healing.

Sometimes information is inadvertently omitted that may be critical to patient care. Perhaps a nurse on a busy medical-surgical floor has a patient with an unexpected cardiac arrest on the unit. That night the nurse mulls over the events of the day and realizes the failure to document a vital aspect of the patient's condition or treatment. In such a case, an addition to the medical record may be appropriate even though it will not be in sequence of time. The appropriate way to make the addition is for the nurse to use the next available blank space in the hospital record to make the notation. The entry should have the correct date and time but should be headed "Addendum or addition to nurse's note of month, day, time." This is an honest addition to the record for purposes of providing the documentation of complete patient care. Such an addition will not injure the credibility of the nurse defendant in the eyes of the jury.

Generalized terms should be avoided. Evaluations by the hospital staff should be based on specific observations. The classic example for nurses is the phrase "patient had a good night." Does this mean that the patient who has not slept in 3 nights finally had 2 hours of sleep? Or does it mean the patient was comfortable and slept well as usual? Or might it mean that the patient was quiet and did not bother the nurses?

If the nurse is unable to perform a treatment, it is important that the chart reflect the omission and the reason for the omission. When a physician is notified, the record should show that he or she was informed, what the physician was told, and what time the notification occurred. An example of this is the situation where the physician orders an intravenous line removed on a patient who is dehydrated and has a poor oral intake. The nurse has a duty to discuss this (the dehydration and poor oral intake) with the physician. If, nevertheless, the order is to stand, the nurse should chart "IV discontinued as ordered by Dr. John. Doctor made aware of patient's oral intake being 100 cc in 24 hours and the inability to retain fluids (emesis two times today)."

If the nurse had deviated from a hospital policy or procedure or from a standard nursing practice in caring for a patient, the record should reflect this deviation and why it occurred. Policies and procedures are admissible in court and are frequently used to establish standards of care as well as to show deviations from such standards. The nurse who deviates from policies and procedures might have to defend this deviation.

Nurses frequently question how to document the situation when a physician does not respond quickly to a call for help. (See Chapter 4 for a discussion of the nurse's obligation to make sure that the patient is receiving medical attention.) The nurse should carefully document the time the physician was called and the time of his response, as well as the content of the conversation. If the situation is serious and the physician has not responded, the nurse should notify her supervisor in addition to properly documenting what has occurred.

Following the birth of her child, the patient began to bleed. The nurse told the physician three times that the patient was bleeding excessively. The physician instructed the nurse to keep watching the patient.

Some time later, the nurse checked, but the patient died from a hemorrhage due to laceration of the cervix shortly after the doctor's arrival.

The appellate court ordered a new trial and stated that evidence was sufficient to support a finding that the nurse who knew the mother was bleeding excessively was negligent in failing to report to her superior the circumstances of the mother's peril so that prompt and adequate measures could be taken to safeguard her life.

Goff v. Doctor' General Hospital, 333 P.2d 29 (Calif.1958).

The nurse should document carefully the method of admission to the institution and the patient's condition on admission. If an elderly patient, following his or her first night in the hospital, is found with bruising and lacerations, it is important to know if the patient was admitted with these injuries.

With the initiation of the prospective payment system resulting in the decreased use of acute care facilities and the earlier discharge of patients, discharge instructions and evaluations are becoming a critical aspect of patient care and should also be thoroughly documented. Documentation regarding health teaching should include what was taught to the patient and how the patient was evaluated to assess his or her understanding of the instructions. If a family member was also instructed, this should be noted.

ALTERING THE RECORD

Records that have been altered for whatever reason should include the date, reason for change, and signature, and position of the person making the change.

If an error is made in charting, the acceptable method of correction is to draw a single line through the error, write "error" above it, the date, time, and initials of the person making the correction. The correct entry should then be made in the next available space in the chart. This entry should describe the correction of the previous entry and should also be signed. The original charting should never be obliterated, for the implication could be that a cover-up has occurred.

Another reason for making the correction in such a manner is that a physician or nurse may have acted on the information contained in the first notation. If a clinical decision has been made based on the erroneous information, it may later be impossible to justify the reason for that decision after the erroneous information has been obliterated or removed from the chart. If the alteration was dishonest or appears to be dishonest, it could result in a charge of fraud or misrepresentation.

A 23-year-old woman was admitted to the hospital's psychiatric unit with a diagnosis of schizophrenia. After being placed in the unit's "quiet room," all furniture including a steel bedframe was removed for safety reasons. The frame remained out of the room for 3 days but reappeared for no explained reason on the fourth day.

A few days later, the nursing staff failed to record an order for antipsychotic medication resulting in no such medication being given for a 3-day period.

The patient was later found in a semicomatose condition after her neck became lodged between the siderails and the mattress of her hospital bed.

A few days following the patient's injury, the director of nursing at the hospital ordered the entire staff who charted the patient's care to rewrite and change the hospital records. The original record was removed, and a "revised" record substituted without the knowledge of the hospital administration and in violation of explicit hospital policy. The substituted record was clearly false and conflicted with other records and the testimony of staff on duty at the time.

The jury was instructed by the judge to consider the substitution of the record as a circumstance indicating the hospital's consciousness of negligence. A $3.6 million verdict was upheld.

Pisel v. Stamford Hospital et al, 430 A.2d 1 (Conn.1980).

The medical record should never be erased or obliterated. In a potential liability situation, it would be prudent to have the notation witnessed by a coworker. The following case is an example of how an alteration in the record may prove devastating in court.

A 6-year-old child was admitted for minor eye surgery. During the administra-

tion of anesthesia, he suffered a cardiac arrest and subsequently severe brain damage.

The evening before surgery, he entered the hospital with a runny nose and was quite apprehensive and uncooperative. He had a temperature elevation when he first arrived that increased up to midnight. The hospital records purport to show that his temperature just before the operation was a little under normal, but expert testimony indicated that there had been a correction and erasure in the record, and what the original record showed did not appear.

The appeals court held that the jury should decide whether the operation should have been postponed. The jury returned a verdict of $4 million against the hospital and physicians.

Quintal v. Laurel Grove Hospital, 397 P.2d 161, 41 Cal.Rptr. 577 (1965).

Use of "white out" on nurses' notes has resulted in a need to x-ray these notes in at least one malpractice case.

Plaintiffs' claims of fraud and mistake received their impetus from an interview by Plaintiffs' counsel of Dr. Terry Gerard in the spring of 1984. At that interview Dr. Gerard, who had been an intern at Doctors Hospital at the time of Gary's birth, signed an affidavit stating that he had placed certain progress notes in the child's hospital chart which are no longer there. He said these entries were critical of Dr. Greenwald, a Defendant in the medical malpractice action. Primarily, he said the notes documented his unsuccessful efforts to get Dr. Greenwald to come to the hospital to treat Gary.

Following the interview with Dr. Gerard, Plaintiffs' counsel discovered "white outs" in Gary Ahrens' hospital chart which also are alleged to have been part of a fraudulent scheme.

The court first dealt with the alleged missing progress notes and then with the white outs.

Dr. Gerard testified that during the afternoon of Gary's birth (July 12, 1979), he was the intern on duty. Three infants were in the nursery under his care—Gary Ahrens, Jeffrey Ahrens, and Misty George. He said he made notes during the afternoon on a pad and that that evening, he transferred these notes onto "Progress Record" forms in Gary Ahrens' and Misty George's hospital charts. The charts do not contain any such notes however. Dr. Gerard testified that he made no progress notes with respect to Gary Ahrens' twin brother, Jeffrey (there is a Progress Record form in Jeffrey Ahrens' chart which contains two entries dated July 13 and 16, 1979 signed by Dr. Nickelsen, the attending pediatrician). Dr. Gerard testified that it was unnecessary for him to make progress notes on Jeffrey Ahrens, because he was not having any problems. There is no Progress Record form at all in the charts of either Gary Ahrens or Misty George. Witnesses for both sides stated this was not unusual in a case where the patient was at the hospital for less than a day. Jeffrey

Ahrens' post-delivery course was uneventful, but Misty George had hyaline membrane disease, and Gary Ahrens developed hypoglycemia.

Pursuant to a request made by the pediatrician (the request was made by Dr. Neil Nickelsen, partner of Dr. Greenwald) for the George and Ahrens infants, Misty George and Gary Ahrens were picked up by a transport team. The transport team had been called to pick up Misty George. However, when they arrived mid-evening at the Hospital, Dr. Nickelsen asked them to transfer Gary Ahrens also on the evening of July 12, and they were taken to special high-risk nurseries at Grady and Egleston Hospitals respectively. Standard procedure in such cases is to send a copy of the transported infant's chart with him to the new hospital, but no copy was sent with Gary Ahrens to Egleston Hospital. Gary Ahrens' hospital chart does not contain a parental authorization for a copy of his chart to be sent. Misty George's chart, however, reflects a signed consent for a copy of her chart to be sent to Grady Hospital on July 12, 1979. No evidence was presented addressing whether Grady has a copy of Misty George's file, and if so, whether it contains any progress notes by Dr. Gerard.

A few days after Gary Ahrens' transfer to Egleston Hospital, he developed necrotizing enterocolitis which required removal of his colon. The reason necrotizing enterocolitis developed is a major issue in the case. Plaintiffs have alleged a number of contributing causes. For one thing, they allege that Gary's premature delivery by elective cesarean section was a causal factor in his developing hypoglycemia. The hypoglycemia in turn allegedly caused or contributed to the necrotizing enterocolitis. In addition, Plaintiffs allege that the pediatricians responsible for Gary's care—Dr. Greenwald and Dr. Nickelsen—negligently failed to be present in the nursery on the afternoon following his birth. This failure is alleged to have caused a delay in treating his hypoglycemia, thus contributing to the later development of necrotizing enterocolitis.

Finally, there is evidence that when Dr. Gerard inserted an umbilical vein catheter in Gary while caring for him, that the catheter was misplaced and became curled up inside the child's liver. Dr. Greenwald contends that he instructed Dr. Gerard to give oral feedings of glucose only. Dr. Greenwald's contention is that Gary's hypoglycemia was not severe enough to require intravenous glucose, and that Dr. Gerard acted improperly when he allegedly decided on his own to administer intravenous glucose.

Since there is an absence of documentary evidence and no testimonial evidence except Dr. Gerard's affirming his creation of progress notes on July 12, 1979, the fate of the petition depends entirely on Dr. Gerard's credibility.

Dr. Gerard is not a disinterested witness. Rather, he participated in Gary Ahrens' care during a critical time following the child's birth. He admits that as the intern on duty, he had the obligation to place appropriate progress notes in the hospital charts of his patients. Yet, there is no tangible evidence that he put any progress notes in the charts of any of the three patients he treated.

Dr. Gerard's stated perspective on the events of July 12 is that until he inserted the umbilical vein catheter in Gary Ahrens (at about 6:00 PM), the child was in a great deal of distress. He explicitly testified that Gary was lethargic and that he had to be fed through a nasogastric tube. This particular part of his testimony was very unconvincing. Indeed, Dr. Gerard admitted uncertainty as to whether he had reported any lethargy or physical symptoms to the attending pediatrician during their phone conversations. After some equivocation, he testified he probably had told the pediatrician that the child was a "little bit listless." Tr.69. At another point in his testimony he testified that he was uncertain that he was capable of identifying lethargy in a newborn.

Other evidence contradicted Dr. Gerard's testimony about the lethargy and the nasogastric tube. The nurses' notes in Gary Ahrens' chart do not reflect that he was lethargic or in distress (the nurses' notes on the George infant, on the other hand, do reflect a distressed infant). The notes reflect that Gary was fed orally, not through a nasogastric tube: Further, Sue Peterson—the only nurse who had an independent recollection of the events of July 12—testified credibly that Gary Ahrens had not been lethargic and that he had been fed orally, not through a nasogastric tube. (She testified that Misty George had had a nasogastric tube, however.) Dr. Gerard's contrary testimony, therefore, is not credited.

The fact that Dr. Gerard's testimony was impeached in certain respects lessens the court's confidence in his testimony that he placed progress notes in the file which are not now there. Also, the fact that his testimony is uncorroborated, and the fact that he is not disinterested weigh negatively. Thus, the court is unable to find that the evidence is of "clear, unequivocal, and decisive" quality. This failure is fatal to both the fraud and mistake theories.

After Dr. Gerard's testimony came to light, Plaintiffs' counsel reviewed Gary Ahrens' original hospital chart and found "white outs" on certain portions of the nursing notes. The allegation is that these white outs were part of a fraudulent scheme to hide relevant facts concerning Gary Ahrens' treatment, or alternatively the cause of a mutual mistake concerning Gary Ahrens' course of treatment.

Analysis of these contentions is simplified by the fact that the parties have determined with x-ray equipment what the original notes said prior to the white outs. The line in the nursing notes which originally said "1628 results of RBS–1628–Dr. Gerard notified—" was changed to delete the intermediate reference to "1628" and to substitute "21%," so that the line as altered now reads: "1628 Results of RBS–21%—Dr. Gerard notified."

Another line in the nursing notes originally read: "1745 Scalp vein IV started per Dr. Fund with C̄ # needle." This entry was whited out and over that, the following entry was made: "1750 glucagon τ mg IM given RAT as ordered. Took and retained 10cc D5W Has fair suck reflex."

Beth Tiller, the nurse who made the original entries, the white outs, and the "write overs," testified at the September 13–14 hearing. Her testimony was credible. She stated that the white out/write over procedure was not in accordance with correct nursing standards and that the proper procedure would have been for her to line through the erroneous material, mark it "error," and then make a correct entry beneath it. She said she could not remember why she had used the white out fluid instead. It was clear that she lacked an independent recollection of the events of July 12, 1979, but the nature of the material "whited over," taken in conjunction with other material in the chart, fails to suggest a fraudulent or guilty motive. First, the substitution of the figure of 21 percent for 1628 was an obvious correction of an inadvertent repetition of the time of day. Secondly, it seems likely that Nurse Tiller made the entry concerning the scalp vein IV as Dr. Funk tried to start the IV. When he failed because the patient's veins were too small, Nurse Tiller decided to change the entry. The white out procedure was improper, but the court again is unable to infer a fraudulent or guilty motive. Therefore, the white out made by Nurse Tiller was not significant to meaningful review of the chart.

For the foregoing reasons, the court finds no fraud or mistake relievable in equity under applicable Georgia law, and the judgment in favor of the Hospital stands.

Ahrens v. Katz, 595 F.Supp.1108 (1984)

The destruction of records may prove to be even more devastating in a malpractice case.

A man appeared at the hospital emergency room with severe pain. The nurse refused to call a physician, and the patient returned home where he died a short time later.

The nurses testified that they had taken the patient's vital signs, but the records had been destroyed.

The court held that the jury could find the hospital to be negligent.

Carr v. St. Paul Fire and Marine Insurance Co., 384 F.Supp. 821 (1974).

A patient underwent a tubal ligation and subsequently suffered ruptured ectopic pregnancy. The patient brought suit against the hospital where the tubal ligation took place, alleging that the procedure was performed negligently. The hospital moved for summary judgment on the basis that plaintiff had failed to present expert testimony to establish that the procedure was negligently performed or that such negligence was the proximate cause of her injuries. Plaintiff conceded that she was unable to meet this burden but pointed out that the reason her expert witness was unable to evaluate the treatment was that there were no records of it. The trial court granted the hospital's summary judgment motion, and plaintiff appealed.

The appellate court reversed, holding that the burden of proof should be shifted to the defense in malpractice actions where the defendant has failed to maintain treatment records. Such records are essential to proving a malpractice claim, the court pointed out, and health care providers have both a statutory and a moral duty to maintain them. Relying on principles of fairness and public policy, the court wished to avoid a rule which would allow a health care provider to benefit from its own misconduct. Thus, the court held that where a health care provider negligently fails to maintain treatment records, a presumption of negligent treatment arises and burden of proof on this issue shifts to the defense. The court further held that where the failure to maintain treatment records is intentional, the health care provider should be foreclosed from rebutting the presumption of negligence. In such a case, therefore, the treatment would be deemed negligent and the claimant will be left only with the burden of proving damages. The court also ruled that the burden of showing that the failure to maintain records was negligent rather than deliberate should rest with the health care provider, since the evidence regarding the reason that the records are unavailable would be peculiarly within the health care provider's knowledge.

The court went on to rule that although it is the duty of the physician, rather than the hospital, to make a record of a patient's treatment, the hospital has an independent duty to assure that such records are kept.

Valcin v. Public Health Trust of Dade County, 473 So.2d 1297 (Fla.App.1985).

In 1979, a patient was admitted to Cedars of Lebanon Hospital for study and evaluation of his coronary arteries. Several days later, after a determination that a triple bypass operation was required, he went into surgery. At some point during the administration of anesthesia, he suffered a cardiac arrest and despite a concerted and indisputably nonnegligent effort by all present to save his life, died.

The patient's wife sued the hospital, the Florida Patients' Compensation Fund (the Fund), and the anesthesiologists. Her multicount complaint charged that the anesthesiologists' negligence caused the cardiac arrest; that the hospital was negligent in its selection and supervision of these anesthesiologists; and, of particular pertinence to this appeal, that the hospital was negligent per se by failing, contrary to Section 395.202, Florida Statutes (1979), to provide the patient with requested medical records, thus "[frustrating] the plaintiff's ability to pursue certain proof which may be necessary to establish her case"; and, that the hospital intentionally interfered with Mrs. Bondu's right of action in that it "purposely and intentionally lost and/or destroyed," among others, the anesthesiology records, again "[frustrating] the plaintiff's ability to pursue certain proof which may be necessary to establish her case."

The hospital's duty to maintain and furnish such records to a patient or the patient's personal representative upon request (implicit in which is the duty to make such records in the first instance) is found in Section 395.202, Florida Statutes (1979):

"395.202 Patient records; copies; examination.—

"(1) Any licensed hospital shall, upon request, and only after discharge of the patient, furnish to any person admitted therein for care and treatment or treated thereat, or such person's guardian, curator, personal representative, or anyone designated by such person in writing, a true and correct copy of all records in the possession of the hospital, except progress notes and consultation report sections of a psychiatric nature concerning the care and treatment performed therein by the hospital, provided the person requesting such records agrees to pay a reasonable charge for the copying of said records, and further shall allow examination of the original records in its possession, or microfilms or other suitable productions of the records, upon such reasonable terms as shall be imposed to assure that the records shall not be damaged, destroyed, or altered.

"(2) The provisions of this act shall not apply to any hospital whose primary function is to provide psychiatric care to its patients."

Since the patient's wife alleges that this duty was breached by the hospital when it failed to furnish Mr. Bondu's records to her, and that this breach caused her damage in that she lost "a medical negligence lawsuit when [she] could not provide expert witnesses," her complaint states a cause of action. Since the complaint does not allege that the records were intentionally removed or destroyed, the hospital need not prove otherwise.

Bondu v. Gurvich, 473 So.2d 1307 (Fla.App.3 Dist. 1984).

In addition to the presumption that if an action was not documented, it was not done, a second presumption is that anyone who signs a document has read it. Sometimes physicians will countersign verbal orders that were interpreted incorrectly and fail to note the error. The physicians cannot successfully defend themselves by saying that they did not read the orders but signed them.

When a nurse is asked to sign a nurse's note of which she or he has no personal knowledge, the nurse may have to defend a claim of negligence. For example, if one nurse adds a medication to an intravenous solution, and another nurse records the medication, both nurses will be subject to an allegation of negligence if a problem arises regarding the administration of a wrong medication.

Some institutions, by policy, require that only registered nurses document observations on the medical record. In these hospitals, nurses chart the observations of other personnel. To avoid confusion, the nurse should chart these notes as accurately as possible. For example, "Bed bath administered by nursing assistant Edwards."

Some hospitals also require a countersignature by a nursing instructor when a nursing student charts. If this is the policy, it should be made clear whether the instructor is countersigning to validate the activities of the student or to check the quality of the documentation itself.

SOCIAL SERVICE

Social service workers are also concerned about their liability exposure and the need for appropriate documentation.

Social workers, as professionals, are accountable for their own actions. The nature of this profession requires attention to the social status of the patient as well as behavioral characteristics that tend to be more subjective in nature.

Some institutions require their social service department to maintain separate departmental records. A preferable policy allows the social service worker to chart pertinent observations on the patient's medical record. This recognizes the role of the social worker as a member of the health care team and the unique contribution that can be made through the assessment and perspective of this professional.

Each social service note should reflect all social service activity on behalf of the patient including the results of contacts. For example, "discussed case with physician yesterday" would be a more valuable note if it read "discussed case with Dr. White yesterday, who feels that home care is indicated."

The general rules of documentation noted in this chapter apply to social service notes. The most important of these rules as they apply to social service include the need to be objective and to display thought processes when decisions are being made. Recommendations made to the physician or patient should be documented. The provision of alternatives or options regarding community agencies and nursing homes should be documented. Discharge or closing notes are particularly important. This note should indicate whether the discharge plan has been carried out. It should also include, when appropriate, such facts as the ambulance company name and expected time of pick up as well as family and professional notification.

INTERNAL REPORTS

Internal reports, such as incident reports and committee minutes, are a second type of documentation found in hospitals.

Questions are often raised by nurses as to the type of documentation appropriate on such reports. A second concern frequently expressed is the potential for use of these documents in a malpractice case.

INCIDENT REPORTS

The document traditionally known as an *incident report* is one example of an internal report used to identify problems within the institution. An incident report should be used to document any unusual occurrences whether or not harm has occurred to the patient. In some states these reports are called *event occurrence* or *situation reports*. Documentation of the incident report must follow the same guidelines as those of the patient's medical record (see Chapter 12). Opinions should be avoided. For example, a patient received too much intravenous solution, and one nurse stated on the report that another nurse was negligent. This is a judgment based on one person's perspective. In this case, the patient had received too much solution because the patient had readjusted the flow.

Judgments such as this should be avoided in the patient's record as well as on the incident report. The incident report should be a reflection of the documentation on the medical record. All information regarding the incident correctly belongs on the medical record and on the incident report as a means of notifying the administration and the risk management office. The incident report is a management tool that provides for the reporting of important occurrences in a convenient manner.

In some states, incident reports may be used in court as evidence and can be used as evidence in litigation. Therefore, opinions rendered on this report could be very damaging. The incident report should not be part of the medical record. In some instances, an investigative report is needed to clarify the incident. This should also not become part of the medical record but must be filed in the risk management office together with the incident report. The purpose of the investigative follow-up is to determine what can be done to prevent a similar problem in the future. Thus, the incident report serves two purposes. The first purpose is to prevent similar problems in the future. The second is to provide notice of potential litigation.

COMMITTEE MINUTES

Committee reports are often requested in malpractice cases. These reports may contain information regarding a particular patient as that included in a mortality or tissue committee report. A committee report may also be used to identify problem areas within the institution as in the infection or audit committee report.

Because of the need to encourage hospital and medical staffs to have a frank and honest evaluation of problems, most states have specifically enacted laws to prevent the use of these reports in malpractice cases. Many states completely protect all information that is designated for use in peer review activities. This may include risk management and quality assurance data as well as incident reports depending on the wording of the particular state statutes.

An infant was born prematurely and allegedly became blind due to prolonged overdoses of oxygen.

As part of the malpractice suit, the plaintiff's attorney requested minutes of various committee meetings.

The court interpreted the Texas statute to preclude the use of these documents for court.

Texarkana Memorial Hospital, Inc. v. Jones, 551 S.W.2d 33 (Texas 1977).

In the previous case, the court observed that the improvement of medical treatment can only be served through uninhibited discussions.

On the contrary, a Colorado court recently permitted the use of the hospital's infection control committee reports.

A patient was treated for a compound fracture of the leg. The leg became infected.

In the malpractice case that followed, the patient's attorney requested the hospital to provide the infection control committee report.

The court, in ordering the hospital to produce the document, stated that this report was not protected by the Colorado statute. The court did not feel that the production of this report would inhibit the committee's activity.

Davidson v. Light, 79 F.R.D. 137 (Colorado 1978).

As the two previous cases indicate, it is difficult to predict whether the court will permit such documents as hospital committee reports for use in malpractice cases. The statutes of the particular state play a significant role in these rulings.

PROBLEM-ORIENTED RECORDS

In recent years, efforts have been directed toward the establishment of new systems of charting. It is generally believed that more effective mechanisms are needed to provide better records.

One such system is the problem-oriented approach. There are, at present, no legal standards as to how charting must be accomplished. The court cases have addressed the issues of what should be documented. The profession must determine the best method for accomplishing the goal of accurate and complete documentation.

Any approach that places the emphasis on providing a mechanism for systematic charting and that allows no omissions of important data should be advocated. Since all health care providers may be held liable for their omissions of data, as well as commissions, some systematic evaluation that allows for individualized patient care is greatly needed.

PATIENT ACCESS TO RECORDS

Hospital records are normally considered the physical property of the hospital. The contents of the patient's medical record, however, belong to the patient. Therefore, it is the patient who should control the access of others to the medical record.

For years, patients have been denied the right to review or have copies of their records, while others (insurance companies, physicians, nurses) had total access to these records. Both courts and legislatures have realized that the confidential information contained in the record must be protected. If a copy of the patient's record is requested, the patient must sign an authorization indicating that this is a valid release of the record.

Sometimes patients request an opportunity to read their records while in the hospital. This may reflect a breakdown in communication between the health care providers and the patient, or it may simply be a matter of curiosity. In general, the patient does have the right to review their record. Only where the contents of the record may prove injurious to the patient should a restriction exist. Some states have provided for this exception through legislation. However, if the contents of the record may be injurious to the patient based on a determination by the physician, an alternative may be to allow the patient's next-of-kin to review the record. The patient's permission must be obtained before such a review may occur.

A practical reason for permitting patients to see their own records is to give them an opportunity to determine that their records are correct. Errors may occur despite the best efforts of health care providers.

This procedure also allows the patient to become a more complete participant in his or her own care. It may be recommended to the patient that having a physician or nurse present during the review will aid in the interpretation of the medical contents of the record. Copies of records should be released to the patient or their designee, including their attorney, for a set fee and with reasonable requirements.

Certain records may be protected by specific federal statutes. The information on these records should only be released with a specified release from the patient or on a court order. These records include information related to drug and alcohol use.

All health care providers should be cautioned about releasing patient information without the permission of the patient, for example, in response to a telephone inquiry (see Chapter 4).

SUMMARY

A significant portion of the medical record for legal purposes is the area of the record identified as nurses' notes. The nurses' documentation presents the most complete picture of the patient. Frequently, an omission in a patient's record leads to an allegation that the nurse has breached the standards of care.

Nurses' notes should be factual, honest, and without opinions. If a deviation from usual procedure is necessary, the nurse should document the reason. Medical records should never be altered or destroyed.

Other documentation may exist in the form of incident reports and committee minutes. These documents may be used in court as evidence in a malpractice case depending on the state laws.

In recent years, patients have gained increased access to the contents of their medical records. Most states permit patients to review their own medical records. Before the contents of a record can be released to a third party, the patients should provide the appropriate written authorization.

CHAPTER **12**

ALTERNATIVES TO MALPRACTICE LITIGATION

RISK MANAGEMENT

When the malpractice crisis arrived at the doors of health care institutions in the 1960s, efforts to prevent malpractice claims began in earnest. In 1969, hospitals borrowed the term *risk management* from the insurance industry.

The concept of risk management has been used by the insurance industry since the early 1950s. Insurance companies entered the premises of their clients to evaluate where potential risks were present and to advise on how to prevent injuries from these risks. A primary principle was loss prevention.

Although the insurance industry was primarily interested in the concept of preventing financial loss, hospitals have adapted the concept, with a shift in emphasis, to the prevention of "people" loss— death and disability to patients and employees resulting from preventable incidents. By preventing the injury from occurring, the financial loss is also prevented.

The risk management process is used basically to assess areas in which claims can be prevented. This process includes the identification, analysis, and treatment of risks. Claims that have already been brought may be handled by the risk manager. This management may occur as part of a self-insurance mechanism or may be done in conjunction with an outside insurance company. Claims management, one element of risk management, involves the risk management department in the witness interviews, evidence presentation, depositions, settlement negotiations, and trial preparations.

Recent additions to the Joint Commission of Accreditation for Hospital Standards have included a recognition of risk management programs, and emphasis upon their use for the improvement of patient care. In institutions where safety standards are easily met, the area of concentration is usually the delivery of professional services. The professional delivery of health care services is directly related to the concept of quality assurance. Institutions must know whether patients receive the quality of care in their institutions that they expect. Mechanisms must be in place to evaluate how care is given.

A good risk management program has many components. Every hospital employee plays a role in the risk management process. To be successful, each program must be individually molded to meet the needs of the institution. The background and experience of the risk manager help to determine the direction of the program. Many nurses have assumed the risk manager's position in various types of health care facilities. The experienced staff nurse has much to offer in such a position because of his or her familiarity with direct patient care.

Some institutions have chosen people with an insurance background to direct risk management activities. If so, the financial aspects of risk management are usually emphasized, that is, what is insured and how to finance the risk.

Other institutions have designated the director of engineering as risk manager. This step may be appropriate in older facilities that must emphasize basic safety needs. An organized and functioning safety committee is an absolute necessity for every risk management program regardless of the type of institution. With the growth of corporate liability as discussed in Chapter 2, the risk management program is even more vital for the protection of corporate assets.

SAFETY PROGRAM

A comprehensive safety program is essential to risk management. This program is responsible for meeting the basic safety needs of patients, employees, and visitors. The institution through its safety committee must provide safe premises. The area of law known as premises/general liability operates somewhat differently than the malpractice area. Sometimes patients are injured by falls that are totally unrelated to their professional care and treatment. They may initiate a claim based on the failure to provide safe premises. These claims will be successful only if the dangerous condition is unknown or not obvious. The owner or occupant is under no legal duty to reconstruct or alter the premises so as to obviate known and obvious dangers, nor is he or she liable for injury to a visitor resulting from a danger that was obvious or should have been observed in the exercise of ordinary care.

A woman tripped over a television antenna cord as she was gathering her belongings to check out of the hospital. The television had been installed in the room for another patient 4 or 5 days before her fall. The cord extended from the window near her, around the foot of her bed, to the portable television set near the foot of the other patient's bed. At the point where she tried to step over it, the cord was about a foot off the floor, as it usually had been. The patient testified that she had three choices: she could step over the cord, walk around the television set, or push it aside, since it was on rollers. Nurses who had been in the room had rolled it out of the way or had stepped over the cord. The patient had usually walked around it. When the set was installed she had been aware of the danger of having the cord up in the air and had so advised the installer. She stated at the time of her fall that she knew the set was there, she knew she could have walked around the set, but she attempted to step over the cord because she "was anxious to go home." The court did not permit recovery.

Charrin v. The Methodist Hospital, 432 S.W.2d 572 (Tex.1968).

The hospital's engineering department in helping to meet basic safety needs of patients must be alert to any area that might cause injury to the patient.

A hospital's roof leaked, and a patient's bed became wet. The patient's suit alleged that both the leak and leaving her in a wet bed for 2 hours, which caused pneumonia, were the institution's negligence. The court allowed her recovery of damages.

Tulsa Hospital Associates v. Juby, 175 P.519 (Okla.1918).

A patient left her room to go home from the hospital, slipped and fell in the hallway. The floor had just been washed, waxed, and buffed. The area was also poorly lighted. The court held that a cause of action was stated against the hospital.

Starr v. Emory Hospital University, 93 S.E.2d 399, (Ga.1956).

The hospital must comply with basic fire control procedures in order to receive approval from external agencies including insurance companies.

A patient dying with cancer received second and third degree burns during a fire in his hospital room and died a short time later. The response of the nurses to a call of "Fire" was to run empty handed to the room and then to run back to the desk and pick up the wrong fire extinguisher. The court found hospital personnel were inadequately trained in fire control. However, in this case fire spread so quickly, there was no proof that proper training would have made a difference.

Mahavier v. Beverly Enterprises, 540 S.W.2d 813 (Tex.1976).

After her baby was delivered, the patient was transferred to the psychiatric ward of the hospital. While she was locked in her room, a fire began. She received second and third degree burns over 95 percent of her body and died 2 weeks later. Apparently, she had been given a lighted cigarette by a hospital employee shortly before the fire.

The plaintiff's attorney demanded copies of the rules and regulations of the hospital in regard to fire drills and training and education of personnel in dealing with fires.

The appeals court held that these reports must be produced.

Shibilski v. St. Joseph's Hospital of Marshfield, Inc., 266 N.W.2d 264 (Wisc.1979).

The question of whether or not general liability exists extends to the hospital's parking lot. A hospital was found free from fault when a visitor fell in the hospital parking lot.

The woman tripped over a bumper guard or median in the lot. No expert testimony was presented to show that the design, construction, or maintenance of the parking lot created a hazardous condition. Evidence did show that the premises were kept in a "reasonably safe condition."

Ryle v. Baton Rouge General Hospital, 376 So.2d 1024 (La.Ct.of App., Oct.1979).

A parking lot operator, as other possessors of business premises, is not an insurer of the safety of customers using the lot but does owe them a duty of reasonable care.

A visitor accompanied by her boyfriend came to the hospital. She was riding on the back of his motorcycle; as they approached the gate to the hospital parking lot, the wooden bar that blocked the entrance rose to let them pass.

However, before they could get past the gate, the bar came down and hit the face shield of her helmet. The impact caused the bar to break in two, but it also knocked the face shield off, injuring the visitor.

> **The appellate court held that the case should go back to be heard by a jury.**
> McPherson v. High Point Memorial Hospital, 258 S.E.2d 410 (N.C.App.1979).

In another parking lot case the plaintiff based his claim on the hospital's failure to make traffic control devices (the painted letters on the roadway) sufficiently visible to the other driver.

> **The plaintiff was approaching a T intersection in the defendant hospital's parking lot from the shaft of the T. Another driver was approaching along the top of the T. The plaintiff stopped before reaching the intersection and was struck from the side by the other driver. The other driver was not aware that there was a traffic control signal painted on the roadway because of its faded condition.**
>
> **The jury was permitted to conclude that the hospital negligently failed to maintain the traffic control signals in the parking lot.**
> Chernov v. St. Luke's Hospital Medical Center, 601 P.2d 284 (Ariz.1979).

The two previous cases appear to require the hospital to provide continuous maintenance of its parking lot and the equipment connected with it.

Liability for injuries may be based on a breach of duty in regard to the activities of a third party on the premises as well.

PRODUCTS LIABILITY

Along with a sound safety program, the institution has a duty to provide safe and adequate equipment for use. This provision for equipment is monitored by the risk management department.

Hospitals may be held to a higher standard of care than other corporations in an equipment case based on negligence.

The hospital has an obligation to provide safe equipment for use on its patients. Many hospitals employ equipment maintenance personnel to evaluate and maintain the equipment.

If the equipment malfunctions or is defective, the area of law known as product liability is involved. This action is somewhat distinct from the malpractice or negligence action. A lengthy discussion of these differences is beyond the scope of this book, but the student of nursing law should recognize that such a distinction exists. The hospital and the manufacturer of the equipment may both be held liable in a product liability suit.

When a product is involved, negligence does not always have to be proven. In other words, the injured party may not have to prove that a deviation from proper standards of care has occurred. A product may be held to a higher level of liability, one that is sometimes referred to as strict liability. This legal concept means that the product had a defect and caused the injury. These are two basic elements of proof in a product liability case. The same piece of equipment in a negligence case would be discussed in the terms applied to all negligence cases: (1) duty, (2) breach of duty, (3) causation, and (4) damages.

When the hospital furnishes instruments for use by a surgeon, it acquires the duty of using reasonable care to see that such instruments are reasonably fit for the purposes for which they are intended and provided.

A patient was admitted for skin grafting surgery. The surgeon was to remove a patch of skin from the front of her right thigh where she had previously sustained electrical burns. An alleged defect in the electrical surgical instrument, consisting of a bent spring impairing the usefulness of the depth setting adjustment of the instrument, caused deep cuts to the plaintiff.

A judgment of $10,000 was allowed to stand against the institution. The court stated that the surgeon should be able to rely on the hospital to furnish safe equipment.

South Highlands Infirmary v. Laura Camp, 180 So.2d 904 (Ala.1965).

In a recent case, a Pennsylvania court extended the hospital's responsibility for examining equipment that is purchased for use in the operating room.

A patient was admitted to a medical center for an anterior cervical fusion. Because of a mishap involving equipment used during surgery, she became a quadriplegic. The surgical resident used a Stryker plug cutter to remove bone from the vertebrae. When he removed the instrument, he found it had taken a full depth of vertebrae tissue and penetrated to the cortex. A scratch was noted in the instrument that could have caused a screw to slip.

The court stated that preoperative checks should be made on surgical equipment to prevent patient harm.

Grubb v. Albert Einstein Hosp. 387 A.2d 480 (Pa.1978).

An area that nursing personnel often fail to recognize as being within their scope of responsibility is that of equipment usage.

If the article furnished were obviously unfit for its intended use, the nurse would be in violation of the usual standards of nursing practice if he or she were to use it.

A loose belt caused the head of an x-ray machine to fall on a patient.

The patient alleged that following the accident her vision had changed and that she had difficulty with her teeth. Her physician testified that as a result of the accident the patient experienced excessive tearing from her eye and limitation of the side motion of her lower jaw. The court found that the hospital and physician were negligent in failing to inspect and maintain the machine in a safe operating condition.

The court held that both the physician and the hospital were liable, since the defect was obvious and should have been detected.

Nelson v. Swedish Hospital, 64 N.W.2d 38 (Minn.1954).

In many malpractice cases the allegation is made that a particular piece of equipment has caused a patient to be injured (see Chapter 4).

A patient with a fractured hip and a past history of a stroke and diabetes was brought into the hospital. His physician ordered an aqua pad to be applied. The following evening, the patient had a reddened, blistered area where the pad had been applied. As a result, the patient's surgery was delayed until the lesions were treated.

The appellate court held that the jury should be allowed to determine if the nurses were negligent.

Hale v. Holy Cross Hospital, 513 F.2d 315 (1975).

A patient had surgery for stomach ulcers. Postoperatively, the patient progressed normally for 4 days.

The fifth day, he was raising the head of the electric bed when the bed jerked and fell a short distance. The next morning, he complained of pain in his stomach. That evening, emergency surgery indicated that the patient's spleen had ruptured. The patient believed the fall of the bed had caused the rupture.

During the trial, evidence indicated that the bed had been thrown away without inspection by hospital personnel. The court found the hospital could be held liable for the malfunctioning of the bed.

Arterburn v. St. Joseph Hospital and Rehabilitation Center, 551 P.2d 886 (Kansas 1976).

As the previous case illustrates, it is extremely important to retain equipment that may be defective and responsible for a patient's injury or complication. The hospital often loses a valuable defense if such equipment is discarded. The risk manager may assist with evidence preservation.

A patient had injured his right knee and had surgery. Postoperatively, he was provided with crutches by a hospital orderly. They were sold to him by the hospital for his use while hospitalized. When he used the crutches for the first time, the handle of one of the crutches collapsed causing him to fall and sustain injuries necessitating further surgery. The fall was caused by the collapse of the handle of one of the crutches when a bolt and a wing nut fixing the handle to the crutch parted. The crutches had been fully assembled before leaving the manufacturer's factory.

The court held the defendants not negligent. The manufacturer was able to prove that extensive strength tests were done on the crutches and that none of the bolts had ever stripped. Evidence also indicated that during various stages of the manufacturing procedure, checks were made to determine if the wing nuts were properly tightened.

Hally v. Hospital of St. Raphael, 294 A.2d 305 (Conn.1972).

Liability may result if the machine is known to be malfunctioning and its use is continued or if continuous knowledge of a problem exists.

A patient received an infection from contaminated sutures furnished by the hospital and used by the surgeon, both of whom knew of the problem from past experience.

The court held that continuous knowledge of a problem constituted negligence.

Shepherd v. McGinnis, 131 N.W.2d 475 (Iowa 1964).

Sometimes an injury occurs because the patient's response to the equipment is not adequately observed.

A 3-day-old infant had been placed in an incubator at birth because she was premature. Because the infant felt cold, the nurses caring for her turned the heat up in the incubator. The infant suffered central nervous system disorders, cerebral palsy, and mental retardation.

The court held that the hospital could be held negligent, but that no evidence was found to hold the manufacturer of the incubator liable.

Horowitz v. Michael Reese Hospital, 284 N.E.2d 4 (Ill.1972).

As the previous case illustrates, legal actions involving equipment frequently include the manufacturer as a codefendant. The rationale for this additional defendant is that the equipment could have malfunctioned or could have been defective.

Sometimes the hospital is named as a defendant when the patient is injured by a piece of equipment that breaks or dislodges. The allegation may be that hospital personnel misused the equipment or failed to notice an obvious problem. Courts are reluctant to allow evidence of a change in equipment made after the incident since this would discourage the improvement of products.

Records of actions taken as precautions in a product liability suit may be important to the defense. Such records provide tangible evidence of technical competence and an attitude of due care. Test reports as well as written procedures involving inspections are very important. These records should be retained, at a minumum, until the products' anticipated useful life span is over plus 2 to 5 years.

In addition to equipment, the area of law known as product liability encompasses other products used within the hospital, such as drugs.

The cases involving drugs frequently deal with whether sufficient warnings had been given regarding the hazards of the drugs. A whole series of cases were litigated in the late 1960s through the 1970s regarding the use of the antibiotic chloramphenicol.

A 7-year-old child died of aplastic anemia induced by chloramphenicol. Her pediatrician had prescribed the drug once for tonsillitis and 9 months later for a staphylococcus infection. He did not order blood tests or a throat culture.

The jury returned a total verdict of $215,000 against the physician and the manufacturer of the drug.

Incollingo v. Ewing, 282 A.2d 206 (Pa.1971).

The question of the liability of the manufacturer usually involves the sufficiency of warnings provided to the medical profession. Once these warnings are provided, the burden shifts to the physician to respond appropriately and to warn the patient.

QUALITY ASSURANCE AND RISK MANAGEMENT

It is quite clear to hospitals that because of court decisions (see Chapter 10), hospitals can and will be held liable for failing to provide monitoring systems to evaluate the management of patient care. Although a strong interrelationship exists between the concepts of quality assurance and risk management, they do not serve the same purposes.

Quality assurance evaluates the role of the deliverer of health care services, whereas risk management emphasizes the perception of the patient regarding the incident or situation, since this is the ultimate determinant of whether a claim is brought.

For example, if an 82-year-old patient fell out of bed because siderails were needed and not used, the risk management department would assign this incident a low priority depending on extent of injury and other circumstances. It is unlikely that a malpractice claim would be brought due to the age of the patient. However, the quality assurance department would certainly consider the health care provider's activities in failing to meet the proper standards of care.

Another distinction lies in the application of legal standards to the situation by the risk management process. Risk management identifies the situation for claim potential based on current legal standards and future projections of how the courts might decide a particular case. This is a minimum standard. Quality assurance applies a higher standard, analogous to an ethical standard rather than a legal standard. Quality assurance refers to the quality of care we want to provide for our patients rather than what we are required by law to provide.

There are also similarities between the two concepts. Both quality assurance and risk management evaluate systems breakdowns within the institution. Essentially, the same data is reviewed by both departments in order to identify such systems breakdowns. But the departments split in function when the quality assurance department takes the same data and uses it to evaluate the care delivered by the health care provider, while the risk management department uses the data further to identify the individual patient who may have a malpractice claim. Quality assurance looks for patterns or trends. Risk management focuses on the isolated incident that may lead to a $1 million lawsuit.

IDENTIFICATION OF RISKS

The initial step in the risk management process is the identification of risks. While identification can be accomplished in many ways, the familiar document known as the incident report is used extensively.

The concept of the incident report has changed over the years. Traditionally, it was viewed as a tool used only by the nursing department and primarily when an injury had occurred to a patient. In many institutions, the report was filed with the patient's medical record. Some hospitals filed the reports in the personnel folders of the nurses who were responsible for the incidents. The incidents then formed a basis for the annual evaluation of the employee.

The new definitions of the term *incident* are much broader and meant to involve all hospital departments. In many states the term *incident* has been changed to *event* or *occurrence*. An example of the new definition is that used by the Pennsylvania Hospital Insurance Company (PHICO):

> An event is any happening which is not consistent with the routine operation of a hospital or the routine care of a particular patient. It may be an accident or a situation which might result in an accident. This might involve patient, visitor, or other (eg., employee).

Since PHICO insures the majority of hospitals in Pennsylvania, this definition of an event has become the one adopted by most Pennsylvania hospitals. It is a broad definition and is meant to include areas that provide a potential situation for injury as well as for the actual injury.

For example, the nurse who finds a medication in her patient's medication drawer or cassette that had not been ordered for the patient but that has a similar name to one that has been ordered (Isordil for Inderal or vice versa is a common example) has identified an incident. No injury has occurred, and, in fact, the drug has not been given. An investigation will be made to determine why the incident occurred. Perhaps the pharmacy department has made an error in ordering the medication. Perhaps this mistake has happened several times and is indicative of a breakdown in a system. This is the true value of a risk management program—it identifies a system breakdown that has occurred repeatedly but has not as yet harmed anyone.

Examples of incidents are endless and involve all departments and aspects of patient care. Falls are the most common event, but medication errors are the more serious in terms of injury. Some falls are preventable. Proper housekeeping techniques to prevent slips on wet floors and good nursing judgment to determine when restraints and extra precautions are necessary are two areas that contribute to a reduction in falls.

Another example of a system breakdown occurs when the wrong patient is sent to the operating room or the right patient has the wrong procedure performed.

A woman was brought into the hospital for a condition of the cervix. She was taken into the operating room by a surgical technician and was thought to be another patient who was to have a thyroidectomy. Within a short time, the

surgeon was informed that he had the wrong patient on the operating table, and the surgery was terminated. The thyroidectomy was not completed, and such incisions as had been made were sutured and repaired. The patient had a 4-inch incision along her neck that became infected and required cosmetic surgery.

The court held that the jury's verdict of $100,000 was not excessive in view of the critical duty placed on the surgeon, the anesthesiologist, and the surgical technician to establish with absolute certainty the identity of a surgical patient. All parties admitted that they did not check the identity of the patient against the name on the bracelet. The fact that the patient responded to the wrong name was not accepted as a defense by the court.

Southeastern Kentucky Baptist Hospital v. Bruce, 539 S.W.2d 286 (Kentucky 1976).

The previous case is a classic example of a system breakdown. Not just one person made an error, but several people did. A basic check and balance system within the institution has failed when this type of serious incident occurs; an investigation invariably indicates that many people have failed to meet a proper standard of care. Unfortunately, mistaken identity is not as rare as we would desire. Many risk managers become concerned when they see an operating room schedule with two patients having the same or similar names scheduled for surgery on the same day.

An escort removed two patients from their hospital rooms to the operating rooms. The hospital charts of the patients were mixed and each patient was placed in the operating room scheduled for the other. The result was that the patient who had been scheduled for a hemorrhoidectomy received instead an orchidectomy and hernia repair by a different surgeon. At the same time, the patient scheduled for the orchidectomy and hernia operation had a hemorrhoidectomy. The errors were not discovered until after the operations.

The plaintiff received a verdict of $100,000 against the surgeon and hospital.

Huggins v. Graves, 337 F.2d 486 (1964).

The gross negligence that leads to these types of errors has led courts to consider the question of whether punitive damages (see Chapter 6) should be allowed in compensating the patient who has been identified incorrectly.

A woman was admitted to the hospital for a breast biopsy. She was confused with another patient admitted for gall bladder surgery, which was scheduled at the same time. A mixup in the charts occurred, and each patient was subjected to the surgery scheduled for the other. When the surgeon opened the patient and discovered a normal gall bladder, he inspected the chart and wrist band and found the error. Later he performed the breast biopsy.

The jury awarded damages against the hospital and physicians. The award included an additional sum for punitive damages based on their belief that such damages were warranted. However, the court on appeal disallowed the additional damages.

Ebaugh v. Rabkin, 22 Cal.App.3d, 99 Cal.Rptr.2d 706 (1972).

Laboratory

Another example of the type of systems breakdown just described occurs when an incorrectly identified specimen arrives in the pathology laboratory or when a specimen fails to reach the laboratory. If the specimen is a blood sample and the problem can be easily remedied by obtaining another blood study from the patient, no serious harm will result. However, if the lost specimen is a tissue sample and the only tissue available to determine if the patient has a malignancy, a more serious problem arises.

Sometimes a slight change in circumstances, as in the specimen example, may result in a more serious problem despite the fact that a similar breakdown in the system has occurred in both instances.

Dietary

Breakdowns in the systems of any hospital department may also lead to patient injury. The hospital will be held liable for the negligence of any of its employees (see Chapter 4). Every institution, for example, supplies patients with food through a dietary department with a dietitian supervising the diets of patients. This is to ensure that the diet provided is in accordance with the physician's instruction about a particular type of diet. Frequently, the patient's diet is a significant aspect of the treatment to be given. In some institutions, a procedure specifies that the nursing staff must check the patients' trays when they arrive on the floor before the patients are served. This procedure verifies compliance with important dietary restrictions (for example, that of a diabetic patient). If this system is not operating properly, both the nurse and the person directing the preparation of the food may be held liable.

A patient had a subtotal gastrectomy for a duodenal ulcer. He was to have only water and intravenous solution for 5 days. However, he was given solid food during this period by mistake and died of peritonitis. A practical nurse caring for the patient testified that a nursing assistant had given the patient a tray of food, and the patient had eaten milk and cake.

The hospital was held liable for wrongful postoperative care.

McNerney v. New York Polyclinic Hospital, 238 N.Y.2d 729 (1963).

Although the dietitian was not named as a defendant in the previous case, it is obvious that the duty of due care would extend to hold the person liable for the initial incorrect preparation of the patient's tray.

Even when the incorrect diet is served, the injured party must be able to prove that the food was the probable cause of his or her injury.

As a result of erroneous instructions given by the hospital's night charge nurse, the dietary department sent trays of solid food to a patient's room for all three meals on one particular day. The patient, who had a colon resection, protested eating this food and asked that his physician be called.

The nurse stated she would not "bother" the physician and assured him that the food would not have been sent to his room for him to eat unless it were appropriate. He then ate most of the food.

A short while later it was discovered that the two ends of the colon, which were sutured together during surgery, had come apart.

However, the testimony at trial did not prove that the ingestion of solid food was the probable cause of the patient's complication. Therefore, the patient did not recover damages.

Lenger v. Physicians' General Hospital, 455 S.W.2d 703 (Texas 1970).

If it can be proven that the patient was fully alert and aware of any dietary restriction but chose to eat the food anyway, it is less likely that a hospital employee will be held liable for serving the food.

Physical Therapy

Sometimes an injury is related to treatment received by a patient in the physical therapy department.

A patient had hip surgery and subsequently needed physical therapy. For her therapy, she was placed on a tilt table. She slid downward from it, and her hip became flexed causing her injury. Evidence indicated that the patient had pulled herself downward, therefore contributing to her injury.

No award was granted to the patient.

Gilles v. Rehabilitation Institute of Oregon, 498 P.2d 777 (Oregon 1972).

The preceding case illustrates an important concept in the definition of an incident. Hospital personnel may not characterize the above situation as an incident, since it did not involve the traditional incidents such as falls, burns, or medication errors. But the patient who does not receive the anticipated result of treatment will often view litigation as an answer.

Other Sources

Although the incident report is the traditional method of collecting data for risk management purposes, many other sources of data exist in the institution.

The claims history is an important aspect of risk management. Evaluating what the institution has already been responsible for will help to prevent future injury to patients.

Surveys provided by the Joint Commission on Accreditation of Hospitals, State Departments of Health and insurance companies will assist in identifying potential problems.

Committee reports supply valuable information. The risk manager may identify problem areas through the infection control, safety, and medical records committees as well as many other institutional committees.

As was previously mentioned, patient communication is of prime importance for the identification of potential liability claims. The patient representative, the patient advocate or ombudsman, as part of the risk management team, will provide input into this area. The patient representative acts as liaison between the patient and the institution. Since the initial prerequisite for a malpractice claim is a dissatisfied patient, this communication is vital.

Complaints frequently are presented by patients who have had personal property lost or damaged. The patient who does not receive the anticipated result of treatment and who has lost property may have extra incentive to visit an attorney.

Damage to a patient's property that is the fault of hospital staff is a common incident. The hospital clearly assumes this responsibility and should offer to repair or replace the article. Some institutions have patients sign a release from responsibility for loss or breakage of items. This should serve as notice to the patient that if property is kept against hospital advice, there will be no reimbursement from the hospital if the property is lost or damaged. However, such a form will not excuse the institution if negligence has occurred. For instance, if an escort knocks a patient's watch off the bedside table after being alerted to the watch's presence by the patient, the hospital could be held liable.

In cases in which the hospital is clearly not liable for the damage, the decision may be made by the risk manager to reimburse the patient based on other factors. If the patient already has had an incident that could result in a liability claim, to add to the patient's unhappiness by refusing to reimburse for lost or damaged property would be counterproductive.

Patient comments may also be communicated into the risk management system from the business office. At times patients refuse to pay bills because they believe their treatment and care was unsatisfactory. Any health care provider who talks to patients may supply such information to the risk management team.

The medical records department may be used to provide information from the patient's records. This information usually supplements what the risk management office has received from other departments. Attorney requests, received by the medical records administrator, are reviewed to determine if this request for records is related to a potential malpractice case.

The risk management process would be incomplete without the identification of incidents involving physicians and their treatment of patients. A successful risk management program must emphasize the prevention of malpractice claims against physicians. This is in recognition of two basic facts. The hospital will usually be named as a joint defendant in any case in which the incident occurs while the patient is hospitalized, even if the incident involves only the physician's direct treatment of the patient. Second, the large dollar judgment and settlements are usually paid in the cases in which the physician is the primary defendant but in which the hospital is a defendant as well. For example, these cases are often complications of surgery. Although the hospital is named as a primary defendant in cases involving the traditional hospital incidents (falls, burns, medication errors), these cases do not usually result in large monetary judgments. Physicians should be encouraged to communicate situations involving their treatment of patients to the risk management office. This will enable the system to work on their behalf as well as that of the institution.

EVALUATION AND TREATMENT OF RISKS

After the data is received by the risk management office, the process of evaluation begins. The department where the incident occurred usually completes the investigation of the incident under the supervision of the risk manager. If the risk is viewed as serious and involving a potential liability claim, the insurance carrier will be notified. Often portions or all of the patient's bill will be absorbed by the institution. In most states, this is not viewed as an admission of liability. It often serves to defuse an angry patient or family. The patient representative will visit the patient and family and listen to what they have to say about the incident. Their perceptions will then be communicated to the physician, administration, and risk management. The medical records will be reviewed for accurate and complete documentation.

If the incident is not serious, it will be filed and used for statistical studies and analyses. Repetitive incidents are indications of system breakdowns and should be addressed before a patient is injured.

Educational programs are a basic thrust in risk management. These educational efforts should include one-to-one instruction whenever this is indicated. Also included will be programs for all hospital departments involving specific areas of risk management and liability programs for all professional groups.

Documentation of the process of risk management as applied to a patient's potential claim will often provide a valuable asset in the defense of a case. In many states, risk management investigations are protected from discovery for litigation purposes if they are made part of the peer review process.

Departmental educational programs should include a presentation on how to document the patient's medical record for risk management purposes. It is important for personnel to document not only what is done for the patient but also the reason. The follow-up to an injury should be documented as well.

Nationally, risk management is too new a concept to evaluate in terms of its total effect on the malpractice problem. However, it is viewed with enthusiasm and optimism by many health care providers as a sensible mechanism with great potential to benefit the consumers of health care.

LIABILITY INSURANCE

Despite the best risk management efforts, malpractice claims will be instituted. The necessity for malpractice insurance coverage is evident in today's legal climate. Nurses should be familiar with the basic terminology used in insurance contracts.

In general, professional liability policies cover liability arising out of the rendering of or failure to render professional service, including (1) medical, surgical, dental, or nursing treatment; (2) provision of food or beverages to patients; (3) furnishing or dispensing of drugs or medical, dental, or surgical supplies or appliances; or (4) performance of autopsies.

Two forms of malpractice coverage may be purchased. The claims-made policy protects against claims made during the policy year. The occurrence policy protects against all incidents that occur during the policy term, regardless of when a claim arising out of the incident is made. Because many claims are not made until several years after the incident has occurred, the occurrence form offers more complete protection. However, a claims-made policy will offer comparable protection with the addition of a separate policy known as *tail insurance*.

Regardless of the type of policy purchased, incidents and occurrences should be reported to the carrier promptly. This enables the insurance carrier to begin an investigation while the facts are clear in the minds of personnel involved in the incident.

Since the nurse is increasingly likely to be a named defendant in a malpractice case, nurses should be encouraged to purchase their own liability insurance. These policies will provide coverage for the nurse in some cases that the institution's policy does not cover, for example, a nurse offers advice to a friend or neighbor and a lawsuit results. Hospital coverage is provided for the nurse as long as the nurse is acting "within the scope of employment." Clearly an act by the nurse outside of working hours and away from the employing institutions would not be covered (see Chapter 7).

ARBITRATION SYSTEMS

Some state legislatures have enacted laws formulating malpractice arbitration panels as an alternative to the trial by jury. The purpose of these panels is to eliminate the need for lengthy jury trials, particularly in cases where a nuisance claim is involved. Nuisance claims are those that do not have a valid legal basis. Most arbitration panels are composed of physicians, lawyers, and/or lay members of the community. Primarily, they screen cases so that only cases where liability might exist are actually heard by a jury.

HOME CARE RISK MANAGEMENT

As health care expands to more outpatient services and less inpatient, risk management has developed to meet the needs of this revised delivery system.

In many ways the risks of liability are similar. The primary difference is the absence of control in the home care environment. This absence of control is often frustrating for the health care provider.

Potential problem areas include inappropriate referrals, lack of communication among health care providers who are geographically separated, auto accidents, providers injured by patients or accused of theft, and difficulty with supervision because of distance.

SUMMARY

As a means of preventing malpractice claims from being initiated, many institutions have developed risk management programs. The process of risk management is designed to identify potential liability claims and breakdowns in systems that could lead to liability.

Most hospitals have the necessary components for a good risk management program—functioning safety and equipment monitoring programs. What is frequently missing is a centralized office or person responsible solely for the risk management function. Emphasis in risk management is placed on educational programs.

Identification of risks is the initial step to a successful program. All departments in the hospital, as well as many other sources of information, will be used for this purpose. Evaluation and treatment of risks are the next steps in the process.

Quality assurance principles overlap the risk management concept. In smaller institutions, the same person may coordinate quality assurance and risk management.

If risk management efforts fail and a malpractice claim is filed, it is increasingly likely that a nurse will be a named defendant in the case.

A recent development in malpractice litigation provided by a number of states is arbitration panels. One purpose of such panels is to screen cases so that nuisance claims are dismissed.

CHAPTER **13**

ETHICAL/LEGAL ISSUES

Nurses often express concern regarding their responsibilities for various ethical issues. The nursing profession should be aware that their legal and ethical responsibilities are not identical. In some areas, the courts have not reviewed a case involving a particular ethical issue. Therefore, a legal standard does not exist. In the absence of a court decision, the nurse must be guided by the ethics of the profession and by personal moral standards.

Where the courts have reviewed an ethical area, some guidelines do exist. However, these guidelines are not comprehensive and do not answer many of the questions posed by the nursing profession. The law requires a basic minimum standard; whereas the ethical standards of the health care professional may require a higher standard of care in a particular situation.

TERMINATION OR REFUSAL OF TREATMENT

Health care professionals who care for the terminally ill patient are continually faced with conflict in regard to the termination of treatment. The written or nonwritten order not to resuscitate, as also discussed previously, poses special problems for the professional nurse.

The cases dealing with the issues of withdrawing life support and those discussing when and what kind of treatment should be initiated provide some guidance to these difficult issues.

Many hospitals have adopted the following classification system for critically ill patients in an attempt to provide some definition and consistency to the care rendered.

1. Class A. Maximal therapeutic effort with no reservation.

2. Class B. Maximal therapeutic effort with no reservation, but with daily evaluation because probability of survival is questionable.

3. Class C. Selective limitation of therapeutic measures.

4. Class D. All therapy can be discontinued. Any measures indicated to ensure maximum comfort of the patient may be continued or instituted. These patients are brain dead or have no reasonable probability of return to a cognitive and sapient life.*

The Karen Quinlan case is a well-publicized example of the values a court considers when evaluating the ethical-legal areas.

Karen Quinlan was admitted to the hospital in a coma from which she never awakened. She had an irreversible brain injury and no hope of recovery, but she had not experienced brain death.

Her parents wished to have the life support mechanism withdrawn. The physicians caring for her refused to do this without court support.

The Supreme Court of New Jersey held that if the decision to withdraw life support was approved by the hospital's ethics committee, the patient's attending physician, the patient's guardian, and the patient's family, life support could be withdrawn. *The patient's previously expressed wishes weighed heavily in the court's decision.*

In re Matter of Karen Quinlan, 355 A.2d 647 (New Jersey 1976).

Since the *Quinlan* case in 1976, the courts of numerous states have dealt with issues concerning the discontinuation of life-sustaining treatment from terminally ill patients.

A Florida court dealt with the disconnection of a respirator from a competent patient.

A 73-year-old man suffered from amyotrophic lateral sclerosis (Lou Gehrig's disease) and was being kept alive by a respirator.

He sought a declaration from the court of his right to remove himself from the respirator.

The court found that his right was protected by a constitutional right to privacy and that neither the medical profession nor the court was entitled to substitute its judgment for his.

Satz v. Perlmutter, 362 So.2d 160 (Fla. App. 1978).

---

*From an Appraisal of the Criteria of Cerebral Death, *Journal of the American Medical Association*, No. 10 (March 7, 1977):982.

When the patient is able to speak for himself, as in the previous case, the court will consider whether the patient is competent. Competence, for the purpose of medical decision making, deals with whether the patient seems to understand the nature of the decision that is being made including the effects of that decision.

If the patient is unable to speak for himself, because he is unconscious or incompetent, for example, the court's determination becomes more difficult. The court must always weigh whether the person speaking for the patient is representing what the patient would wish to have happen and whether the decision is consistent with reasonable medical judgment.

A 67-year-old man with an IQ of 10 and a mental age of approximately 2 years and 8 months, was defined by the court as being "profoundly mentally retarded."

In 1976, he was diagnosed as having acute leukemia. He had lived in state institutions since 1923, was unable to communicate verbally, and was disoriented.

His condition was fatal, but with chemotherapy a remission might occur. A guardian for the patient was appointed by the court who determined that because he would experience significant adverse side effects and discomfort that he would be unable to understand, no treatment should be given. The Court upheld the guardian's decision.

Superintendent of Belchertown State School v. Saikewicz, 370 N.E.2d 417 (Mass. 1977).

In *Saikewicz*, the Massachusetts court was dealing with a legally incompetent patient who was terminally ill and for whom there was a possibility of life-prolonging treatment. Based on these specific facts, the decision to withhold such treatment was made by a Probate Court in Massachusetts, which attempted to substitute its judgment for that of the patient.

Subsequent Massachusetts cases have further narrowed this position.

A 67-year-old patient suffered from a degenerative disease of the brain that was progressive and also from a serious life-threatening coronary artery disease. The attending physician, with the family's concurrence, recommended that if a cardiac arrest occurred, resuscitation efforts should not be undertaken.

The court held that the decision not to resuscitate could be written as an order on the patient's record without court approval, as this was a medical and not a legal decision.

In the Matter of Shirley Dinnerstein, 380 N.E.2d 134 (Mass.App.1978).

No health care provider in any United States jurisdiction has been found criminally or civilly liable for withholding extraordinary care from a terminally ill patient.

An 85-year-old woman was the victim of a purse snatching. A bystander found her lying on the sidewalk. On arrival at the hospital, she was able to talk, but her condition quickly degenerated.

Six days later, based on her condition and age, after consultation with other physicians involved in the case, and on agreement by the victim's son, the neurosurgeon discontinued all "heroic measures." She died a few minutes later.

In the criminal trial for the murder of the victim, the purse snatcher (who was 12 years old) alleged that the physician's act in discontinuing heroic measures caused the victim's death.

The court concluded that the physician's act in discontinuing heroic measures to keep the crime victim alive was a reasonable medical procedure and did not insulate the defendant from liability for murder.

In the Matter of J. N., Jr. v. United States, 406 A.2d 1275 (D.C.1979).

REFUSAL OF SURGERY AND BLOOD

The patient's right to refuse surgical intervention has been upheld by the courts in many jurisdictions as long as the patient is competent. Competence refers to medical competence, a determination by a physician that a particular patient at a specific moment in time is able to understand the nature of the explanation and the consequence of refusing treatment. The refusal must be an informed refusal. The patient must clearly understand the ramifications, particularly if death or disability may occur.

A 77-year-old woman had gangrene in her foot and lower leg. Her physician recommended amputation. She refused to consent to the surgery.

Her daughter filed a petition seeking appointment of herself as temporary guardian with authority to consent to the operation on behalf of her mother.

The court held that a competent person can reject proposed treatment even if a reasonable person would have consented. Since the patient was competent, she was permitted to withhold consent.

Lane v. Candura, 376 N.E.2d 1232 (Mass. 1978).

The religious beliefs of patients sometimes forms the basis for their refusal of treatment. This has occurred in cases involving blood transfusions, where a principle of the patient's beliefs is that blood transfusions are unacceptable.

Earlier case law supported the patient's right to refuse blood transfusions when religious beliefs required such a refusal. This principle is generally applied when an adult of sound mind refuses such treatment.

A 23-year-old childless woman who was a Jehovah's Witness refused a blood transfusion.

The hospital sought permission to administer the transfusion, claiming it was necessary to save the woman's life. The patient argued that such an order would interfere with her First Amendment rights.

The court refused to grant the hospital permission to administer the transfusion stating that an adult of sound mind cannot be compelled to submit to medical treatment against her will unless the state can show a compelling overriding interest.

In the Matter of Melido, 88 Misc. 974, 390 N.Y.S.2d 523 (1976).

The patient was a 27-year-old mentally alert and fully competent adult who suffered from kidney disease, which required the regular use of renal dialysis. He was in critical need of a blood transfusion but refused treatment based on his religious beliefs.

The court ruled that the state had not proven a compelling interest that would allow court intervention.

St. Mary's Hospital v. Ramsey, 465 So.2d 666 (Fla. App. 1985).

In the previous decision the various state's interest, analyzed and rejected by the court, were 1) the preservation of life; 2) the protection of the parties; 3) the prevention of suicide; and 4) the ethics of medical practice. The legal system attempts to balance the rights of the individual as it conflicts with basic values of society.

If an unborn child is involved, the courts may intervene on behalf of the child and permit the treatment to be given.

A pregnant patient stated that she would refuse blood transfusions because they were against her religion. Evidence established that at some point in the pregnancy she would probably hemorrhage severely, and both she and the child would die unless a blood transfusion was administered.

The court held that an unborn child was entitled to the law's protection; therefore, blood transfusions should be administered. Here the welfare of the child and the mother were so intertwined that it was impractical to attempt to distinguish between them.

Raleigh Fetkin-Paul Morgan Memorial Hospital v. Anderson, 42 N.J. 421, 201 A.2d 537, Cert. denied, 377 U.S. 985, 84 S.Ct. 1894, 12 L.E.d.2d 1032 (1964).

A hospital was permitted to administer blood transfusions to safeguard the welfare of both a pregnant woman and her unborn child, who was diagnosed as having hydrocephalus and spina bifida. The patient had refused because of her religious beliefs.

The court ordered the blood to be administered.

Crouse Irving Memorial Hospital, Inc. v. Stacey and Scott Paddock, New York Sup. Ct., (January, 1985).

In the previous case the court stated that when a patient puts her doctor in charge of surgical procedures she necessarily makes the physician responsible for the conduct of the operation. Every such grant of responsibility should be accompanied by authority sufficient to properly carry out the delegated responsibilities, the court added. Certainly, if the medical personnel are requested to undertake a delivery that will entail incisions and this is known to the patient, the attending physicians must be permitted to stabilize the patient from the resulting loss of blood. Therefore, in the court's judgment, the physicians in this case may continue to administer blood transfusions to the mother even after the moment of delivery as are necessary to stabilize her condition.

An order for compulsory medical care to a parent may be granted if the state can show an interest in promoting the welfare of children. The rationale for the courts' decision is based on the belief that the state would be encumbered with the care of these minor children if the parent were to die after refusing treatment. Therefore, the state has the right to intervene.

A young woman was brought to the hospital by her husband for emergency care, having lost two-thirds of her body's blood supply from a ruptured ulcer. She was 25 years old, mother of a minor child, and a Jehovah's Witness, as was her husband.

Both husband and wife refused to allow blood transfusions, although they knew the patient would die and that there was a better than 50 percent chance of saving her life if blood were given.

An order was issued by the judge allowing the hospital to administer such transfusions as the physicians should determine were necessary to save her life. The patient had indicated to the judge that if such a course were followed it would not then be her (moral) responsibility.

Application of President and Directors of Georgetown College, 331 F.2d 1000 (D.C.Cir. 1964).

When patients are unable to speak for themselves, it is often difficult to determine what the patient would wish in terms of treatment. *The court may look to prior behavior and statements of the patient.*

An incompetent 94-year-old Jehovah's Witness who requires a life-sustaining blood transfusion may exercise his religious beliefs and refuse the procedure, Massachusetts' Supreme Judicial Court has ruled. The court applied a substituted judgment test and noted that the patient had a history of refusing transfusions. It therefore concluded that the patient's strong religious beliefs would cause him to decline the transfusion if he were competent to decide for himself. The state's interest in preserving life does not overcome the patient's desires, the court added, observing that the patient is without friends and dependents having an interest in his welfare.

In re Soulas, No. 84 289 (Mass. 1984).

In general if patients are unable to speak for themselves, it is better to err in the direction of providing treatment. Sometimes patients who are able to speak do change their decision about refusing treatment.

The patient, a 22-year-old, was transported to a regional trauma center. The patient was in a coma and the parents had telephoned to order that blood should not be administered. They also indicated that the patient had signed a written directive covering this type of situation.

The hospital petitioned the court and received an order to administer blood.

In Re Estate of Darrell Dorone, 502 A.2d 1271 (Pa.Super. 1985).

In the previous case the court indicated that the written directive (which was never produced to the hospital) would have to be weighed very carefully for evidence of the patient's current desires.

If a minor required the medical care that is being refused by the parent due to religious beliefs, courts may intervene to protect the welfare of the child. However, in most cases it must be demonstrated that the child's life is in danger.

A 16-year-old boy had a spinal curvature, and surgery was recommended. His mother consented conditionally with a refusal for blood to be administered.

The hospital asked that the minor be declared a "neglected child" and that a guardian be appointed.

The court refused permission for the appointment of a guardian and stated that the state did not have an interest of sufficient magnitude outweighing a parent's religious beliefs when the child's life is not immediately imperiled by his physical condition.

In Re Green, 292 A.2d 387, (Pa. 1972).

In some cases the refusal of the parents has not been based upon religious beliefs.

A 2-year-old boy suffered from acute leukemia. His parents wanted to discontinue the chemotherapy prescribed by his physician and substitute Laetrile.

The court considered this a child neglect case and ordered that the child be made ward of the court and placed back on the chemotherapy program.

Custody of Minor, 379 N.E.2d 1053 (1978), reviewed and aff'd, 393 N.E.2d 836.

If the competent patient refuses blood and that refusal is permitted, it is clear that the patient must be willing to accept the results of that decision.

A woman who refused blood on religious grounds and who subsequently bled to death after a negligently performed dilatation and curettage had assumed the risk of death.

The woman had suffered a miscarriage. During the operation the surgeon lacerated the uterus. Although the physician warned the patient and her husband that she would probably die without a blood transfusion, they continued to refuse blood.

The physician was not held liable.

Shorter v. Drury, 695 P.2d 116 (Wash. 1985).

In some states, physicians and hospitals have refused to provide care for patients who refuse blood.

The patient alleged that physicians negligently handled his treatment after he refused blood transfusions.

The court found for the defendant. The evidence established that the doctors had acted within their rights in refusing to perform surgery without transfusion authorization and that they were not required to refer the patient to a doctor who would perform bloodless surgery.

Davis v. United States, 629 F.Supp. 1 (D.C.Ark. 1986).

A federal civil rights claim was initiated by Jehovah's Witnesses. California medical licensing officials instituted disciplinary proceedings to discourage physicians from performing bloodless surgery.

Graham v. Deukmajlan, No. 82-5208 (C.A.9, 1983).

REFUSAL OF NOURISHMENT

While the court decisions regarding termination of life support systems tend to be consistent from state to state, the majority of states have not yet rendered any opinion. The current decisions seem to indicate that a national consensus has been reached on the basic legal questions. The most recent refusal of treatment cases have moved from the medical issues of respiratory support to the issues of nutritional support. Whether a patient may, under any circumstances, refuse food and water has been the center of current litigation.

A 28-year-old woman, Elizabeth Bouvia, has suffered cerebral palsy since birth. She is now a quadriplegic, completely bedridden, immobile, and in constant pain.

In 1983, Ms. Bouvia was a patient at Riverside General Hospital. She expressed a wish to die and requested that the feeding tube keeping her alive be removed so that she could intentionally starve to death. The patient was clearly competent.

The lower court refused to grant her request and permitted the hospital to force feed her. Given adequate nutrition, the patient could live 15–20 years.

The Appeals Court unanimously reversed the lower court. The court declared that her decision to forego medical treatment or life support through a mechanical means belongs to her. It is not a medical decision for her physician to make nor is it a legal question to be resolved by lawyers or judges.

Bouvia v. Superior Court of the State of California for the County of Los Angeles, 225 Cal.Rptr. 297 (Cal.Ct.of App., April 16, 1986).

The distinction between termination of ventilator support and nutrition in the case of an incompetent patient was discussed in a case involving a nursing home patient.

A terminally ill, 84-year-old nursing home patient suffered from severe organic brain syndrome, arteriosclerosis, and diabetes and was unable to speak, swallow, or move. The patient's guardian, her nephew, requested the removal of a nasogastric tube supplying nourishment.

The New Jersey Supreme Court defined the parameters under which life-sustaining treatment may be withdrawn or withheld: (1) from an elderly nursing home resident; (2) who is suffering from serious and permanent mental and physical impairments; (3) who will die within approximately one year even with the treatment; and (4) who, though formerly competent, is now incompetent to make decisions about life-sustaining treatment and is unlikely to regain such competence.

The court outlined four commonly identified state interests which limit personal rights. The first is the interest in preserving the particular patient's life and the sanctity of all life. The second is the prevention of suicide. The third interest is the safeguarding of the integrity of the medical profession. The fourth interest is the protection of innocent third parties.

On balance, the court felt that in this case, the right to self-determination outweighs any countervailing state interest.

In the Matter of Claire C. Conroy, A-108 (N.J. Sup.Ct., Jan. 17, 1985).

Following *Claire Conroy*, the New Jersey courts considered this case.

A 90-year-old patient had suffered a severely disabling stroke and needed a feeding tube surgically implanted. The patient's son refused to consent to the surgery.

The court directed that the tube be implanted and ordered that removal of the tube not occur without agreement of the prognosis committee of the hospital.

In the Matter of Elizabeth Visbeck, No. P 29-86 E, New Jersey Superior Court, March 31, 1986.

In the previous case, the court relied upon the *Conroy* court's statement that treatment may not be withheld or withdrawn from an incompetent patient, unless the patient was suffering from recurring, unavoidable, and severe pain.

The plaintiff brought action seeking removal of nutrition from his comatose wife, a nursing home resident. The nursing home opposed the action.

The court rejected the nursing home's argument.

In the Matter of Nancy Ellen Jobes, No. C-4971-85 E, N.J. Sup.Ct., 1986.

Delaware has been added to the list of states with legal decisions involving the termination of treatment.

Mary Reeser Severns, 55 years old, was seriously injured in a motor vehicle accident.

She had remained in a coma for one year when her husband petitioned the court to discontinue treatment including antibiotics.

The court upheld the discontinuance of all medical supportive measures keeping the patient alive in a comatose state.

In Re Severns, 425 A.2d 156 (Delaware 1981).

CHILDREN

One of the most difficult issues faced by health care providers concerns how to handle the situation when a child has serious medical problems and the parents refuse to consent to treatment that could improve the child's condition. These cases that consider the newborn infant are often referred to generally as *Baby Doe* cases.

Baby Jane Doe suffered from multiple birth defects, the most serious of which were spina bifida (a condition in which the spinal cord and membranes that envelope it are exposed), microcephaly (an abnormally small head), and hydrocephalus (an accumulation of fluids in the cranial vault). In addition she exhibited a "weak face," which prevented her from closing her eyes and making a full suck with her tongue, a malformed brain stem, upper extremities spasticity, and a thumb entirely within her fist.

As a result of the spina bifida, the baby's rectal, bladder, leg, and sensory functions were impaired. Due to the combination of microcephaly and hydrocephalus, there was an extremely high risk that the child would be so severely retarded that she could never interact with her environment or with other people.

At the direction of the first pediatric neurosurgeons who examined her, the baby was immediately transferred to University Hospital for dual surgery to correct her spina bifida and hydrocephalus. This would have entailed excising a sack of fluid and nerve endings on the spine and closing the opening, and implanting a shunt to relieve pressure caused by fluid build-up in the cranial cavity. While these dual corrective surgical procedures were likely to prolong the infant's life, they would not improve any of her handicapping conditions, including her anticipated mental retardation.

After consulting with several physicians, nurses, religious advisors, social workers and members of their family, the parents of the baby decided to

forego the corrective surgery. Instead they opted for a "conservative" medical treatment consisting of good nutrition, the administration of antibiotics and the dressing of the baby's exposed spinal sack. The objective of this conservative treatment was to encourage the skin to grow over the exposed spinal sack and to protect it. Because of the parents wishes, no surgery was performed.

The parent's decision caused A. Lawrence Washburn, an attorney from Vermont with no connection to either the parents or the hospital, to commence a proceeding in state court. In his proceeding he sought the appointment of a guardian for Baby Jane Doe and an order that the hospital must perform the surgical procedures. The state court appointed one William E. Weber as the child's guardian and held an evidentiary hearing on October 19 and 20 to determine whether Baby Jane Doe was in need of immediate surgical procedures to preserve her life. Following the hearing, at which University Hospital and the parents were represented, the court concluded that surgery was necessary and ordered that it be performed.

This decision was appealed to the Appellate Division of the Supreme Court of the State of New York on October 21, 1983. The appellate court ruled that since Baby Jane Doe was not in imminent danger of death, the parent's choice of a conservative treatment for their child was a reasonable choice among possible medical treatments. The court concluded that in making this decision the parents had acted in the best interests of the child, and therefore reversed the decision of the trial court and dismissed the suit.

United States v. University Hospital of State University of N.Y. at Stony Brook, 575 F.Supp. 607 (E.D.N.Y. 1983) app'd, 729 F.2d 144 (2d Cir. 1984).

The plaintiffs were parents of Keri Ann McNulty, a child who was diagnosed at birth as having congenital rubella, or German measles. As a result, she had serious medical complications, including cataracts on both eyes, deafness, congenital heart failure, respiratory problems, and some degree of mental retardation. While at first it was thought she would not survive, it became clear that she would survive if properly treated.

A cardiac catheterization was performed, which disclosed that the child had a severe congenital heart problem that required surgery. If the child had the surgery, there was a likelihood that she would survive, although there was a high probability that she would not. However, if she did not have the operation within a short time, she almost certainly would die. The parents opposed the surgery and the guardian favored it. However, a decision had to be made quickly because if the child was not strong enough to withstand the surgery, the operation would not be performed.

After reviewing the medical testimony, the hospital records, the report of the guardian and the arguments of the parents, the judge ruled: "I am persuaded that the proposed cardiac surgery is not merely a life prolonging measure, but indeed is for the purpose of saving the life of the child, regardless of the quality of that life." He therefore ordered that the surgery be performed.

In re McNulty (Mass, Probate Ct. Essex Cty., February 19, 1978).

In a Georgia case, the child's parents, after consultations with physicians and review by a hospital Infant Care Review Committee, decided to have their child's life-support system removed. The hospital filed a petition with a lower court asking court approval for discontinuance of the life-support system. The court ruled that the hospital and the physicians should not interfere with the constitutional and common law rights of the child and should not interfere with the parents' wishes. After removal of the life-support system, the infant died within 30 minutes.

After pointing out that the case was not moot since similar circumstances could arise in the future, the court explained that the condition of the child was such that she was terminally ill and there was no reasonable possibility that she would ever attain cognitive function. Under such circumstances, the court found that the life-support system was prolonging her death rather than her life.

The court noted that no hospital ethics committee need be consulted, but the diagnosis and prognosis must be made by the attending physician, and two physicians with no interest in the outcome of the case must concur in the diagnosis and prognosis.

Since it found that there is no legal difference between the situations of infants and incompetent adults, the court took the opportunity to extend its holding to incompetent adults with no living wills.

In re L.H.R., Georgia Supreme Court, No. 41065, October 16, 1984).

The Georgia Supreme Court has determined that the family of a terminally ill infant in a chronic vegetative state with no hope of recovery may make the decision to remove life-support equipment without court approval.

Because most states have not dealt with these issues, internal policies or guidelines within hospitals and nursing homes should be established to assure a consistent approach to the resolution of conflicts.

The establishment of Ethics Committees will also help to achieve consistency and proof of a deliberative decision-making process to review these cases.

LIVING WILL AND DURABLE POWER OF ATTORNEY

A number of state legislatures have introduced legislation to permit a person to declare what should be done if terminal illness and incapacitation occur. The document known as *the living will* permits a person to determine how he or she should be cared for in the future while he or she still has the capacity to make such a decision. Since living wills are not yet legally binding in many states, they serve as guidelines to reflect the patient's wishes.

This legislation is also referred to as *right to die* legislation. A secondary objective of these laws is to relieve physicians and health care facilities from liability for honoring the wishes of patients to have treatment terminated.

In 1976 California became the first state to adopt a right to die law. By 1985 at least 35 states and the District of Columbia had enacted Natural Death Acts which authorize and recognize the use of living wills.

Some states require that the document be executed only after a patient is diagnosed as terminally ill. Other states allow the patient to appoint another person who would make the necessary medical decisions when the patient became incapacitated, using the durable power of attorney. Health care providers are generally more familiar with the power of attorney document that deals with financial issues. The financial power of attorney allows an individual to appoint a representative to handle his or her financial matters. The durable power of attorney allows an individual to appoint a representative to handle medical decisions. This appointed person may be a relative or friend of the patient. In states where the durable power of attorney exists, it is a legally binding document that specifies the individual who is to make decisions for the patient rather than what specific treatment the patient desires to have or to refuse. Durable means the document continues in effect after the patient is incapacitated.

Some states recognize both documents as legally binding authorizations.

While there are differences in the particulars of each state's legislation, the general concept of allowing a competent person to decide whether he or she wants extraordinary measures is consistent.

States without the statutory authorization of living wills may have court decisions dealing with the issue.

Brother Fox, an 83-year-old priest, became permanently comatose during hernia surgery in October 1979. When hospital officials and physicians refused a request to terminate the respirator, court proceedings were initiated.

Although Brother Fox did not have a written living will, there was evidence that he had made his views known orally.

The court held that these statements were sufficient to authorize the termination of life-sustaining procedures, since Brother Fox was clearly capable of realizing the consequences of his statements.

Eichner v. Dillon, 426 N.Y.S.2d 517 (1980)

Selma Saunders, 70 years old, suffers from emphysema and lung cancer. She is currently confined to the home of her daughter where oxygen is administered almost continually. Her condition is progressive without any currently known medical cure.

Mrs. Saunders had previously executed a living will while living in another state. She now petitioned the Supreme Court of New York for a prospective determination as to whether the directive would be followed in New York in the absence of a state law dealing with the issue.

The court held that the document was valid as an informed consent directive based on the patient's right to refuse medical treatment under the New York law regarding Patient's Rights.

Saunders v. State of New York, 492 N.Y.S.2d 510 (New York 1985)

The nurse who has knowledge is under a legal duty to reveal the existence of a living will or its revocation. The nurse must reveal statements made by the patient that may be interpreted as revocation of the living will. The nurse who receives a copy of a living will from a patient or family should notify the attending physician and place the document in the medical record.

The hospital may wish to establish a mechanism to handle living wills of prospective patients. In many communities prospective patients will mail these documents to the hospital. The hospital may decide to return this document to the individual if a patient medical record does not exist. The individual should be informed that his or her family physician and at least one relative should be given the document. As a service to the community, the hospital may choose to retain these documents on file. If the latter alternative is selected, it is important to assure a retrieval system that will produce this document when the patient arrives at the hospital. This could be accomplished with a computer program listing names of individuals who have filed these documents with the hospital.

Judicial decisions involving these documents have occurred in some states.

The wife of terminally ill, comatose Francis B. Landy, asked the hospital to implement her husband's directive, executed 6 years before his illness.

The hospital petitioned the court, which ruled against the request.

A subsequent decision by the court of appeals admitted the living will as evidence, but stated it was not sufficient in itself to guarantee immunity to physicians acting in accordance with it and that life support could be withdrawn only if a court-appointed guardian had obtained court approval.

The Florida Supreme Court subsequently struck down this decision. It affirmed the significance of the living will, gave the right of decision to a comatose patient's family, and removed the necessity for court intervention before life support could be terminated.

John F. Kennedy Memorial Hospital v. Bludworth, 452 So.2d 921 (Fla. 1984)

In a state with a mandatory Natural Death Act, guidelines may exist for the treatment of patients who have not executed an advance directive.

Bertha Colyer suffered massive brain damage from a cardiopulmonary arrest and was in a persistent vegetative state with no reasonable prospects of recovering significant brain function.

A lower court allowed the removal of life-support systems.

This was upheld by the Washington Supreme Court. The court provided guidelines for the exercise of the right to refuse treatment by an incompetent person who has not executed an advance directive under the Washington Natural Death Act as follows: 1) concurrence of three physicians, including the attending physician, that the patient's vegetative condition is irreversible; 2) the court appointment of a guardian; 3) a belief that the patient, if competent, would choose to withdraw the treatment.

In the Matter of The Welfare of Bertha Colyer, 660 P.2d 738 (Wash. 1983)

A 70-year-old man suffering from emphysema, chronic respiratory failure, arteriosclerosis, an abdominal aneurysm, and a malignant tumor of the lung was placed on a mechanical ventilator when his lung collapsed during a tumor biopsy.

Despite requests from the patient and his family that the ventilator be removed, the hospital and physicians refused, claiming that the patient could live for up to a year if he were weaned from the ventilator. Because the patient had on several occasions attempted to disconnect the ventilator tubes himself, his wrists were forced into soft restraints.

The court upheld the patient's right to refuse treatment.

A second suit filed by the patient's wife following his death is currently pending. The suit seeks $10 million in punitive damages and $5,000 per day for pain and suffering while the patient was on life-support equipment from April to November of 1984.

Bartling v. Superior Court, 209 Cal. Rptr. 220 (Cal. App. 1984)

Paul Brophy, Sr., a 46 year old Massachusettes fire fighter, suffered a subarachnoid hemorrhage from an aneurysm. Two weeks later he had a craniotomy and never regained consciousness following the surgery.

In December, 1983, Mrs. Brophy authorized surgical creation of a gastrostomy for feeding purposes.

One year later, she requested that all life sustaining treatment be discontinued including artificial nutrition and hydration.

Mr. Brophy's children, siblings, and mother supported the decision. His physician refused to comply with this request and was supported by the medical and nursing staff as well as the hospital Board of Directors.

The court found that it was medically and ethically appropriate to enter a "do not resuscitate" order and to implement a nonaggressive treatment plan. However, the court ruled that it would be ethically inappropriate to deny nutrition that could be provided in a nonintrusive, painless manner despite the substituted judgment of the patient not to live in a vegetative state. The court indicated that if Brophy were terminally ill or dying and receiving no benefit from the noninvasive provision of food and water, then it might be permissible to withhold feeding.

Brophy v. New England Sinai Hospital No. 85E0009-G1 (Norfolk County) Oct. 21, 1985

This decision is being appealed to a higher court in Massachusetts.

NDA (NATURAL DEATH ACTS)

A determination of who has authority to terminate treatment for a patient is sometimes difficult.

A severely mentally retarded 42-year-old hospital patient suffered a cardiorespiratory arrest which completely destroyed his cerebral cortical activity.

The trial court authorized the hospital to: (1) withhold resuscitation in the event of further arrest, (2) withhold antibiotics, and (3) withdraw use of the ventilator.

The patient had no relatives; the physician had asked the guardian to consent to termination because the patient was in a vegetative state with no reasonable hope of recovery. The guardian, the Foundation for the Handicapped, believed it did not have the authority to consent.

The Washington Supreme Court held that the guardian did have authority to consent since it was possible to conclude that the patient's best interests would be served by such action.

The court stated that these decisions must be made on a case-by-case basis with particularized consideration of the best interests and rights of the specific individual. The court also stressed the distinction between treatment that is expected to result in some measure of recovery and that which merely postpones death.

The court dismissed the argument that the state's Natural Death Act prescribed the exclusive method for determining the issue of withdrawal of life support systems. Hamlin's mental disability had precluded him from executing a valid directive under the Act. The court held that the Act was not exclusive since an incompetent patient does not lose his right to consent to termination of treatment by virtue of incompetency.

The court went on to discuss the issue of guardianship pointing out that guardianship proceedings are sometimes used in cases where patients are incapable of making decisions concerning medical treatment. The court did not feel that guardianship proceedings were a necessary predicate to effective decision making if family members were available. If there is no family, the court will be involved in the appointment of a guardian but not necessarily in substantive decision making.

In re Hamilton, 689 P.2d 1372 (Wash. 1984).

A 42-year-old patient with multiple sclerosis suffered a respiratory arrest. She was placed on a ventilator with only brain stem functioning.

The court held that the family was entitled to act as her substitute decision maker in deciding to discontinue the use of a respirator and other artificial devices and that neither civil nor criminal liability would be incurred by physicians or hospital employees who complied with the decision.

Foody v. Manchester Memorial Hosp. (Conn. Super. 1984).

In general, if the patient is unable to make his or her own medical decisions, the right to decide transfers to the next-of-kin. Generally, the next-of-kin is the spouse followed by adult children, parents, then siblings.

The controversial ethical decisions being made in the health care delivery system sometimes have criminal implications. Recent criminal cases have been initiated through nurses who were uneasy with medical decisions that had been made by physicians.

Clarence Herbert, 55 years old and a former security guard, had a heart attack and went into a coma following surgery on August 26, 1981. Three days later his doctors removed a respirator in keeping with his family's wishes and believing the patient would die within minutes. Herbert continued to breathe on his own.

On August 31, doctors removed tubes supplying nutrition and intravenous fluids. The patient died on September 6.

Information supplied by a nurse prompted a grand jury investigation and murder charges filed against the physician.

The court held that withdrawal of care was not murder. The appeals court said that the doctor's decision to remove the life-support equipment and IVs was intentional and with knowledge that the patient would die, but was not an unlawful failure to perform a legal duty. The court stated that the physician had no duty to continue treatment once it proved to be ineffective.

Barber v. Superior Court, 195 Cal. Rptr. 484, (Cal.App. 1983) 1983)

ABORTION

The right of a patient to self-determination has been extended by the abortion cases. The United States Supreme Court has recognized the right of a woman to privacy and to be the final arbitrator in matters relating to her own body. However, the Supreme Court has also recognized the interest of the state in protecting potential life and has placed certain limitations on her right in relationship to that of the unborn child.

In the first trimester of pregnancy, the state is virtually powerless to restrict or regulate the abortion procedures. During the second trimester, the state may stipulate the medical conditions under which the procedure can be performed. During the final state of pregnancy, due to the interest in protecting the rights of the unborn child, the state may justify stringent regulations and prohibition of abortions.

Courts have also held the need for either spousal or parental consent to an abortion to be invalid.

A minor has the right to refuse to consent to an abortion, even though her parents may request that one be performed.

A 16-year-old unmarried teenager had run away from home twice and was found hitchhiking on the highway with a 16-year-old boy. She was pregnant, and her mother wanted her to have an abortion.

The court found her to be a child in need of supervision, and she was placed in the custody of her mother under the supervision of the Department of Juvenile Services. However, the court held that the mother could not compel her daughter over her daughter's objection to submit to an abortion.

In Re Smith, 295 A.2d 238 (Md.1972).

STERILIZATION

Court decisions involving sterilization procedures have dealt with two general issues.

One group of decisions is related to the allegation of negligence when a sterilization procedure is performed unsuccessfully.

The defendant physician performed a vasectomy on a patient. The physician did not order a postoperative test to determine if semen was being produced. The patient's wife became pregnant shortly thereafter. The infant was delivered without any problems.

The court held the injured party was not permitted to recover damages for the birth of a normal child.

Ball v. Mudge, 391 P.2d 201 (Wash.1964).

If the child is born with some deformity or if the mother has some injury, courts are not as reluctant to award damages.

A second group of sterilization cases deals with the questions of consent to sterilization.

The question of whether a sterilization procedure may be done on a minor who is retarded is a changing legal concept.

A 13-year-old girl was severely mentally retarded. Her parents, who cared for her at home, wanted to obtain the court's approval for a sterilization procedure.

The judge refused to enter the order authorizing the sterilization because of prior cases holding that a judge who orders a sterilization without specific legislative authority does not receive judicial immunity for his act.

In the Matter of S.C.E., 178 A.2d 144 (Del.1977).

The parents of an 18-year-old woman who suffered from Down's syndrome requested a tubal ligation, but their request was rejected by the hospital unless authorized by the court.

The trial court said it would grant the parents' application based on findings that (1) the daughter was incompetent and incapable of understanding the nature of the sexual function and reproduction; (2) the incompetency was in all likelihood permanent; (3) the daughter was presumably fertile and capable of procreation; (4) all procedural safeguards had been satisfied, including appointment of a guardian and full court hearing, and (5) the parents had demonstrated their genuine good faith and shown that their primary concern was for the best interests of their daughter.

In the Matter of Grady, 405 A.2d 851 (N.J.Super.Ct., July 12, 1979).

In general, courts are reluctant to support the sterilization of an incompetent patient. The previous mechanism of securing a court order to allow this procedure to be performed may no longer be upheld when challenged.

An open issue exists as to the need for the consent of the spouse to a sterilization procedure.

While courts have stated that in an abortion, the woman's right to make the decision unilaterally prevails, such a statement has not clearly defined the question with sterilization. A strong public policy argument may be made supporting the need for the spouse's concurrence.

Once a sterilization procedure is complete, a permanent change has occurred, affecting the right of the nonsterilized spouse to have children. The completion of a sterilization procedure on one spouse is the permanent deprivation of a marital right affecting the other spouse. Based on this argument, both partners should consent to the procedure.

However, one jurisdiction has determined that the consent of the spouse is unnecessary.

A hysterectomy was performed on a woman with her consent but not her husband's consent.

He brought an action for $100,000 based on [her] loss of the ability to reproduce a child.

The court held that he had no right to recover damages, stating that a husband does not have a right to a childbearing wife as an incident to marriage and that the right of a person who is capable of competent consent to control her own body is paramount.

Murray v. Vandevander, 522 P.2d 302 (Okla.1974).

CHILD ABUSE

The incidence of child abuse continues to rise annually and has become a well-recognized cause of morbidity and mortality among children in the United States.

The health providers role in the area of child abuse involves the duty to report suspected child abuse victims. Many states require nurses and physicians to report known or suspected cases of child abuse. Emergency room personnel should be especially alert to evaluating the possibility of child abuse. Failure to detect this problem may impose liability on the health care provider, including possible criminal prosecution. The majority of the mandatory reporting laws grant immunity from civil suit to those who are requested to report, if they have reported in good faith.

HUMAN EXPERIMENTATION

In order for medicine to advance, research must be done. At some point during the research process, it becomes necessary to use human subjects. Sometimes this experimentation occurs in a hospital setting. All of the elements of informed consent discussed in Chapter 8 apply to the experimental situation. In addition, the patient must be told that the treatment is experimental in nature.

A mother with Rh negative blood was asked to participate in a study to determine the shelf life of a drug used to prevent the blood sensitization of patients following the delivery or miscarriage of a pregnancy with an Rh factor problem.

The patient, aware of the danger to subsequent pregnancies because of Rh sensitization, refused the experimental drug and requested the alternative drug known to be effective.

However, despite her wishes, she was given the experimental drug. When this was discovered months later, the patient developed anxiety, depression, and anger.

Subsequent tests indicated the experimental drug had been effective. The patient was permitted to recover damages for emotional injury, even though she had suffered no direct physical harm from the drug.
Blanton v. U.S., 428 F.Supp.360 (D.C.1977).

The nurse who participates in experimental projects should act in accord with research protocol. This protocol should be provided by the physician responsible for the research project, reviewed by a hospital committee of physicians, and be made readily available to nurses.

NURSING ETHICS

The nurse's right to raise objections about patient care issues seems to revolve around situations where the ethical issues are those which society generally has identified as being problematic.

If the patient care issue crosses the line into perceived criminal conduct or neglect, nurses have been instrumental in having those cases brought into a public forum. In the controversial abortion issue, the nurse is usually permitted to decide whether he or she wants to work with abortion cases.

However, when the nurse makes an individual, independent decision not to care for a particular patient, the court's review of the situation may not lend support to the nurse's position. For example, if the nurse refuses to care for an AIDS patient because of a value judgment about the patient's lifestyle, the court will not permit such a refusal. But if a nurse refuses because she is pregnant and fearful of the effects of communicable disease exposure, the court may permit that decision. Generally the court will evaluate whether a rational basis exists for the decision.

An RN refused to dialyze a terminally ill patient. The nurse refused because of moral and ethical objections. She was terminated from employment and sued for reinstatement.

Guidelines from the American Nurses Association Code of Ethics were presented into evidence.

"The nurse provides services with respect for human dignity and the uniqueness of the client unrestricted by considerations of social or economic status, personal attributes, or the nature of health problems."

"The nurse's respect for the worth and dignity of the individual human being applies irrespective of the nature of the health problem. It is reflected in the care given the person who is disabled as well as the normal, the patient with the long-term illness as well as the one with the acute illness, or the recovering patient as well as the one who is terminally ill or dying . . ."

"If personally opposed to the delivery of care in a particular case because of the nature of the health problem or the procedures to be used, the nurse is justified in refusing to participate . . ."

"If the nurse must knowingly enter such a case under emergency circumstances or enters unknowingly, the obligation to provide care is observed. The nurse withdraws from this type of situation only when assured that alternative sources of nursing care are available . . ."

This argument was rejected. The court stated that the code of ethics defined a standard of conduct beneficial only to the individual nurse and not to the public at large.

Warton v. Toms River Community Hospital, 488 A.2d 229 (N.J.1985).

SUMMARY

Although the practice of nursing is frequently guided by legal standards, ethical considerations are of primary importance.

Legal standards are a minimum standard, whereas ethical requirements may be more rigorous.

Termination or refusal of treatment is an example of such an ethical issue. A competent adult is usually permitted to determine if his or her treatment can be terminated or refused. Courts will be inclined to uphold such a decision if it is based on religious considerations. However, a strong state interest such as concern for children or for an unborn child may cause the court to overrule the patient's decision.

While the document known as the Living Will may have limited legal effect, it does provide some guidance as to what the patient has chosen.

Abortion, sterilization, child abuse, and human experimentation are further examples of ethical issues that have significant implications for nurses.

CHAPTER **14**

CRIMINAL LAW

As described in earlier chapters, a tort is a civil wrong. Some torts result from lack of due care and are commonly referred to as negligence cases. This chapter, is an introduction to nurse-related aspects of criminal law. *A type of deviation from proper conduct other than a civil wrong is a criminal wrong.*

Technically, a crime is a wrong punishable by imprisonment and/or fine and is an injury to the state rather than an injury to a person. The same action may be both a criminal and a civil wrong. For example, if a driver who caused a car accident was intoxicated, the injured party would have a claim for damages against the driver, and also the state could bring criminal charges against the driver. In a criminal case, the court considers the intent of the defendant as well as the defendant's actions. In a civil action the court does not consider the state of mind (intent) of the defendant.

MISDEMEANOR AND FELONY

A *misdemeanor* is a general name for any less serious criminal offense. A *felony* is a crime punishable by death or imprisonment in a penitentiary.

TYPES OF CRIMES

Homicide is the killing of one human being by another. Not all homicides are illegal. A killing may be justifiable or excusable or it may be a felony.

An example of justifiable homicide is a killing occurring to prevent the killing of another. An excusable homicide might be a killing done in self-defense.

One kind of felony-homicide is *murder*, the unlawful killing of a human being with intent to kill. *Euthanasia*, the act of putting to death those who are suffering from a disease, is murder according to the law.

The following cases illustrates the concept of a felony-homicide.

A chiropractor was convicted of felony-homicide in the death of an 8-year-old child. However, the judgment was reversed on appeal because of improper jury instructions.

The chiropractor had falsely represented to his patient his ability to cure a particular form of cancer. The child needed his cancerous eye removed, but the chiropractor convinced the family to forego treatment.

People v. Phillips, 42 Cal.Rptr. 868 (1968).

A nurse's aide was convicted of first degree murder based on charges that he injected an elderly hospital patient with a fatal dose of lidocaine.

Evidence indicated that the patient died of an overdose of the drug, that lidocaine was missing from an emergency crash cart on the night of the victim's death, that defendant had access to both the victim and the drug just prior to the patient's death, that the defendant had previously administered medication to two other patients without authority, and that defendant had told a cellmate that he had "killed people for kicks."

Hargrave v. Landon, No. 83-8405, (D.C., Va. 1984).

A nurse working in a pediatrician's office was convicted of murder for causing respiratory arrest in children by injecting them with succinylcholine. She was suspected of injecting five other children during a 1-month time period.

She had told another nurse that she wished the town would provide a pediatric intensive care unit. When the second nurse stated that there were not enough cases to justify such a unit, the accused nurse allegedly had replied "Oh, they are out there; all you have to do is go out and find them."

Jones v. State, 716 S.W.2d 142 (Texas 1986).

Manslaughter is the unlawful killing of another without malice aforethought. Nurses may be found guilty of manslaughter.

A surgeon ordered a nurse to prepare a 10 percent cocaine solution with epinephrine for a tonsillectomy patient as an anesthetic. The patient convulsed and died. The physician had meant procaine. Even though the nurse repeated the order, she was found guilty for not questioning it. The nurse was convicted of manslaughter.

Somera Case, G.R. 31693 (Philippine Islands, 1929).

A registered nurse transfused a patient with incompatible blood intended for another patient.

The evidence indicated that following the patient's death, the nurse had taken steps to conceal her conduct by disposing of the remainder of the blood and changing notations on the patient's chart.

State v. Winter, No. A-35, Sept. Term 1983 (NJ 1984).

Involuntary manslaughter refers to a killing that is both unintentional and without malice. The following cases illustrate how a nurse may be found guilty of involuntary manslaughter.

A registered nurse was in charge of a state hospital for the mentally retarded. She gave four times the correct dose of paraldehyde to a patient. As a result, the patient became ill, was taken to another hospital, and died 5 days later of pneumonia.

However, the criminal conviction was reversed, because it could not be proven that the medication was the direct cause of death due to the lapse of time.

State v. Comstock, 70 S.E.2d 648 (W.Va. 1952).

The son of an incapacitated woman hired a practical nurse to live with his mother and take care of her.

The practical nurse grossly neglected the patient. By the time the inadequate care was discovered, the patient was dying of an extensive infection resulting from serious bedsores.

The nurse was found guilty of involuntary manslaughter.

People v. Montecino, 152 P.2d 5 (Calif. 1944).

Where nurses have deviated from prescribed treatment and failed to adhere to appropriate standards of practice, they may not only be in violation of Nurse Practice Acts but also may be subject to criminal charges.

The Director of a Nursing Home, the charge nurse, and the nursing home were charged with second degree assault for injecting Thorazine which caused the patient's death. The medication had not been ordered for the patient, but the nurses administered it for sedation because the patient was upset.

People v. Nygren, 696 P.2d 270 (Colorado 1985).

Health care providers have also been named defendants in rape cases.

A female patient was admitted to the hospital with migraine headaches. Later she was transferred to the intensive care unit.

The night charge nurse was found guilty of inserting his hand into the patient's vagina and of having sexual intercourse with her.

State v. Raines, 344 S.E.2d 138.

The defendant was a physician convicted of rape with three young female patients on several different occasions while examining them in his office.

People v. Minkowski, 23 Cal. Rptr. 92 (Calif. 1962).

Attempts have been made to extend liability to the hospital for the criminal actions of an employed nurse.

An obstetrical nurse delivered a baby girl while on duty at the hospital without the assistance of a physician. The nurse substituted a dead fetus for the live baby she delivered and reported a stillbirth. She then took the baby to her own home.

A few months later the nurse murdered another woman. The court addressed the issue of whether the hospital should have known of the first incident and therefore have been on notice that the nurse was dangerous.

The court held that even assuming an investigation had disclosed the nurse's switching the dead fetus for the live birth, the hospital would have had no indication that the nurse's criminal impulses would focus on the murdered woman. Therefore the hospital had no liability.

Hooks v. Southern California Permanente Medical Group, 165 Cal.Rptr. 741 (Cal. Ct. of App., June 25, 1980).

Cases involving the termination of life-support systems have also sometimes evolved into criminal proceedings. When the health care provider believes that an unethical or illegal practice is occurring, one course of action has been to go out of the hospital for advice and assistance in handling the case.

Adequate policies and open communication lines within the institution will diminish the need for outside intervention. Ethics Committees, newly formed in many institutions, as discussed in Chapter 13, are one mechanism through which these controversial cases can be addressed.

Clarence Herbert had undergone surgery for closure of an ileostomy. He suffered a cardiorespiratory arrest in the recovery room and was placed on life-support equipment.

Upon the family's request, the physicians ordered removal of the respirator. Mr. Herbert continued to breathe but showed no signs of improvement. After several days, the physicians ordered removal of the intravenous tubes. Dr. Barber wrote in the patient's medical record "family wants IVs stopped." The patient died 6 days later.

A nurse took the medical record to the district attorney, who charged the physicians with murder as an attempt to cover up malpractice in the operating room.

The court dismissed the charges stating, "We view the use of intravenous administration of nourishment and fluid as being the same as the use of other forms of life-support equipment. A murder prosecution is a poor way to design an ethical and moral code for doctors who are faced with decisions concerning the use of costly and extraordinary life-support equipment."

Barber v. Superior Court of the State of California, 195 Cal. Rptr., 484 (Calif. App. 1983).

NON-HEALTH CARE PROVIDER CRIMINAL ACTIONS

Non-health care providers may also face liability for criminal charges. This liability may occur when family members do not provide reasonable access to medical care on behalf of a family member who is unable to care for himself or herself.

The defendant was convicted of involuntary manslaughter for failing to provide medical care for his wife after she had been injured at home.

The court pointed out that even though his wife was chronically and seriously ill, his failure to obtain help for her hastened her death.

State v. Mally, 366 P.2d 868 (Mont. 1961).

Even though a person may be at the threshold of death, if the spark of life is extinguished by a wrongful act, it is sufficient for a conviction.

The large majority of these types of cases involve a failure to provide medical aid involving a parent-child relationship. A person of mature years is generally not in a helpless condition. However in the above case, the evidence clearly indicated that the patient could not have rationally refused medical aid because of the nature of her injuries.

After a child died of acute bronchial pneumonia, a jury found the parents guilty of reckless homicide on the basis of evidence that the child had been ill for some 5 days but that the parents, because of their religious beliefs, had failed to seek medical care for him.
Hall v. State, 493 N.E.2d, 433 (Ind. 1986).

When a health care provider becomes aware of such gross negligence, the duty to intervene through communication with a child services agency generally arises under the mandatory child abuse reporting laws in most jurisdictions.

A 27 year old California woman has been charged with a criminal misdemeanor for contributing to the death of her baby by failing to follow her doctor's advice before the infant's birth.
   She is accused of failing to summon prompt medical help when she began to hemorrhage the day she gave birth. She also was accused of taking amphetamines and smoking marijuana during pregnancy.
   Her son was born with massive brain damage and died 6 weeks later.
State v. Monson, (Calif. 1986).

THE NURSE'S CRIMINAL LIABILITY FOR FOLLOWING DOCTOR'S ORDERS

In the civil liability chapters we have discussed the nurse's potential civil liability exposure for following doctors' orders that are inappropriate and will harm the patient if followed, or for failing to follow appropriate physician orders resulting in harm to the patient. An important word needs to be added with regard to the same issue as it is decided in the criminal court room.

   If a criminal act is involved, the nurse may be guilty even though the physician has expressly directed the nurse's actions.

A nurse served as the office manager for a physician who specialized in weight control.

She was convicted of aiding and abetting him in his unlawful diversion of large quantities of controlled substances. Prior to trial, the physician was ordered to have a psychiatric examination that proved he was not competent to stand trial. The nurse was found to have an excellent factual and national understanding of the charges against her.

She was convicted and sentenced to prison for one year, with 6 months suspended and a 5-year probationary period.

United States v. Vamos, 797 F.2d, 1146 (NY 1986).

Recently a number of criminal cases have been initiated involving the failure to resuscitate a viable fetus following an abortion. In these cases, despite the physician's direct order not to provide care, the nurse who follows the order as well as the physician may face criminal charges.

SUMMARY

Most lawsuits brought against nurses are based on negligence or the intentional torts. Criminal offenses are defined as either felonies or misdemeanors. Examples of crimes that nurses may become involved in include homicide and manslaughter. Criminal Cases involving nurses are being reported more frequently. An interesting new issue emerges in the cases dealing with a criminal charge against a family member for failing to obtain medical care for one who is unable to obtain his or her own care.

CHAPTER 15

WILLS

Most hospital nurses have been asked at some point in their careers to witness a patient's will. This is almost inevitable since many people do not decide that a will is necessary until they become ill.

Nurses should not feel uncomfortable when faced with this request, nor should they automatically refuse all such requests. It is hoped that hospitals will not adopt policies discouraging nurses from complying with such requests. Some hospitals seem to feel that this is yet another factor taking the nurse away from her primary duty—providing bedside nursing care. This attitude fails to reflect an equally important aspect of nursing care—the duty to provide emotional support to patients. For the patient with terminal cancer who is dying, this act of witnessing may be the final act of compassion and caring that the nurse can provide.

FACTORS NECESSARY FOR A VALID WILL

Nurses will feel more comfortable with the request to witness a will if they are familiar with the factors necessary to execute a valid will. Each state has specific rules that explain what elements are necessary for a will to be valid.

In general, for a will to be valid the person making the will, known as the testator, must be of sound mind and free of duress. Some states recognize a handwritten will that is signed by the testator. These states may not require witnesses. However, most states require two witnesses and some, three. The testator must sign the will in the actual presence of the witnesses. It is not necessary for the witnesses to see the document. The purpose of the witness is to witness the signature itself. This is similar to the witness to the signature on an operative consent form. The witness can then later testify that this person signed this document but can not testify as to the content of the document or the testator's exact understanding of the contents. The will must be dated, and the testator must sign at the end of the document. Any writing added after the signature of the testator may be considered invalid in court.

The purpose of a will is to allow the testator to dispose of his property as he wishes. When a person dies without a will, property is passed according to the laws of the state. For example, some states allow one-half of all property to be inherited by the surviving spouse and the other half to be divided evenly among their children. If a person dies without a will and with no surviving relatives, the property will belong to the state.

THE NURSE'S ROLE

One of the most important factors for the nurse involved in witnessing a will is the question of the patient's ability or capacity to consent. Particularly since these are wills made during periods of serious illness, the issue of whether the patient was mentally competent to make a will may be questioned.

The degree of mental competence required to make a will is not necessarily the same as that required for a signature on an operative consent or on a contract, for example. In order to have legal capacity to make a will, the testator must be of legal age and must understand the type and amount of his or her property, who his beneficiaries are, and what disposition he or she is making of the property. Old age, severe illness, great weakness, and even the fact that the testator may have a legal guardian does not necessarily prevent him or her from validly executing his or her own will.

Besides witnessing the will, the nurse can provide a valuable service to the patient by documenting in the patient's medical record the apparent mental and physical condition at the time the will was signed. The fact that the will was made should also be noted. These records will be very important if the will is later contested by relatives who believe they should not have been excluded.

GIFTS

Sometimes nurses are asked to witness a gift just as they might witness a will. The person giving the gift must know what he or she is doing and must do so freely without undue influence or fraud.

If the nurse is the recipient of a gift from a patient that is valuable, there is a presumption in the law that undue pressure may have been present. This is in recognition of the fact that hospital patients may be under emotional pressure that is not normally present. Legally, there is no reason for a nurse to refuse a gift from a patient, particularly if it will cause distress to the patient. However, if it appears that the patient and/or relatives subsequently wish to retrieve the gift, the nurse should comply with their request.

SUMMARY

The hospital-based nurse is sometimes asked to act as a witness to a patient's will. There is no legal reason for the nurse to refuse such a request. A knowledge of some basic principles regarding wills may help the nurse feel more comfortable when this request is made.

CHAPTER 16

EMPLOYMENT ISSUES

CONTRACTS: DEFINITION AND REQUIREMENTS

A contract is an exchange of promises between two persons who are legally capable of making a binding agreement. In order for a contract to be valid, there must be an offer of something and an acceptance of that offer. A third requirement is the need for consideration; that is, something of value must be exchanged between the parties. In some cases money may be the consideration. In other contracts, a promise to do something or to refrain from doing something may be the consideration.

A contract may be oral or written. In certain situations, the law requires that a contract be in writing, for example, a contract that cannot be completed within 1 year. This type of contract must be in writing and includes a contract for employment.

Although an oral contract is valid, in some cases it is preferable to have all contracts documented in writing. This documentation is valuable when a question about the interpretation of a contract arises at a later date.

Breach of contract occurs when the terms of the contract are not carried out by one of the parties. Depending on the nature of the breach, the other party will be entitled to financial compensation or other remedies.

One type of contractual situation with which the nurse must become familiar is the employer-employee contract under which the nurse frequently practices nursing.

For instance, a breach of contract may exist when a private duty nurse severs her relationship with the patient without giving reasonable notice.

CONTRACTUAL BASIS OF LIABILITY

The law recognizes that medicine is not an exact science. Physicians do not ensure cures or guarantee recovery to their patients. Therefore a contract to cure does not usually exist in the physician-patient relationship as is often alleged by the patient in sterilization and plastic surgery cases.

However, this factor can be altered if the patient is able to prove that a nurse or physician promised a satisfactory result. This allows the patient to base a claim on a contractual basis as well as on malpractice. The advantage of this is the provision of additional damages as well as the elimination of the need for expert testimony.

The statute of limitations for contracts is usually longer than for torts. Using this basis for claim, the patient will have a longer period of time to initiate a suit.

THE NURSE AS AN EMPLOYEE

An employer has certain legal responsibilities to employees whether or not these duties are specifically outlined in a written contract. These duties may be implied from the employer-employee relationship.

A recent case involving a student nurse offers an illustration of an implied contract.

A former nursing student alleged that her school of nursing had breached its contract by taking actions unauthorized by and contrary to its own rules. As a result of the alleged breach, she claimed she was improperly forced out of the nursing department and was graduated with a psychology degree instead. She was seeking monetary damages and a mandatory injunction reinstating her in the nursing program.

The student missed some classes and clinical experiences while accompanying an ill friend to the hospital. Previously, she had received As and Bs in nearly all of her classes. She received an F in the class rather than the "incomplete," which she believed the instructor had told her she would receive. She appealed this grade through the appeals process of the school. The appeals committee recommended that the grade of "incomplete" be given as well as an opportunity to complete the work.

The associate dean, after receiving the recommendation, overruled the decision and denied the grade appeal. The student was then dropped from the nursing program.

The rules provided that the committee would submit its recommendation to the dean. Both parties agreed that these rules constituted a contract. The issue was whether the dean had the authority to reject the recommendation of the committee. This authority had to be an implied term of the contract, since the dean's action, based on this recommendation, was not specifically stated.

The court stated that it had to look beyond the words of the contract to determine the intent the appeals committee's recommendation was to have. A letter from the dean was offered into evidence indicating to the student that the committee's decision would determine the issue. Therefore, the court held that the recommendations of the appeals committee were to be final.

The student was reinstated.

Lyons v. Salve Regina College, 422 F.Supp. 1354 (U.S.D.C. Rhode Island, 1976).

An employer has a legal duty to furnish employees with a safe place to work. The employer is under an additional duty to protect reasonably those employees who, due to youth or inexperience, may be assumed unlikely to use due precautions.

A 19-year-old orderly contracted serum hepatitis after his skin was punctured by hypodermic needles that had been thrown into trash bags, which he was removing. Evidence indicated that the orderly was not given any special precautions as to how the bags should be handled.

The orderly appealed a judgment for the defendant hospital and was given an opportunity for a new trial.

Walker v. Graham, 343 So.2d 1171 (La.1977).

If an employee of the hospital is unable to work because of a work-related injury or illness, the issue of whether this employee is entitled to worker's compensation becomes significant.

A nurse discovered she had contracted hepatitis. However, she was unable to prove that her case of hepatitis arose from her employment at the hospital. She did not prove that she had come in contact with any hepatitis or that any patient in the hospital had hepatitis during the period in which she claimed she contracted the disease. Therefore, the nurse was not entitled to worker's compensation.

Sacred Heart Medical Center v. Carrado, 579 P.2d 412 (Wash. 1979)

A nurse was asked by the director of research at the school of nursing to assist in developing a proposal for obtaining funds to study home care of children with terminal cancer. She orally agreed to a lump sum of $9 or $10 per hour to be paid on completion of the project. She was 6-months pregnant and worked on the project at home. While returning home from delivering a final draft of the proposal to a secretary at the school, she was involved in a car accident that rendered her a quadriplegic. The university appealed a workmen's compensation award to the nurse.

The court ruled that the nurse was an employee of the university and that the injury arose in the course of her employment. The award was affirmed.

Kahn v. State of Minnesota, 289 N.W.2d 737 (Minn.1980).

The scope of definition for a work-related injury is frequently a topic for litigation.

A nurse had been Assistant Director of Nurses for 9 years and had served as Director of Nurses whenever the Director was away or ill. Although the nurse had received about average to outstanding performance ratings, there was evidence that her performance had begun to decline.

She testified that there was a movement by some to force her to quit, and the employer requested and received her resignation a short time later.

About 4 years after her termination, the nurse filed a claim for worker's compensation based on her depression. The Worker's Compensation Board affirmed the insurance company's denial of her claim and the nurse appealed.

The court reversed and remanded the case and held that stressful events and conditions of the nurse's employment, including her termination were the major contributing causes of her mental disorder.

Elwood v. State Accident Insurance Fund Corp., 676 P.2d 922 (Oregon 1984).

Worker's compensation is intended to be an exclusive remedy for work-related injuries. Sometimes an employee will attempt to sue for negligence rather than to accept the standard financial award allowed under the state's worker's compensation laws.

An employee arrived at her hospital approximately 30 minutes prior to the beginning of her shift. As she waited in the lobby for her shift to begin, she was assaulted by a patient.

She sued her employer for negligence. The court held that her exclusive remedy was under the worker's compensation law because the employee was not outside the course and scope of her employment.

Johns v. State Dept. of Health, 485 So.2d 857 (Florida 1985).

Worker's compensation is set by state law and differs in each jurisdiction. These acts replace the employee's common law remedy that required the employee to sue the employer for negligence, which was usually an unsuccessful process. Originally, compensation was given only when an employee could prove that a traumatic injury had occurred in a job-connected accident. These laws have been broadened to include diseases that result from hazardous occupational environments. Recent cases dealing with payments for asbestosis are an example. *At the time of the injury the employee must give written notice of injury to the employer.*

Unemployment compensation is another important employment issue for nurses. Generally, an employee must be furloughed to qualify for unemployment compensation. If a person is fired or leaves a job voluntarily, he or she must prove that there was "good cause" for leaving in order to be eligible for unemployment compensation.

A staff nurse voluntarily resigned from the hospital because of intolerable working conditions including confusion over job assignment, lack of procedures for coordinating treatment among shifts, and inadequate record-keeping.

The court held that this resignation was not for "good cause" so as to justify an award of unemployment benefits.

Sohler v. Director of Division of Employment Security, 388 N.E.2d 299 (Mass. 1979).

A registered nurse was discharged from employment for deliberately violating a hospital policy by changing the prescribed amount of medication she administered to a patient without the permission of a physician. She administered meperidine 50 milligrams rather than 100 milligrams prescribed by the physician.

The court held that she was appropriately discharged for misconduct and therefore not eligible for unemployment compensation.

Davis v. California Unemployment Insurance Bd., 117 Cal.Rptr.463, 43 Cal.App.3d 71 (1974).

A finding of willful misconduct generally will result in a denial of unemployment compensation.

A nurse's aide was informed by her supervisor that she would not be relieved from duty on a given weekend. She told her supervisor that she could "take the job and shove it." The court held that a single instance of the use of unprovoked vulgarity with a superior was sufficient to constitute willful misconduct.

Therefore, unemployment compensation was denied.

Losch v. Commonwealth, Unemployment Compensation Bd. of Rev. (Pa. Cmwlth. 1983), 461 A.2d 344.

A nurse's aide was discharged by a nursing home for leaving a patient unrestrained on a commode and for using the private property of another patient.

The finding that the aide had been guilty of deliberate misconduct in willful disregard of her employer's interests was supported by sufficient inquiry as to whether the aide had been well enough trained and instructed so as to eliminate the possibility that her acts might have resulted from incompetence or good faith lack of understanding of the employer's policies or practices.
Starks v. Director, Div. of Employment Security, 391 Mass. 640 (1984).

Failing to renew a nursing license may be a legitimate basis for discharge as well as for denial of unemployment compensation.

A registered nurse failed to obtain renewal of her license, despite her knowledge that renewal of the license was required by her nursing home employer.
The court upheld this as willful misconduct.
Adams v. Commonwealth, Unemp. Comp. Bd. of Rev. (Pa. Cmwlth. 1984) and 484 A.2d 232.

Other hospital employees such as radiology technologists have attempted to secure these benefits.

A hospital radiology technologist refused to sign or accept a written warning with respect to his conduct at the hospital and did not give any explanation for this refusal. Evidence also indicated that he had refused to work weekends and became insolent to his supervisor.
Because he lost his employment due to misconduct, it was held that unemployment benefits were properly denied.
Herwig v. Ross, 414 N.Y.S.2d 797 (N.Y.App.Div.1979)

LABOR RELATIONS

Labor law is becoming increasingly significant to the nursing profession as nurses begin to unionize. Although it is too early to assess the total impact of unionization on the nursing profession, it is quite clear that nurses need to be aware of basic labor law concepts.

Before 1974, the Taft-Hartley Act exempted nonprofit hospitals from the jurisdiction of the National Labor Relations Board (NLRB). A union organized within the hospital did not have the support of the NLRB to compel the employer to recognize the union or to bargain.

After 1974, hospitals became subject to the NLRB. Employees now have the right to bargain collectively. The Act now covers all health care institutions, including hospitals, health maintenance organizations and nursing homes, without regard to whether the facility is proprietary or nonprofit. The Act protects the rights of employees to band together. It states that employees have the right to self-organization, to form, join or assist labor organizations to bargain collectively through representatives of their own choosing, and to engage in other concerted activities for the purpose of collective bargaining. The rights that are protected include the right to complain about working conditions with, to, or on behalf of other employees; the right to discuss, advocate, and actively strive toward unionization by soliciting other employees and/or distributing literature, subject to consistently enforced "no solicitation", "no distribution" policies and the right to strike on their own behalf.

In the health care industry, unions must give at least ten (10) days advance notice of the date and time for a threatened strike.

Unfair labor practices, such as discrimination against employees because of union activities, are now under the jurisdiction of the NLRB.

An issue that frequently arises for consideration by the NLRB is the question of union solicitation for membership. Since solicitation in a hospital may disrupt the rendering of health care, the problem is more complex than in an industrial setting.

Many hospitals have developed "no solicitation" and "no access" rules that have the effect of inhibiting union solicitation. These rules are usually upheld by the courts if they are reasonable and uniformly applied in a nonarbitrary manner. However, if the rules seem to violate rights of free speech, which are constitutionally guaranteed by the First Amendment, the rules will not be upheld.

An off duty hospital employee began distributing union literature to other employees outside the hospital entrance at about 6 AM, before her scheduled work hours, beginning at 8 AM. At 7 AM she was ordered to cease because of a hospital no access rule prohibiting off-duty employees from being on hospital premises.

The union attempting to organize the medical center initiated a lawsuit charging that enforcement of this rule was an unfair labor practice.

The hospital argued that the no access rule was appropriate, because the hospital had arrested three employees on suspicion of taking drugs and 12 for nondrug thefts during a 6-month period. Also, 5 employee-owned cars were stolen from the employees' parking lot during the same period.

The no access rule stated: "Employees are not to be on hospital premises except during assigned working hours or while attending an authorized hospital function. It is expected that employees will not visit areas other than those where they work during duty hours, unless with the specific approval of their supervisors."

The court determined that the hospital rule could not be applied to prohibit access to outside nonworking areas of the hospital.

NLRB v. Presbyterian Medical Center, 586 F.2d 165 (Kansas 1978).

A hospital banned solicitation by its employees at all times in any area of the hospital that was accessible to or used by the public. The ban extended to lobbies, the gift shop, cafeteria, and entrances on the first floor as well as corridors, sitting rooms, and public restrooms on other floors.

The court permitted the hospital to ban solicitation in corridors and sitting rooms on patient floors. However, the hospital was to allow solicitation in the cafeteria, gift shop, and lobbies on the first floor.

NLRB v. Baptist Hospital, Inc., 442 U.S., 61 LEd.2d 251, 99 S.Ct.2598 (1979).

The issue of whether nurses may be terminated for union activity is frequently raised by nurses. A recent case illustrates this question.

Four union organizing nurses were terminated for the bizarre fashion in which they prepared a sedated patient for transportation to surgery.

The patient was isolated before surgery due to possible infectious hepatitis. He was the husband of a nursing supervisor at the hospital. One of the nurses dressed him in a disposable yellow gown on which she had lettered the words "Yellow Bird Express." Another nurse placed a brown plastic bag over the patients feet, a surgical mask over his face, and a plastic shower cap on his head. The patient's wife complained to the director of nursing about this conduct. The nurses were subsequently discharged.

The nurses filed a grievance with the National Labor Relations Board and complained that they were fired because of union activities. The court held that proof was insufficient to show that antiunion feelings were the primary motive for discharge of the nurses. The bizarre treatment of the patient raised doubts with patients and other hospital personnel about the quality of nursing care at the hospital.

Hubbard Regional Hospital v. NLRB, 579 F.2d 1251 (C.A. 1, June 21, 1978).

Individuals who fall within the definition of "supervisor" are not employees for purposes of the Act and, therefore, cannot be included as part of the union. Whether or not an individual who is a charge nurse can be considered a supervisor depends on an evaluation of a number of factual circumstances including: (1) whether the positions are permanent rather than rotated among numerous nurses, (2) the individual's power to exercise the authority to grant time off or to authorize overtime, (3) if they exercise authority to call in replacements to cover absences, (4) if they are compensated at a higher rate of pay than non-supervisory nurses, (5) if they exercise the authority to take or recommend disciplinary actions and (6) if they attend meetings not open to nonsupervisory personnel (The Health Care Supervisor's Legal Guide, Pg. 51).

Under what circumstances a nurse's employment can be terminated is an important issue to all nurses.

A nurse-anesthetist assisted in a D & C procedure. During the procedure she observed a fetus being removed from the patient's uterus part by part. Afterwards she learned that she was scheduled to participate in a bilateral tubal ligation. She advised the hospital administrator that she would not participate in the procedure, based on moral grounds. Another nurse-anesthetist was obtained, and the operation went ahead as scheduled.

The nurse then received a letter stating that she was terminated for her refusal to participate in the sterilization procedure. The court held that the nurse's decision was protected by the State's conscience statute that granted health care personnel the right to refuse to engage in such procedures.

Swanson v. St. John's Lutheran Hospital, 597 P.2d 702 (Montana 1979)

TERMINATION

A private duty nurse was informed that she was no longer allowed to practice private duty nursing at the hospital because of her abusive criticism of certain members of the medical staff, which had a disruptive and disharmonious effect on staff operations.

She sued for monetary damages and an injunction. The court dismissed her complaint and the decision was upheld on appeal.

Ashley v. Nyack Hosp., 412 N.Y.S.2d 388 (1979).

Whether civil rights laws can be the basis for liability has also been considered.

A nurse was employed for 9 years and was head nurse of the hospital's emergency room. Her dismissal allegedly arose from statements made by her at a meeting of the County Government Sub-Committee on Emergency Medical Services. She was representing the hospital at the meeting and allegedly made derogatory remarks regarding some of the hospital's doctors.

The nurse was given the option of resigning or being fired; she chose to resign. She then initiated an action under the civil rights law alleging violation of her constitutional rights.

The court held that the hospital and its employees were not so closely connected with the state or government so as to subject themselves to liability under this law.

Bach v. Mount Clemens General Hosp., 448 F.Supp.686 (Michigan 1978).

However, in a more recent case the court sent the case back for further proceedings so that both parties could present additional evidence.

The nurse, a Director of Nursing, noted irregularities in the hospital's nursing department. After she produced evidence of this, she was transferred and then fired.

A federal trial court dismissed her civil rights action against the hospital corporation, finding her evidence insufficient to demonstrate the existence of corporate policy.

On appeal, the federal court found that the nurse had a long and distinguished career and that her treatment could only be explained as retaliation.

Rookard v. Health & Hospitals Corp., 710 F.2d 41 (N.Y.Ct. of Appl. 1983)

The case of an employee who is terminated after having filed a worker's compensation claim may require special scrutiny.

An operating room technician for more than 13 years was terminated. The previous year she had filed a claim for injury to her thumb and was granted benefits for temporary total disability. During the next two years, she was absent for 249 days.

The hospital discharged her for excessive absenteeism and she sued for wrongful discharge. She alleged that her discharge was motivated by the hospital's desire to penalize her for claiming worker's compensation benefits.

The discharge was upheld because Maryland State law required that the sole reason for discharge be the filing of a worker's compensation claim in order for an employee to maintain that the discharge was retaliatory.

Kern v. South Baltimore General Hosp., 504 A.2d 1154 (Md.App. 1986).

Because state worker's compensation laws differ, a similar result to the previous decision would not necessarily occur in a different state.

Following the termination of a nurse's employment, the employer is faced with the difficult problem of providing references.

A nurse and her daughters were employed by a nursing home. The mother clocked her daughters in and out of work when, in fact, they were absent. The employee handbook listed "clocking someone else in or out of work" as conduct leading to dismissal. The nurse was dismissed.

Approximately one year later she applied for employment at another nursing home and signed a form authorizing the release of information from her previous employer. Subsequently the factual information regarding her termination was sent.

The nurse then filed a complaint disputing the findings and asserting that she was deprived of due process because she was terminated without a hearing.

The court concluded that the nursing home's statements to the prospective employer were true and accurate and that the plaintiff had suffered no infringement of any constitutionally protected interest.

Pollock v. Baxter Manor Nursing Home, 536 F.Supp. 673 (Arkansas 1982).

DISCRIMINATION

Section 703 of Title VII of the Civil Rights Act of 1964 deals with employment and states in part:

Civil Rights Act of 1964: 42 USCA Section §2000e-2. Unlawful employment practices. "It shall be an unlawful employment practice for an employer—(1) to fail or refuse to hire or to discharge any individual, or otherwise to discriminate against any individual with respect to his compensation, terms, conditions, or privileges of employment, because of such individual's race, color, religion, sex, or national origin; or (2) to limit, segregate, or classify his employees or applicants for employment in any way which would deprive or tend to deprive any individual of employment opportunities or otherwise adversely affect his status as an employee, because of such individual's race, color, religion, sex or national origin. 42 U.S.C. Section §2000 e.2 (1981)."

There are a number of cases in health care law dealing with the various types of discrimination.

Racial discrimination is sometimes alleged in this line of case law.

A nurse brought suit against the hospital claiming that she was discriminated against because of her race and was forced to resign her position as head nurse.

The hospital was found not guilty of racial discrimination.

Barbara K. Glymph v. Spartanburg General Hosp., 783 F.2d 476 (Fourth Circ. 1986).

A hospital employee sought a position as Word Processing Director.

The court found that the hospital's failure to offer the position to the woman, who is black, constituted illegal discrimination.

Evidence indicated that she was a superior candidate for the position based on her educational background, experience, and employment history with the hospital.

Children's Hospital of Pittsburgh v. City of Pittsburgh Commission on Human Relations, Comm. Ct. of Pa., No. 2815 C.D. 1984 (1986).

A black female was employed as a staff pharmacist. She prepared prescriptions for a patient and erroneously placed instructions on the vial for the patient to take an anticoagulant every 6 hours rather than one time a day. The patient died of internal bleeding from the drug overdose.

The pharmacist was reprimanded and reassigned to nondirect care activities. She resigned and initiated an action claiming that she was functionally demoted because of her race.

The court held for the defendants and the decision was upheld on appeal.

Earlie v. Jacobs, 745 F.2d 342 (Texas 1984).

Religious discrimination may also be alleged by employees.

A supervisory security guard was terminated from employment for refusing to work on Saturdays due to his religious beliefs.

The Pennsylvania Human Relations Commission ordered reinstatement of the discharged officer.

However, the court reversed this decision finding that the medical center did not discharge the sergeant because of his religious beliefs, but because of his refusal to work on Saturdays. The employer was able to demonstrate that it could not reasonably accommodate the employee's religious beliefs without undue hardship to its business operation. The court considered the nature of the hospital's business, the weekly frequency and permanent duration of the accommodation, and the nature of the employee's work. The court found that the other employees would be unduly burdened by such an accommodation.

Pennsylvania State University, Milton S. Hershey Medical Center v. Commonwealth of Pa., No. 3490 (Commonwealth Ct. of Pa. 1986).

SEXUAL HARASSMENT

The Equal Employment Opportunity Commissions Guidelines on Discrimination Because of Sex, 29 C.F.R. Section 1604.11 (1981) specifically address sexual harassment and are the EEOC's interpretation of how the 1964 Civil Rights Act prohibits sexual harassment.

Section 1604.11 Sexual Harassment

"(a) Harassment on the basis of sex is a violation of Sec. 703 of Title VII. Unwelcome sexual advances, requests for sexual favors, and other verbal or physical conduct of a sexual nature constitute sexual harassment when (1) submission to such conduct is made either explicitly or implicitly a term or condition of an individual's employment, (2) submission to or rejection of such conduct by an individual is used as the basis for employment decisions affecting such individual, or (3) such conduct has the purpose or effect of unreasonably interfering with an individual's work performance or creating an intimidating, hostile, or offensive working environment.

(b) In determining whether alleged conduct constitutes sexual harassment, the Commission will look at the record as a whole and at the totality of the circumstances, such as the nature of the sexual advances and the context in which the alleged incidents occurred. The determination of the legality of a particular action will be made from the facts, on a case by case basis.

(c) Applying general Title VII principles, an employer, employment agency, joint apprenticeship committee, or labor organization (hereinafter collectively referred to as "employer") is responsible for its acts and those of its agents and supervisory employees with respect to sexual harassment regardless of whether the specific acts complained of were authorized or even forbidden by the employer, and regardless of whether the employer knew or should have known of their occurrence. The Commission will examine the circumstances of the particular employment relationship and the job functions performed by the individual in determining whether an individual acts in either a supervisory or agency capacity.

(d) With respect to conduct between fellow employees, an employer is responsible for acts of sexual harassment in the workplace where the employer (or its agents or supervisory employees) knows or should have known of the conduct, unless it can show that it took immediate and appropriate corrective action.

(e) An employer may also be responsible for the acts of nonemployees, with respect to sexual harassment of employees in the workplace, where the employer (or its agents or supervisory employees) knows or should have known of the conduct and fails to take immediate and appropriate corrective action. In reviewing these cases the Commission will consider the extent of the employer's control and any other legal responsibility which the employer may have with respect to the conduct of such nonemployees.

(f) Prevention is the best tool for the elimination of sexual harassment. An employer should take all steps necessary to prevent sexual harassment from occurring, such as affirmatively raising the subject, expressing strong disapproval, developing appropriate sanctions, informing employees of their right to raise and how to raise the issue of harassment under Title VII, and developing methods to sensitize all concerned.

(g) Other related practices: Where employment opportunities or benefits are granted because of an individual's submission to the employer's sexual advances or requests for sexual favors, the employer may be held liable for unlawful sex discrimination against other persons who were qualified for but denied that employment opportunity or benefit.

SUMMARY

The law of contracts has a limited but extremely important impact on the practice of nursing.

One type of contractual situation with which the nurse should become familiar is the employer-employee contract under which the nurse practices nursing. A private duty nurse generally functions under a more specific contract than does a hospital staff nurse.

Regardless of whether a written contract exists, an employer has certain legal responsibilities to employees. Whether the nurse is entitled to worker's compensation or unemployment compensation is a question that is frequently raised.

Labor law is becoming an increasingly more important legal area for nurses.

A contractual basis for liability is sometimes asserted in a malpractice case. Health care providers should be cautious in guaranteeing results to their patients.

CHAPTER **17**

SPECIALITY NURSING

The general principles of nursing liability described throughout these chapters apply to the speciality areas of nursing. But in addition to these principles, certain issues are unique and specific to the varied settings in which a nurse may practice.

This chapter will outline many of the issues that nurses may encounter in speciality areas such as obstetrics, psychiatry, anesthesia, and emergency department.

OBSTETRICS

Since 1980 the rate of growth of malpractice claims filed in the obstetrical area has exceeded suits filed in other areas of medicine. Speculation as to why this has happened includes unrealistic consumer expectations. With the phenomenal growth in technology including new transplant programs and the media attention to these issues, the public has learned to expect perfection in all aspects of medicine. When a baby is born with brain damage, a frequent response seems to be the need to find someone to blame. Perhaps this is a reflection of a general societal attitude that suggests fault must be present in any untoward circumstance.

The large dollar amounts awarded in settlement or judgment of a case involving an impaired infant or the death of a mother are another aspect of the problem. In all malpractice cases damages are partially based on the life expectancy of the injured patient. With the age of these plaintiffs, financial damages may be very high.

In general, while malpractice claims in obstetrics tend to occur more frequently than other specialty areas, these claims are more often related to the physician's care of the patient rather than the nurse's care.

Many nursing malpractice obstetrical cases deal with a failure to adequately assess and monitor the pregnant patient or with the failure to communicate significant findings.

Following the birth of her child, the patient began to bleed. The nurse told the physician three times that the patient was bleeding excessively. The physician instructed the nurse to keep watching the patient.

Some time later the nurse checked the patient and found that she was bleeding. She did not call the physician because, in her opinion, he would not have come anyway.

Finally the physician was notified, but the patient died shortly after his arrival from a hemorrhage due to laceration of the cervix.

The appellate court ordered a new trial and stated that evidence was sufficient to support a finding that the nurse, who knew the mother was bleeding excessively, was negligent in failing to report to her superior the circumstances of the mother's peril so that prompt and adequate measures could be taken to safeguard her life.

Goff v. Doctor's General Hospital, 333 P.2d 29 (Calif. 1958).

In the previous case the court pointed out that the nurse involved had sufficient time to report the facts and circumstances of the patient's peril to a superior in the hospital corporation for the purpose of taking prompt and adequate measures to safeguard the patient's life.

A difficult problem facing many nurses is the physician who fails to respond to a patient's complaint or responds only in a perfunctory manner. If the lack of response results in poor care for the patient, what can the nurse do? Legally, it is clear that courts will impose a duty on the nurse to advise hospital administrative officers when the patient's care is jeopardized.

A woman was admitted to the hospital for surgical correction of a hammertoe deformity. After surgery the tips of her toes were left exposed to facilitate postoperative care.

When she complained of severe pain, the nurses called this to the attention of the doctor. In response he ordered an x-ray but found nothing. After discharge, however, infection developed at the site of incision. When antibiotics failed to control the infection, the surgeon decided to debride the area. The procedure resulted in loss of tissue and additional bone from both toes.

The court found the nurses had satisfied their duty by informing the physician of the patient's complaint. However, the court added that failure of an attending physician to act on information from nurses regarding a patient's complaint would warrant the nurses' advising hospital administrative officers of the physician's refusal to act.

Brown v. St. John's Hospital, 367 N.E.2d 155 (1977).

The patient's history, which should be noted carefully in obstetric cases, may provide significant clinical information.

A woman was about to have her second child. Her husband and mother were in the labor room with her. The husband repeatedly asked the nurse to call the physician, but the nurse refused and said that the patient was dilated only 7 centimeters. The husband told the nurse that the birth of their first child occurred soon after his wife was dilated 8 centimeters. The nurse said she was in charge and would do what was necessary. After about 10 minutes the patient screamed that she was going to have the baby.

Evidence indicated that the nurse delivered the baby and asked a physician, who was walking down the hall, to suture lacerations which had resulted from the birth. The patient experienced pain, discomfort, and a reduction in sexual activity.

The court decided that the jury had reviewed sufficient evidence to find that the nurse had been negligent in her duties and that the hospital was liable for her negligence.

Hiatt v. Grace, 523 P.2d 320 (Kan.1974).

Sometimes the question is whether a particular procedure falls within the scope of nursing practice, such as a vaginal examination performed by a nurse.

The patient, who was 9-months pregnant, was examined in her doctor's office and sent to the hospital. The nurses were busy with a complicated delivery when she arrived. Evidence was presented that some hospitals in the vicinity require a vaginal examination by a nurse on the arrival of a pregnant patient for delivery. The evidence did not clearly show that this was generally true and also whether this was necessary when the patient had been examined by the doctor immediately before entering the hospital.

The court said that whether the failure to examine by the nurses was negligent would be determined in the light of all the surrounding circumstances. The patient was not permitted to recover damages for the death of her stillborn baby.

Nelson v. Peterson, 542 P.2d 1075 (Utah 1975).

Gynecological surgery cases are not as frequent as obstetrical cases. In some states, such as Florida, physicians are eliminating obstetrical practices and deciding to practice gynecology solely. The most prevalent claims in gynecology are those related to complications of a procedure such as severing a ureter during a hysterectomy and the retention of a foreign object following surgery such as a sponge or instrument. In the foreign object cases, often both the surgeon and the nurse are liable for malpractice. For example if an institution has a count policy and the physician directs the nurse not to follow it, both the physician and the nurse may be held liable if damage to the patient occurs.

The patient had a cesarean section. After the incision was closed, one sponge was missing. X-ray films were taken, but the hospital failed to have them properly reviewed. The patient was sent home and 3 days later returned with symptoms. She also needed a third procedure to treat an abscess that had localized where the sponge had lodged.
  The jury awarded the patient $36,000.
    Kirshnan v. Garza, 570 S.W.2d 578 (Texas 1978).

While the majority of medical malpractice claims currently are based on in-hospital care, there are a minority but increasing number of cases occurring in the outpatient setting. As outpatient care continues to grow, the claims experience in this area will also grow significantly. In obstetrics the claims usually relate to failure to diagnose a complication of pregnancy or a high-risk mother before labor and delivery. A missing amniocentesis report or an unnoticed sonogram order may result in injuries of severe magnitude to the mother, fetus, or newborn. Abortion clinic problems may arise from complications related to incomplete abortions. Pathology reports showing that no products of conception were removed may pass unnoticed. Sometimes the results are noted but the patient is never notified.

A punitive damage award of $7 million dollars was allocated against the hospital for failure to hire a competent nursing staff. The nurse was not trained to read the fetal monitoring system.
    Olsen v. Humana, Inc., no. 107480, Kansas, 1984.

Adequate staffing may be an issue in obstetrics as in other areas of nursing practice.

Allegations of corporate negligence will also increase the cost of obstetrical malpractice awards as in other areas of malpractice.

PATERNAL RIGHTS

An issue unique to obstetrics centers around the presence of the father at the birth of his child. Recent advances in obstetrics concentrating upon the emotional impact of birth and its effect upon the family have resulted in the invitation and, in some cases, the encouragement of fathers' participation in the birth process.

Courts have established that the presence of fathers in the delivery room is a privilege, rather than a right.

Porter Memorial Hospital, a public hospital, maintains and enforces a policy "prohibiting the presence of any person or persons in the Delivery Rooms located in the obstetrics ward other than members of the medical staff and nursing staff."

Plaintiffs are married couples who have completed training courses in the psychoprophylactic or Lamaze methods of childbirth. At the timing of filing this claim, each couple was either expecting the birth of a child or had recently given birth at Porter Memorial. In each case, the hospital had either indicated that pursuant to the policy, it would not permit the husband in the delivery room or had actually prevented the husband from participating in the delivery.

The court upheld the rule stating: "There is a difference of opinion within the profession as to the desirability of such a rule. This is a classic example of the kind of situation in which individual hospitals should be permitted to make individual choices, rather than having an inflexible rule imposed upon all hospitals in the nation by federal judicial decision."

Fitzgerald v. Porter Memorial Hospital, 523 F.2d 716 (7th Cir. 1975).

An action was initiated by prospective parents, the attending physician, and an association that advocates Lamaze against the hospital for an injunction that would require the hospital to allow the husband in the delivery room for the birth of his child and to allow the obstetrician thereafter to permit other husbands to be with their wives in the delivery room.

The court held that "licensed hospitals have the authority, acting on the advice of their medical staffs, to adopt rules of self-regulation governing the hospital's physicians. Licensed physicians must live according to the rules adopted by their colleagues even though the physician has direction over his patient."

The court concluded that the hospital's adoption of the rule was not arbitrary and capricious because it was based upon the increased possibility of infections, concern about malpractice suits, inadequate physical facilities, increased costs, greater tension in the delivery room, lack of privacy to other women who are preparing to deliver, and the strict policy concerning visitors in surgical areas that is favored by the state board of health.

> Hulit v. St. Vincent's Hospital, 520 P.2d 99 (Mont. 1974).

Plaintiffs initiated suit against Woman's Hospital Foundation to allow plaintiff-husband, upon completion of a Lamaze course, to attend the delivery of his child despite a hospital rule to the contrary.

The trial judge heard the witnesses, visited the operating suite, and found that there was nothing unreasonable about the rule excluding husbands.

The appeal court noted that there was nothing in the record or in the law which compelled the defendant hospital to accept the patient much less accede to her demands.

> Baier v. Woman's Hospital Foundation, 340 So.2d 360 (La. 1977).

Hospitals that do not wish to allow fathers or significant others in the delivery room are legally able to support this decision. However, many hospitals do permit this participation. If this policy is in effect, consent of the doctor, the patient, and her husband should be obtained. An adequate explanation should be given before the onset of labor so that events and procedures in the delivery room will be understood.

Hospitals and medical staffs should understand that the adoption of this policy may lead to increased liability exposure.

In a California case two sets of parents brought suit against a hospital and several physicians for the wrongful death of their unborn child and for their own emotional distress in witnessing these deaths.

Each husband was present in the delivery room in close proximity to his wife. One plaintiff alleged that he saw the manipulation of the fetus with forceps and by hand as well as the emergency procedures performed on his wife in connection with the attempted caesarean section.

The other plaintiff husband alleged that he was aware of the diminution of fetal heart tones and observed the nurse's anxiety at her inability to monitor them. He also said he was aware of the resulting emergency and failure of the physician to respond promptly when called.

The court ruled that the plaintiffs could not recover for emotional damages and stated: "We must assume that each husband was in the delivery room by his own choice. Surely, a layman who voluntarily observes a surgical operation must be prepared for the possibility of unpleasant or even harrowing experiences. This is no less true of the procedure of childbirth which, although unlikely to be traumatic, is always subject to complications."

Justus v. Atchison, 139 Cal.Rptr. 97 (Cal.1977).

PSYCHIATRY

Both psychiatric and nonpsychiatric hospitals have been involved in litigation based on the suicide or attempted suicide of a hospitalized patient.

Hospitals are not automatically held liable merely because a suicide takes place on the premises. Suicidal intent is not always foreseeable. However, nursing personnel are often in the best position to observe and report behavior that may predict a suicide attempt.

The high volume of cases involving patient suicides should serve to remind nurses of the need to observe patients for potential suicidal symptoms and to act to prevent suicide.

In cases involving suicidal patients, the duty of hospital personnel, at a minimum, is to effectively carry out the physician's orders pertaining to suicide precautions. If the physician has examined the patient and determined that precautions are unnecessary, hospital personnel will not be held liable for a failure to institute precautions. However, if the patient later exhibits behavior that would raise a suspicion of suicidal intent, the nurse has the duty to communicate this to the physician.

A patient jumped from the 11th floor of the hospital. The patient had been admitted to the hospital for psychiatric care but was not placed in the more secured area with locked doors and windows covered with heavy mesh screens.

The court held that hospital personnel had a right to rely on the physician's evaluation of the patient.

Dimitrijevic v. Chicago Wesley Memorial Hosp., 236 N.E. 2d 309 (Ill. App. 1968).

However, if orders are given and are not followed, hospital liability is much easier to establish.

A patient had been temporarily released from the hospital and had attempted suicide during the time he was outside. Upon readmission the physician entered a written order for 24-hour attendance. Hospital personnel neglected to tell the private attendant of the physician's order or of the patient's suicidal tendencies. The patient jumped to his death while the attendant was out of the room.

The hospital was held liable.

North Miama General Hosp. v. Krakower, 393 So.2d 57 (Fla.App. 1981)

The patient was a registered nurse admitted for evaluation of epilepsy. She was found dead after ingesting a large number of tranquilizers.

The hospital was not held liable. There was no indication that the patient had ever had suicidal thoughts or intent.

Bornmann v. Great South West General Hosp., 453 F.2d 616 (5th Cir. 1971)

The nurse's reliance on verbal orders, as discussed in Chapter 4, may place the nurse in a difficult position for the defensibility of a claim.

A patient had been admitted to the psychiatric unit of a military hospital for 5 days when he committed suicide by jumping out of a 7th floor window. The patient had been treated for his obsessive preoccupation with suicidal ideas.

The admitting physician ordered "S-1" status, the hospital's most restrictive status, which was automatically assigned to new patients. There were no subsequent notations in the chart by a physician changing this status.

Four days later, the nursing staff began to treat the patient as if he had been reassigned to the less restrictive S-2 status. These patients were permitted to leave the ward in the company of either a staff member or another patient. This level, according to policy, was appropriate for patients who were not considered suicidal.

The following day the patient jumped from a 7th floor window of an unsupervised area of the hospital.

The court noted that the nursing staff apparently assumed that the patient's status had been changed by his physician.

Following the discovery of his death, a nurse added an entry to the chart which indicated that the patient's status had been changed.

The court held that the note entered after the patient's death could not be accepted as a change of status order.

The physician testified that he must have verbally authorized the change of status but he was unable to recall any specific circumstances surrounding the alleged verbal authorization.

The hospital was held liable.

Abille v. United States, 482 F.Supp. 703 (N.D. Cal. 1980)

A number of recent psychiatric decisions involve the allegation that a psychiatrist engaged in a sexual relationship with a patient during therapy.

The patient alleged that from June 1968 through February 1974 the psychiatrist engaged in a sexual relationship with her during therapy and improperly administered drugs causing permanent psychiatric damage.

The jury awarded the patient $275,000 in compensatory damages and $300,000 in punitive damages.

Greenberg v. McCabe, 453 F.Supp. 765 (Pa. 1978).

As discussed in Chapter 3, in cases where gross negligence has been established, this type of damage award may not be covered in most professional liability insurance policies.

The patient was hospitalized with catatonic schizophrenia.

About two weeks later she mentioned to a nurse that she had a pain in her arm. The arm was red and swollen and a fracture was diagnosed.

The patient alleged that a fall must have occurred and caused the injury and that the nurses should not have left her unattended.

The court held that there was no proof that negligence had occurred.

Wees v. Creighton Memorial St. Joseph's Hosp., 231 N.W. 2d 570 (Nebraska 1975).

In the previous case the court stated that there was no evidence of a standard requiring a constant, one-to-one attendance and observation by nurse, technician, or aide for every patient.

However, failure to observe a patient with psychiatric problems may lead to liability.

A patient was admitted to a locked psychiatric unit for evaluation. She had a long history of treatment by a number of facilities and therapists. The patient told a registered nurse specializing in mental health nursing for 12 years that she wanted to take a tub bath. The patient asked to be left alone to relax in the tub.

When the nurse returned a short time later the patient was lying in the tub with her face in the water.

The issue before the court was whether the nurse had breached a duty of care by leaving the patient alone in the bathtub.

The court held that expert testimony should have been required to establish the nurse's duty of care.

Kanter v. Metropolitan Medical Center, 384 N.W.2d 914 (Minnesota 1982)

As discussed in Chapter 2, under Corporate Liability, the hospital has a distinct duty to provide safe premises for its patients.

The issue of the installation of security windows in the upper floors of hospitals has been addressed in cases involving both psychiatric facilities and general hospitals.

The patient was admitted to a closed psychiatric ward of a general hospital with a history of mental illness and instability. The next day he slipped through the closed section into the open section where he was spotted by the staff. While being escorted back to the closed section, the patient suddenly jumped through an unbarred window to his death.

The fact that the hospital had considered the risk of patients leaping from the windows was instrumental in the court's decision to dismiss the portion of the patient's complaint, which alleged negligent window construction. The testimony of the architect and psychiatrist was that this decision was consistent with the hospital's adoption of the "open door" concept of treatment for mental illness.

Lucy Webb Hayes National Training School v. Perotti, 419 F.2d 704 (D.C. Cir. 1969).

The psychiatric patients right to refuse antipsychotic medication has been addressed in a number of state decisions.

The patient was a 21-year-old man diagnosed as suffering from paranoid schizophrenia since his middle teens. His father was appointed as permanent guardian.

The issue was whether the guardian had the authority to consent to the forcible administration of antipsychotic drugs to his son or whether a specific court order was needed for this administration.

The Massachusetts Supreme Court determined that the guardian did not have this authority.

Matter of Guardianship of Richard Roe III, 421 N.E.2d 40 (Mass. 1981)

In the previous case the court outlined a number of factors which persuaded it that a court order was necessary to ensure objectivity. These factors included the intrusiveness of the proposed treatment, possibility of adverse side effects, and absence of an emergency situation.

False imprisonment lawsuits based upon false imprisonment in hospitals are brought infrequently and are rarely successful.

The patient was having difficulty sleeping and was overwrought. At the recommendation of her psychologist she decided to enter the hospital for several days of rest. She voluntarily admitted herself to the hospital where she was placed in the psychiatric wing. She was introduced to the psychiatrist and began treatment. During one of the first sessions she began throwing things at the doctor; she was then placed in restraints after which she began screaming and singing in order to annoy people. On her fourth day in the hospital she signed a release that would mandate her release within 5 days. She testified that several days later the physician ordered her to sign a document withdrawing that form or she would be committed to a state hospital.

The court felt that her belief that she was being unreasonably restrained was a jury question.

Marcus v. Liebman, 375 N.E.2d 486 (Ill. App. 1978).

In the previous case the court stated that a claim of false imprisonment was established by showing that the words or actions of one person have unlawfully restrained another's liberty or freedom of movement and where the apprehension of threatened force is reasonable.

ANESTHESIA LIABILITY

The origin of nurse anesthesia in the United States can be traced to the latter part of the nineteenth Century. In 1877, Sister Mary Bernard entered St. Vincent's Hospital in Erie, Pennsylvania for training as a nurse. Within a year she was called upon to assume the duties of administering anesthesia. Alice Magaw (1860–1925) administered anesthesia at the Mayo Clinic and reported 1,042 cases of ether anesthesia in 1900.*

As this speciality developed, an initial and continuing issue concerned whether the administration of anesthesia constituted the practice of medicine. Nurse anesthesia was the first nursing speciality to seek independent recognition in education and certification.

Interpretation of Nurse Practice Acts may lead to clarification of the

---

*Mannino, Mary Jeanette, CRNA, J.D., *The Nurse Anesthetist and the Law*, Grune & Stratton, New York, 1982.

nurse-anesthetist's scope of practice. However, the following two cases illustrate how these interpretations may differ.

The obstetrician administered the initial epidural injection and waited a few minutes to observe the effect. He instructed the nurse to reinject the anesthetic as needed in specific amounts and at specific times. The physician then departed from the hospital, remaining available within minutes if problems arose. This was according to hospital policy.

The Arkansas State Department of Health sought a declaratory judgment to determine whether the hospital could continue this practice of requiring registered nurses who were not specifically qualified in the field of anesthesia to administer epidural anesthesia to obstetrical patients.

The court held that the Arkansas Nurse Practice Act had to be strictly construed. The Act specifically required that a licensed physician or dentist be present when any nurse administered anesthesia.

Therefore, the court held that the hospital's practice of allowing nurses to provide the reinjection should have been discontinued.

Arkansas State Dept. of Health v. Drs. Thibault & Council, 281 Ark. 297, 664 S.W.2d (1984)

A malpractice action was filed against the hospital for the death of a patient following a surgical procedure performed under general anesthesia. The anesthesia was administered by a registered nurse-anesthetist. The plaintiff alleged that the hospital was at fault, since it did not require a physician to supervise the nurse in either the selection or method of anesthetizing a patient.

The court disagreed, concluding that the Louisiana legislation did not intend to require that degree of supervision over a person possessing the skill and training of a registered nurse-anesthetist.

Brown v. Allen Sanitarium, 364 So.2d 661 (La. App. 1978).

As Chapter 5 illustrates, an important and difficult element to prove in a malpractice case is causation. The following case illustrates how this element was established in an anesthesia case.

A 32-year-old, healthy patient underwent gall bladder surgery. During the process of removing the gall bladder, the surgeon noted an abnormally short cystic duct that was embedded in the liver. The surgeon removed a small wedge of the common bile duct and then attempted to repair it. A stab wound was made and the inferior portion of the raw liver began bleeding. The surgeon attempted to control the bleeding by applying posterior pressure to the vena cava.

The anesthesiologist, noticing the bleeding, ordered extra units of blood and requested that an EKG monitor be brought in. Even though the patient received blood, her blood pressure dropped and she eventually suffered a cardiac arrest. An assistant surgeon began cardiac massage and was able to restore function, but the patient never awoke from a coma.

In the medical malpractice action, the appellate court upheld the jury verdict for the plaintiff. They found that the evidence was factually and legally sufficient to support the jury's finding that the anesthesiologist's negligence in failing to recognize the patient's cardiac arrest in time was a proximate cause of her death.

Garza v. Berlanga, 598 S.W.2d 377, (1980).

The following case illustrates multiple defendants and the issue of causation.

The patient was admitted to the hospital May, 1968, for elective surgery on her submaxillary gland. Endotracheal intubation was difficult and was successful only after two attempts by an anesthesiologist, after two other attempts by the anesthesia resident had failed. The time from induction to intubation was about 20 minutes. About 5 minutes after intubation, the surgeon noted that the patient was cyanotic. The chief anesthesiologist entered the room, and while he was working on the patient, the surgeon left the OR. After 5 minutes, while the anesthesiologist was preparing to check the endotracheal tube, the patient suffered a cardiac arrest. The anesthesiologist immediately removed the tube, and the surgeon began external heart massage. The patient's skin color and heartbeat returned to normal, but she had already suffered permanent brain damage.

The ensuing legal action brought about a jury verdict of $1,000,000 for the patient's husband and $500,000 for the patient. The appellate court upheld the trial court decision and, on the issue of causation, said that the surgeon's conduct had been a proximate cause of the patient's injuries.

At the trial, the expert witness testified that the surgeon should have given orders to cancel the anesthesia when it was apparent the patient was in trouble. The hospital and chief anesthesiologist were also found negligent.

Schneider v. Albert Einstein Medical Center, North Division, 390 A.2d 1271, (1978).

The breach of duty in anesthesia cases involves the violation of reasonable standards of care as they have been established by the anesthesia profession.

A 5-year-old, in excellent health, was admitted to the hospital for a T & A. A nurse anesthetist supervised by an anesthesiologist administered the anesthetic. During the procedure, the anesthesiologist was called to an emergency in another OR. When he returned, he noticed that the child was cyanotic with no apparent heartbeat. The nurse-anesthetist was still administering a full concentration of anesthetic agent and was not using precordial monitoring. Emergency resuscitation restored the patient's heartbeat, but, because of the prolonged cardiac arrest, he suffered severe brain damage and died about 7 weeks later.

The child's father filed suit on behalf of his son's estate for wrongful death. The jury awarded the estate $455,199 and the hospital appealed.

The Pennsylvania Supreme Court said that "the trial court had instructed the jury that it could consider pain and suffering and compensation for loss of future earnings and loss of amenities or pleasures of life. In the higher court's ruling, they said loss of life's pleasures or amenities was not one of the elements of recovery for wrongful death and survival action (author's emphasis)."

Willinger v. Mercy Catholic Medical Center of Southern Pennsylvania, 393 A.2d 1188 Pa. (1978).

The amount of damages to be awarded against a surgeon who operated on the wrong patient was at issue in the following Kentucky case.

The patient, Gladys Bruce, was scheduled for a conization of the cervix. She had an identification bracelet on her wrist, but none of the parties involved checked her identification with her bracelet. Since Mrs. Bruce answered to the name of "Smith," a patient scheduled for a thyroidectomy, the surgeon proceeded with a thyroidectomy on Mrs. Bruce. When it was realized that she was the wrong patient, the incision was closed.

Mrs. Bruce brought legal action against the hospital, anesthesiologist, the surgical technician, and surgeon for malpractice. The court ruled that the fact that the patient answered to the name of another patient did not excuse the failure of the surgeon, anesthesiologist, and surgical technician to determine the identity of the patient by examining her identification bracelet.

The following damages were awarded: $10,000 against the surgeon and $90,000 against the hospital, anesthesiologist, and surgical technician.

Southeastern Kentucky Baptist v. Bruce, 539 S.W. 286 (1976).

Documentation is an issue in anesthesia cases just as it is in all other specialty areas.

The patient, a 49-year-old female registered nurse, was having gall bladder surgery. About 2 hours into the operation, the surgeon advised the anesthesiologist that he could not feel a pulse. Emergency procedures were begun; the patient's heart responded almost immediately and then resumed its normal beat. From the operative notes, it appeared that her heart was at arrest for 5 minutes. The patient suffered permanent brain damage which left her partially blind, spastic, and unable to care for herself.

A negligence suit was filed against the anesthesiologist for failing to note that her heart was beating weakly and failing to take remedial measures before the cardiac arrest occurred.

Before the suit was filed, the anesthesiologist was notified by the patient's attorney that he wanted to examine the records of the operation. The anesthesiologist then began adding to the chart until he was advised by a clerk in the record room that his actions were improper.

The trial court judge instructed the jury that changes made on the chart were not material in determining the cause of the cardiac arrest. A verdict for the anesthesiologist was rendered by the jury. On appeal, the verdict for the anesthesiologist was reversed because the instructions regarding changes on the chart were in error. A new trial was ordered.

Seaton v. Rosenberg, 573 S.W 2d 333 Ky. Sup. Ct. (1978).

Whether or not a physician is responsible for the acts of negligence of a nurse-anesthetist has been determined differently depending upon the jurisdiction.

In general, the surgeon is not held liable for the acts of the nurse-anesthetist.

A surgical patient suffered ulnar nerve damage due to poor positioning of her arm during major surgery. A nurse-anesthetist admitted that it was her duty to carefully monitor the surgical patient's arm while administering general anesthesia.

Expert testimony indicated that the surgeons were at the base of the operating table during a vaginal hysterectomy. An operating drape inhibited the physician's opportunity to inspect the patient's upper body.

A North Carolina appellate court found both the chief surgeon and assistant surgeon free from liability. The court determined that neither had a duty to monitor the patient's arm nor a duty to supervise the nurse-anesthetist's work.

Parks v. Perry, 66 N.C. App. 282, 314 S.E.2d 287 (1984).

In Chapter 10, disciplinary actions involving nurses are discussed. Of particular interest to the nurse-anesthetist is the following decision.

The nurse-anesthetist apparently induced anesthesia by needle without the supervising anesthesiologist being present, although the surgeon was physically present in the operating room. The Board of Nurse Examiners ordered a formal reprimand against the nurse-anesthetist for "willfully violating" one of the regulations.

The Pennsylvania Commonwealth Court upheld the Board's reprimand and stated: "The record clearly supports the Board's determination that appellant willfully violated a regulation of the Board. It established that appellant was aware of his responsibility to secure the presence of a directing physician; that he knew that the physician whom he ought to have present was not, in fact, present during the administration of the anesthetic, and that appellant was aware that the physician who was present did not know that he was about to administer the anesthetic."

In footnoting their opinion, the court also said: "It is significant that even though appellant admitted that this physician was not present, appellant nevertheless noted in the anesthesia record, in his own handwriting, that the physician was present and supervising.

"The physician's (surgeon's) deposition . . . makes it abundantly clear that the appellant made no effort to make the physician aware of what was happening, that the physician had absolutely no inkling of what was happening, and that the physician, in fact, had his back to the appellant when the anesthesia was administered."

McCarl v. Commonwealth of Pennsylvania State Board of Nurse Examiners, 39 Commonwealth Court 628 Pa. (1979).

EMERGENCY ROOM LIABILITY

The emergency department will also experience its share of common nursing malpractice cases that can and do occur in all areas of the hospital.

FALLS

The hospital record regarding the patient's treatment stated: "While in the Emergency Room, pt. fell from stretcher. He was attended at the time but he was extremely heavy. He fell despite efforts to catch him. He injured his lip and chin. Sutures were then used to sew up the laceration before transport to floor." This statement appears next to the signature of a nurse.

A discharge report by the doctor stated: "This patient was brought to ER having imbibed freely in alcohol. Apparently he also had taken 2 milligrams of Valium tablets, then later on had taken a good many Dalmane and some Robaxin, the exact amounts of which were not known. When he arrived at the

ER he was quite lethargic and was responsive to some degree. His stomach was washed out thoroughly and his condition was such that it was felt that he should be admitted. While in the ER he attempted to get off the stretcher and fell striking his face, at which time he lost central incisors and cut his chin. The chin was sutured. He was admitted to my service as I was on call for the day. . . Final Dx: Drug overdose, Dalmane, Valium, Robaxin, Ethanol. Laceration of the chin."

The patient testified to his taking alcohol and drugs. From the time he returned home he recalled nothing until he awoke at the hospital with a tube in his nose. He started to pull the tube, but blacked out. Regaining consciousness, he became aware that his chin was stitched and two of his teeth had been knocked out. He had some recollection of falling to the floor, but could not say how his injuries came about. He described his injuries and the treatment.

The jury held the hospital liable for failing to restrain the patient and awarded $8,000 for loss of teeth and a chin laceration.

Bennet v. Winthrop Community Hosp., 489 N.E. 2d 1032 (Mass. 1986).

In this previous case the court placed great emphasis upon evidence that the patient had been inebriated and rambunctious during the ambulance trip and had to be restrained. The knowledge that is available about the patient to the health care provider is always a significant factor in evaluating the liability of the defendants.

A young male patient cut his thumb while at work and was brought to the emergency department. He began to feel ill, and his mother asked the nurse to assist him. The patient's mother stated that the nurse continued filling out papers. The patient fainted, sustaining a concussion, broken teeth. and a fractured thumb.

The jury awarded $7,000. His thumb injury interfered with his job as an airline mechanic.

McEachern v. Glenview Hospital, 505 SW 2d 386 (Texas 1974).

In the previous case the nurse's failure to respond to the request for assistance is a typical precipitating factor in the initiation of a lawsuit. While not a frequent occurrence, it is not unusual to have patients (and family members) faint in the emergency department and sustain an injury. While it is impossible to predict or foresee who will faint, it is prudent to be alert to signs and symptoms that might suggest an individual who is prone to fainting. Patients who have never been injured previously and who have never witnessed loss of blood are examples of situations where the propensity to faint might be considered.

STANDARDS OF CARE

As with any other area of malpractice, standards of care must be established. Policies and procedures of the institution are frequently utilized to establish them.

A physician on duty in a hospital emergency department instructed paramedics who called from the scene of an accidental shooting to transport the chest wound patient to the hospital. The physician did not contact the on-call thoracic surgeon, because he believed the patient's injury would require only minor surgery. When the patient arrived at the hospital, the physician realized that a thoracic surgeon was needed, but an available specialist could not be located for more than an hour. The patient died during the subsequently performed surgery, and his family sued. They claimed that the failure of the on-call system to reach a thoracic surgeon in a timely manner caused the patient's death and that the hospital's emergency department policy and procedure manual provided evidence of the way in which the on-call system should have worked. A trial court refused to submit the issue or the manual to a jury, ruling that neither the hospital nor the physician under contract to provide emergency department services was responsible for the on-call system failure.

The state appeals court ruled that the patient's family was entitled to a new trial because the lower court had excluded as evidence the hospital's emergency department policy and procedure manual. The manual sets out in detail how the on-call system should operate, the court noted, and it also states that speciality consultation should be available within 30 minutes. The court rejected the argument that no liability could be imposed on the defendants. "The issue concerns who is going to assume ultimate responsibility for the entire on-call system, a system which was designed and operated by the hospital and the doctor who contracted to run the emergency room, when that system fails," the court explained. It therefore concluded that the family should receive a new trial and that the emergency department's manual should be admitted as evidence.

Marks v. Mandel, 477 So.2d 1036 (Fla. Dist. Ct. App. 1985).

While the general trend is a reluctance to award damages for emotional distress, a recent case illustrates a situation in which such damages may be allowed.

The patient, subsequently diagnosed as having Guillain-Barré syndrome, was examined by an emergency department physician who found nothing wrong with the patient. When the physician told the patient he could get up and go home, the patient fell on the floor and could not get up. The physician left the room, instructing the hospital staff not to assist the patient up from the floor where he remained for almost two hours.

The Pennsylvania superior court held that although the physician's conduct did not aggravate, extend, or change the nature of the patient's existing disease, the patient could recover for the intentional infliction of emotional distress without a showing of physical injury. All the patient need prove is that the physician knew that severe emotional distress was substantially certain to result from his conduct. The court concluded that the evidence was sufficient to support a finding of intentional infliction of emotional distress.

Hoffman v. Memorial Osteopathic Hospital, 492 A.2d 1382 (Pa. Super. Ct. 1985).

FAILURE TO DIAGNOSE

Failure to diagnose is a common basis for claim against all physicians in all specialities, but it is especially frequent in emergency department cases.

In some cases the failure to diagnose is malpractice; in others it is not. The issue is whether, despite a reasonable standard of care, a misdiagnosis occurred. If the physician fails to review the patient's prior clinical records, liability may result.

The patient's symptoms included a severe vertex headache of sudden onset, violent nausea, pain behind the eyes and elevated temperature. An examination further revealed elevated blood pressure. It was virtually undisputed among the experts who testified at trial that such a complex of symptoms would have at least suggested to a physician the possibility that the patient had suffered a subarachnoid hemorrhage, and it appears equally clear that a physician, exercising the degree of care required of physicians in 1978, would have sought to confirm or refute that possibility. The plaintiff then established through highly qualified expert testimony that, had the possibility of a subarachnoid hemorrhage been considered, a simple, risk-free, virtually infallible diagnostic test, the lumbar puncture, would have confirmed the diagnosis. Further, plaintiff's expert testified that, had the subarachnoid hemorrhage been diagnosed, plaintiff's decedent would have had a 75 percent chance of recovering and returning to her previous activities.

Standing between plaintiff and that diagnosis was the government's practice of permitting patients to be treated and released from the emergency room at the Naval Regional Medical Center without having a licensed physician see either the patient or the patient's chart. Patients on their first visit would see only a physician's assistant, a person with only two years of paramedical training. Whether or not a physician should be called in was entirely within the physician's assistant's discretion. In the present case, because decedent's symptoms did not precisely fit the complex of symptoms which the physician's assistant had been trained to recognize as suggestive of a subarachnoid hemorrhage, the possibility of hemorrhage was never considered, and a physician was not summoned.

Judgment was for the patient's husband for over $300,000.

The court found the Navy Hospital's policy of not having the records reviewed by a physician was negligent.

Polischeck v. United States, 535 F.Supp. 1261 (1982).

The nurse's assessment of the patient in the emergency department is extremely important. The role of the experienced triage nurse is vital to the initial evaluation of the patient.

A 14-month-old was seen in the pediatrician's office and diagnosed with croup. He was sent to the hospital for treatment.

The patient's mother alleged that she brought him to the hospital emergency room for treatment of croup on November 14, 1969. The mother stated that the emergency nurse placed her and her child in a bathroom for a steam treatment. A short time after being placed in the bathroom, the mother testified, her child stopped breathing and was taken from the bathroom and resuscitated; permanent brain damage and mental retardation resulted.

The emergency nurse gave a highly different picture of events, according to defense attorneys. The nurse stated that Mrs. Hollinger brought her son John to the hospital through the emergency room entrance and asked for the admissions office, to which the emergency nurse directed her. The nurse incidentally noticed that the child was having some respiratory distress and followed the mother and child to the admissions office, where the emergency nurse convinced the mother to let her take the child back to the ED for a steam treatment. As the nurse was about to enter the bathroom with the child, he suffered a cardiopulmonary arrest and was resuscitated; permanent brain damage resulted.

The plaintiff alleged that the child suffered from acute epiglottitis and should have been intubated or had a tracheotomy performed immediately. The hospital contended that any negligence was the responsibility of the family pediatrician, who failed to make a proper diagnosis, failed to telephone the ED resident to alert him to the child's condition and pending arrival, and erred in sending the child a distance of 9½ miles to the hospital. The pediatrician was held not negligent.

The jury rendered a verdict in favor of the plaintiffs and against the hospital and the emergency nurse in the amount of $1 million for their negligence.

The jury reached its decision after a 17-day trial with 29 witnesses, of whom 24 were physicians. The patient is a quadriplegic and mentally retarded.

Hollinger v. Children's Memorial Hospital, No. 70L-10627 (Ill. Cir. Ct., Cook County, July 16, 1974).

On the morning of March 14, 1973, a 6-month-old child was sick and crying, and refused to eat. The parents' concern about their child's illness increased during the morning hours. Thus, at approximately 1:00 p.m., the parents drove to the hospital in search of assistance at the emergency department. While the mother and the baby remained in the car, the father entered the ED and informed the nurse on duty about the baby's sick condition. The emergency nurse refused to examine the baby and also refused to call a doctor. The father searched the hospital physicians' offices, hoping to find a doctor who could help, but was unsuccessful.

The family left the hospital but returned to the ED again at 3:00 p.m. The same emergency nurse was on duty. The father informed the nurse that the child was worse. Upon hearing this, the emergency nurse walked out of the hospital ED to the parked vehicle in which the mother and baby were sitting. She felt the baby's head and declared there was no emergency. Again the parents and the child were turned away even though the child, according to the parents' testimony, was breathing harshly and screaming.

At a little after midnight the child was transported to a different hospital ED and admitted. The admitting physician found the child to be in critical condition, suffering from bronchial pneumonia. Emergency medical procedures were undertaken, but the child died 5 hours after admission.

Despite the fact that the child's admitting physician testified that the chances of recovery would have been substantially better if treatment had been rendered when the child was first presented to the initial hospital, the trial court dismissed the case. The trial court ruled that the parents had failed to show that the nurse's actions caused the child's death. When the case was appealed, the appellate court found that the case should not have been dismissed.

In reversing and remanding the case for further proceedings, the appellate court felt that there had to be a determination of whether the hospital and nurse were negligent in twice refusing hospital admission to the infant when an unmistakable emergency situation may have existed. The appellate court found that liability could clearly be based on a hospital's refusal of care in an emergency situation. Furthermore, in previous cases, an infant's pneumonia was held to constitute an emergency. For these reasons, the appellate court ruled that a jury had to determine whether the hospital and nurse were negligent and whether the child's condition constituted an emergency.

Richard v. Adair Hospital Foundation Corp., 566 S.W. 2d 791 (1978).

Along with the risk of liability, the nurse may face loss or suspension of license.

On the night of March 7, 1979, Mrs. Juanita Valdez, who was 8 months pregnant, awoke in great pain. Her family, assuming she had begun labor, drove her to Gregory, Texas, where a midwife had been engaged to deliver the baby. The midwife examined Mrs. Valdez and concluded that she was not in labor but, rather, was experiencing a more serious problem.

Mrs. Valdez was taken to a hospital, where she was examined by two nurses. After a telephone conversation with a physician, the nurses told Mrs. Valdez to go to the Lyman-Roberts Hospital a few blocks away. On arrival at Lyman-Roberts Hospital, Mrs. Valdez' sister-in-law went into the emergency department and explained the situation to the nurse and a nurse's aide.

The nurse's aide and nurse went outside to the car to see Mrs. Valdez. The nurse checked her pulse and also checked for contractions and bleeding. She then told the family to take Mrs. Valdez to Memorial Medical Hospital in Corpus Christi as fast as possible.

The family requested an ambulance. The nurse informed them that the only ambulance available was from the funeral home and their response time was slow. The nurse offered to call a police escort to take the family to the hospital, but they refused this offer of assistance.

The family decided to take Mrs. Valdez back home to Rockport, Texas. Mrs. Valdez died en route of a ruptured uterus.

Subsequently, a complaint was filed with the Texas Board of Medical Examiners. The complaint charged the nurse with failure to contact the physician on emergency call at the request of the patient's family. It also charged her with failure "to evaluate the status of Juanita Valdez and institute appropriate nursing intervention . . . to stabilize a patient's condition or prevent complications."

During a hearing before the Board, the nurse testified that she did not feel it was necessary to call the physician on emergency call because she knew what he would tell her to do. Both the nurse and the on-call physician testified regarding the limitations of conducting emergency surgery on an expectant mother at Lyman-Roberts Hospital.

The board found that the nurse's activities constituted "unprofessional or dishonorable conduct likely to injure the public" and suspended her license for 6 months. The Board's decision was upheld by the Court of Civic Appeals.

Mary Lorene O'Dell Murphy v. Margaret Rowland, RN, et al., 609 S.W. 2d 292 (1980).

On the morning of December 28, 1978, plaintiff noticed that her daughter was feverish and listless. Plaintiff took the child first to a federal clinic, unaffiliated with the defendant hospital, and received several prescriptions. Three days later when the child showed no improvement, the plaintiff took her to the emergency room of the defendant hospital.

Doctor S. was on duty in the hospital emergency room. During the time the child was examined at the emergency room, she was feverish. Plaintiff also alleged that the child acted as though she did not want to be picked up or touched, and her neck was stiff.

An emergency room nurse, Nurse C., talked to the plaintiff concerning the child and recorded on the record the word "fever." The nurse did not take the child's vital signs.

Doctor S. talked to plaintiff and stated that the plaintiff informed him only that the child had a fever, had been coughing, and had a head cold. Doctor S. examined the child, ordered an X-ray of her lungs, and diagnosed the illness as "bronchopneumonia." He gave plaintiff several prescriptions but did not recommend that the child be admitted to the hospital. According to Dr. S., at that time he was unaware that the child had been examined a few days earlier for the same complaint and had been given prescriptions.

The child's condition did not improve. On January 2, 1979, the child's neck was stiff, and she was not eating. Plaintiff took her daughter back to the hospital emergency room the following day. Another emergency room physician was on duty and, after examining the child, ordered tests made and diagnosed the infant as suffering from spinal meningitis. The child was then admitted to the hospital. Despite hospitalization and medical care, the child's condition deteriorated, and she died on January 6, 1979.

Plaintiff brought suit against the hospital and Dr. S., alleging medical malpractice and wrongful death. Plaintiff alleged that the hospital was liable for the negligence of Dr. S. and also "one or more of its nurses, physician's assistants, agents, servants or employees." Plaintiff contended that Dr. S. was negligent in failing to make a proper diagnosis of the child at a time when the meningitis was treatable, and that he and the emergency room nurse failed to conduct an adequate physical examination and did not observe appropriate standards of medical care.

The nurse was held liable for failing to document vital signs including temperature. The physician testified that it was the responsibility of the nurse to take vital signs without being so ordered.

Reynolds v. Swigert, 697 P.2d 504 (New Mexico 1985).

Communication is a significant responsibility of the emergency department staff. Failure to communicate significant health care information provided by the patient can be a basis for liability.

The Ramseys lived in a rural area of Charles County known as Gallant Green. In early May, 1974, Mrs. Ramsey removed two ticks from her son Kenneth. Several days later she noticed a rash on both Ernest and Kenneth. The rash started on the chest and head and was accompanied by a high fever. This prompted Mr. and Mrs. Ramsey to take their two boys to the emergency room at Physician's Memorial Hospital. While there, Mrs. Ramsey told the nurse on duty that she had removed two ticks from Kenneth, one from his head and one from his stomach. This testimony was confirmed by Mr. Ramsey and not contradicted by other witnesses. According to the attending physician, he asked the parents about ticks and was told nothing. He also ordered a search for ticks which proved fruitless. The nurse did not tell the doctor of the tick history which Mrs. Ramsey had related to her.

In diagnosing their condition, the doctor decided the children were suffering from measles and prescribed that the boys take aspirin and be kept in a darkened room. Two days later the rash had spread to the arms and legs of the two boys and the fever had not subsided.

Four days later the children's condition had greatly worsened, but the Ramseys were unable to reach the doctor. On the following day Ernest was found dead. Kenneth was subsequently treated and cured of Rocky Mountain Spotted Fever. The only injury he sustained was a limp which was gone within six months. The autopsy performed on Ernest showed that he died of Rocky Mountain Spotted Fever.

Ramsey v. Physician's Memorial Hospital, Inc., 373 A.2d 26 (36 Md.App.42).

A frequent documentation problem in the ER is the absence of telephone communication documentation.

A 54-year-old patient complained of both chest and arm pains when she visited the hospital ER. Allegedly, the physician who treated her told the plaintiff's husband that nothing was wrong with the patient. She returned home and died of a massive myocardial infarction an hour later.

During the trial, the physician testified that he had asked the patient to stay overnight in the hospital. He also recommended that additional tests and treatment begin in the morning.

There were no notes in the patient's medical record outlining this part of the physician-patient conversation. Further, the results of tests done while the patient was being treated in the ER were not recorded in her medical record.

The jury awarded $470,000 against the hospital and physician.

Broadway v. South Oklahoma City Hospital, No. CJ-80-5430; Oklahoma City, Dist. Ct., Okla., Feb. 17, 1982.

---

* The significance of discharge instructions for the hospitalized patient has received an increased focus of attention with the advent of the prospective payment system and the earlier discharge of patients from the acute care setting.

This legal duty has received attention in the emergency treatment area. Many emergency departments provide written instructions. Others rely upon oral instructions. Failure to provide instructions may be considered a violation of reasonable standards of care.

SUMMARY

While general principles of nursing liability apply to all specialty areas of nursing practice, each specialty area does involve unique legal questions.

Obstetrics is unique as a high-risk area because of consumer expectations. Psychiatry deals with unusual questions involving a patient's right to privacy balanced against the rights of society. Anesthesia involves the nurse-anesthetist practicing at a high level of independence and corresponding responsibility. The Emergency Department is unique in the short duration of exposure to patients and families and the corresponding lack of ability to establish long-term relationships. Failure to diagnose accurately is a frequent liability exposure.

SUGGESTED READINGS

ARTICLES

Advice, PRN. *Nursing '80*, December 1980, p. 28.

Annas, G. J., Invasion of Privacy in the Hospital. *Nursing Law & Ethics*, February 1981, p. 3.

Bernstein, A. H., Incompetent's Right to Die: Who Decides? *Hospitals*, September 1, 1979, p. 39.

Bernstein, A. H., Law in Brief. *Hospitals*, 1979–1980.

Bernzweig, E. P., Don't Cut Corners on Informed Consent. *RN*, December 1984, p. 15.

Bernzweig, E. P., Go On Record with Nothing but the Truth. *RN*, March 1985, p. 63.

Bernzweig, E. P., How a Communications Breakdown Can Get You Sued. *RN*, December 1985, p. 47.

Bernzweig, E. P., How an Emergency Can Spell Trouble. *RN*, March 1986, p. 57.

Besch, L. B., Informed Consent: A Patient's Right. *Nursing Outlook*, January 1979, p. 32.

Beyerson, S. R., Legal Aspects of Nursing Practice: Charting with a Jury in Mind. *Nursing Life*, July–August 1982, Vol. 2, No. 4, p. 30.

Bicher, M., Five Orders You Must Question to Protect Yourself Legally. *Nursing Life*, January–February 1983, p. 21.

Bliwise, R. J., Medical Ethics: On the Critical List? *Lafayette Alumni Quarterly*, Fall 1983, p. 9.

Boulay, D. D., When the Burdon of Proof Falls on You. *Nursing '86*, February 1986, p. 41.

Brent, N. J., Medication Administration. *Nursing Life,* September–October 1986, p. 52.

Chenowith, S. D., Tips on Giving Pre-Trial Testimony. *RN,* February 1985, p. 67.

Cohen, C. B., Interdisciplinary Consultation on the Care of the Critically Ill and Dying: The Role of One Hospital Ethics Committee. *Critical Care Medicine,* Vol. 10, No. 11, November 1982, p. 776.

Craddick, J. W., The Medical Management Analysis System: A Professional Liability Warning Mechanism. *Quality Review Bulletin,* April 1979.

Creighton, H., Physical Handicaps: Law for the Nurse Supervisor. *Supervisor Nurse,* March 1980, p. 44.

Creighton, H., Terminating Life Support: Law for the Nurse Supervisor. *Supervisor Nurse,* January 1977, p. 66.

Curtis, J., Multidisciplinary Input on Institutional Ethics Committees: A Nursing Perspective. *QRB,* July 1984, p. 199.

Cushing, M., The Legal Side: Failure to Communicate, *American Journal of Nursing,* Vol. 82, No. 10, October 1982, p. 1597.

Cushing, M., The Legal Side: Gaps in Documentation. *American Journal of Nursing,* Vol. 82, No. 12, December 1982, p. 1899.

Cushing, M., Informed Consent: An MD Responsibility? *American Journal of Nursing,* Vol. 84, No. 4, April 1984, p. 437.

Cushing, M., Legal Lessons on Patient Teaching. *American Journal of Nursing,* Vol. 84, No. 6, June 1984, p. 721.

Cushing, M., First, Anticipate the Harm. *American Journal of Nursing,* Vol. 85, No. 2, February 1985, p. 137.

deTornyay, R., Changing Student Relationships, Roles and Responsibilities. *Nursing Outlook,* Vol. 25, No. 3, March 1977, p. 188.

Diosegy, A., A Lawyer Answers 10 Legal Questions About Current Nursing Practice. *Nursing Life,* May–June 1983, p. 30.

Dunn, L., Who "Pulls the Plug": The Practical Effect of the Saikewicz Decision. *The Medical Malpractice Cost Containment Journal,* July 1979, p. 161.

Eccard, W. L., A Revolution in White—New Approaches in Treating Nurses as Professionals. *Vanderbilt Law Review,* Vol. 30, 1977, p. 839.

Edwards, R., An Act of Compassion—Or a Crime? *RN,* January 1986, p. 63

Emanuel, W. J., Nurse Unionization Is Dominant Theme. *Hospitals,* April 1, 1981, p. 121.

Esquedo, K., Hospital Ethics Committee: Four Case Studies. *The Hospital Medical Staff*, November 1978, p. 26.

Fiesta, J., Nursing Liability: The Patient who Falls. *Orthopaedic Nursing*, Vol. 4, No. 3, May–June 1985, p. 59.

Fiesta, J., Risk Management and Quality Assurance Interaction. *DRG Monitor*, Vol. 3, Nos. 8 and 9, April–May 1986.

Fine, E. R., What to do When the Doctor is Wrong. *Nursing Life*, Vol. 2, No. 6, November–December 1982, p. 22.

Fink, J. L., Role of JCAH Standards in Negligence Suits. *American Journal of Pharmacy*, Vol. 38, June 1981, p. 892.

Fink, J. L., Preventing Lawsuits: Medication Errors to Avoid. *Nursing Life*, Vol. 3, No. 2, March–April 1983, p. 26.

Forgey, D. A., Hospital Liability: Taking a Turn for the Nurse. *For the Defense*, July 1981, p. 9.

Fralic, M., The Nursing Director Prepares for Labor Negotiations. *Journal of Nursing Administration*, July–August 1977, p. 4.

Gates, M. S., Are You Too Sure of Your Right to Die?. *RN*, December 1978, p. 74.

Gershon, R., Informed Patient Consent Starts With an Informed Provider. *The Hospital Medical Staff*, October 1978, p. 26.

Gibson, J. M., and Kushner, T. K., Ethics Committees: How Are They Doing?, *Hastings Center Report*, June 1986, p. 9.

Greenlaw, J., Reporting Incompetent Colleagues: "Will I Be Sued for Defamation?" *Nursing Law & Ethics*, Vol. 1, No. 5, May 1980, p. 5.

Greenlaw, J., Communication Failure: Some Case Examples. *Journal of Law and Medicine and Health Care*, Vol. 10, No. 2, April 1982, p. 77.

Greenlaw, J., Documentation of Patient Care: An Often Underestimated Responsibility. *Journal of Law and Medicine and Health Care*, Vol. 10, No. 4, September 1982, p. 172.

Greenlaw, J., Legally Speaking: The Deadly Toll of Communication Failure. *RN*, Vol. 45, No. 1, November 1982, p. 810

Guarriello, D. L., The Legal Boobytraps in Nursing Standards. *RN*, June 1984, p. 19.

Hallowell, E. E., Patient Charting: The Legal Cornerstone of Nursing. *The Journal of Practical Nursing*. Vol. 33, No. 1, January 1982, p. 35.

Hemelt, M. D., and Mackert, M. E., Your Legal Guide to Nursing Practice. *Nursing '79*, December 1979, p. 49.

Hemelt, M. D., and Mackert, M. E., Your Legal Guide to Nursing Practice. *Nursing '79*, October 1979, p. 57.

Hershey, N., The Influence of Charting Upon Liability Determinations. *Journal of Nursing Administration*, March-April 1976, p. 35.

Hershey, N., Nurses Notes—They Can Play a Critical Role in Court. *American Journal of Nursing*, November 1969, p. 2403.

Hershey, N., Pitfalls in Liability Insurance. *American Journal of Nursing*, September 1966, p. 2002.

Hershey, N., Student, Instructor and Liability: The Law and the Nurse. *American Journal of Nursing*, March 1965, p. 122.

Hirsh, H. L., Medico-Legal Implications of Medical Records. *Scalpel and Quill*, December 1975, p. 1.

Holder, A. R., Negligent Selection of Hospital Staff. *Journal of the American Medical Association*, February 12, 1973, p. 833.

Horsley, J. E., When to "Tattle" on Physician Misconduct. *RN*, December 1978, P. 17.

Isler, C., Six Mistakes That Could Land You in Jail. *RN*, February 1979, p. 64.

Jakacki, M., and Payson, A. L., Out of Control. *American Journal of Nursing*, Vol. 85, No. 12, 1985, p. 1335.

Kaiser, B. L., Patient's Rights of Access to Their Own Medical Records: The Need for New Law. *Buffalo Law Review*, p. 317.

Kerr, A. H., Nurses Notes—That's Where the Goodies Are. *Nursing '75*, p. 34.

Kimberly, R. A., et al., What do the Courts Expect from Nurses? *Nursing Life*, Vol. 2, No. 3, September–October 1982, p. 34.

Lysman, M., Informed Consent and the Nurse's Role, *RN*, September 1972, p. 50.

Mamana, J. P., Ethics and Medical Technology: Crossroads in Decision Making. *The Hospital Medical Staff*, November 1981, p. 18.

Mancini, M., The Law and the Occupational Health Nurse. *American Journal of Nursing*, September 1979, p. 1628.

Manta, J. G., A Case for Malpractice Insurance: Don't Get Caught Without It. *Nursing Life*, March-April 1982, p. 44.

McMullan, D., Accountability and Nursing Education. *Nursing Outlook*, August 1975, Vol. 23, No. 8, p. 581.

Millard, R. M., The New Accountability. *Nursing Outlook*, Vol. 23, No. 8, August 1975, p. 496.

Morris, W., 1001 Ways to Land in Court. *RN*, July 1981.

O'Sullivan, A. L., Privileged Communication. *American Journal of Nursing*, May 1980, p. 947.

Perry, S., If You're Called As An Expert Witness. *American Journal of Nursing*, March 1977, p. 458.

Perry, S. E., Managing to Avoid Malpractice. *Journal of Nursing Administration*, August 1978, p. 43.

Podratz, R. O., A Student Sues. *American Journal of Nursing*, September 1980, p. 1604.

Pollock, C., et al., Faculties Have Rights Too. *American Journal of Nursing*, April 1977, p. 636.

Pollock, C., Poteet, G., and Whilan, W., Students' Rights. *American Journal of Nursing*, April 1976, p. 600.

Prigoff, M. L., Straight Talk From a Hospital Attorney. *RN*, November 1985, p. 59.

Rabinow, J., Delegating Safely within the Law. *Nursing Life*, Vol. 2, No. 5, September–October 1982, p. 48.

Randall, J. P., Nursing Law at Your Fingertips. *Nursing Life*, Vol. 2, No. 1, January–February 1982, p. 61.

Regan, W. A., Law Forum. *Hospital Progress*, March 1978, p. 32.

Regan, W. A., No-Code Orders and Incompetent Patients. *Regan Report on Hospital Law*, January 1979.

Regan, W. A., Telephone Medicine: Documentation is Vital. *Regan Report on Nursing Law*, Vol. 23, No. 4, September 1982, p. 11.

Robertson, J., Legal Criteria for Orders Not to Resuscitate: A Response of Justice Liacos. *Medicolegal News*, February 1980, p. 4.

Robertson, J. A., Ethics Committees in Hospitals: Alternative Structures and Responsibilities. *QRB*, January 1984, p. 6.

Rozovsky, F. A., et al., Warning Legally Unsafe: Six Common Nursing Practices You Should Avoid. *Nursing Life*, September–October, p. 47.

Salman, S. L., A Systems Approach Can Assure High Quality Care and Low Costs. *Hospitals, Journal of American Hospital Association*, March 16, 1979.

Salman, S. L., Cause for Concern: Safety Training's Negative Cost. *Hospital Health Care Section Safety Newsletter*, National Safety Council, June 1978.

Salman, S. L., Committee is an Important Tool in Risk Management. *Hospitals*, September 16, 1980.

Salman, S. L., Committees Can Help Oversee Hospital's QA Activities. *Trustee*, June 1981.

Salman, S. L., The Impact of Comparative Negligence on Malpractice. *Hospitals*, March 16, 1981.

Salman, S. L., Incident Reporting/Key Loss Control Program Ingredient. *Hospital Health Care Section Safety Newsletter*, National Safety Council, August 1976.

Salman, S. L., Risk Manager Must Interact With Infection Control Expert. *Hospitals*, March 16, 1980.

Schifrin, B. S., Weissman, H., and Wiley, J., Electronic Fetal Monitoring and Obstetrical Malpractice. *Law, Medicine & Health Care*, Vol. 13, No. 3, June 1985, p. 100.

Skillicorn, S., Quality and Accountability. *Editorial Consultant, Inc.*, California, 1980.

Spaulding, J. A., Risk Management: A Hospital-Wide Approach. *Nursing Management*, Vol. 13, No. 4, April 1982, p. 29.

Thobaben, M., and Anderson, L., Reporting Elder Abuse: It's the Law. *American Journal of Nursing*, Vol. 85, No. 4, 1985, p. 371.

Trandel-Korenchuk, D. M., et al., Legal Forum: Malpractice and Prevention Risk Management. *Nursing Administration Quarterly*, Vol. 7, No. 3, Spring 1983, p. 75.

Wallace, C., Outcry over "Baby Doe" may revive little–used Hospital Ethics Committee, *Modern Healthcare*, June 1983.

BOOKS

Anderson, P., *Children's Hospital*. Harper & Row, New York, 1985.

Beis, E. B., *Mental Health and the Law*. Aspen Systems Corporation, Rockville, Maryland, 1984

Benesch, K., Abramson, N. S., Grenvik, A., and Meisel, A., *Medicologal Aspects of Critical Care*. An Aspen Publication, 1986.

Bruce, J. A. C., *Privacy and Confidentiality of Health Care Information*. American Hospital Publishers, 1984.

Chapman, E., *Supervisor's Survival Kit: A Mid Management Primer*. Science Research Associates, Chicago, 1975.

Crawford, R. E., and Doudera, A. E., *Institutional Ethics Committee and Health Care Decision Making*. Health Administration Press, Ann Arbor, Michigan, 1984.

Fenner, K. M., *Ethics and Law in Nursing*. Van Nostrand Reinhold, New York, 1980.

George, J. E., *Law and Emergency Care*. C.V. Moseby, St. Louis, Missouri, 1980.

Henry, K. H., *The Health Care Supervisor's Legal Guide*. Aspen Systems Corporation, Rockville, Maryland, 1984.

Hollander, P. A., *Legal Handbook for Educators*. Westview Press, Boulder, Colorado, 1978.

Hogue, E., *Nursing Case Law Reporter*. National Law Publishing Corporation, Owling Mills, 1983.

Hogue, E., *Nursing and Legal Liability*. National Health Publishing, 1985.

Langsley, D. G., *Legal Aspects of Certification and Accreditation*. American Board of Medical Specialties, Evanston, Illinois, 1983.

Mancini, M., and Gale, A., *Emergency Care and the Law*. Aspen Systems Corporation, Rockville, Maryland, 1981.

Mannino, M. J., *The Nurse Anesthetist and the Law*. Grune & Stratton, New York, 1982.

Post, B. L., Peters, B. M., and Stahl, S. P., *The Law of Medical Practice in Pennsylvania and New Jersey*. The Lawyers Co-Operative Publishing Company, Rochester, New York, 1984.

Rhodes, A. M., and Miller, R. D., *Nursing and the Law*. Aspen Systems Corporation, Rockville, Maryland, 1984.

Robertson, J. A., *The Rights of the Critically Ill*. Bellinger Publishing Company, Cambridge, Massachusetts, 1983.

Rosoff, A. J., *Informed Consent*. Aspen Systems Corporation, Rockville, Maryland, 1981.

Thompson, M. J., *Antitrust and the Health Care Provider*. Aspen Systems Corporation, Germantown, Maryland, 1979.

Wade, R. D., *Risk Management*. Ohio Hospital Insurance Company Publication, Columbus, 1983.

Walton, D. N., *Ethics of Withdrawal of Life-Support Systems*. Greenwood Press, Westport, Connecticut, 1983.

Ziegenfuss, J. T., *Patients' Rights and Professional Practice*. Van Nostrand Reinhold, New York, 1983.

OTHER PUBLICATIONS

American Hospital Association, *Legal Issues and Guidance for Hospital Biomedical Ethics Committees, Report of the Adjunct Legal Task Force on Biomedical Ethics*, January 1985.

American Hospital Association, *Medical Malpractice Task Force Report on Tort Reform and Compendium of Professional Liability Early Warning Systems for Health Care Providers*, May 1986.

HEW Study—Elements in Successful Risk Reduction Programs. A Study of Hospital Patient Injury Programs Developed by Applied Management Sciences, Inc., under grant from HEW. *Hospital Progress*, July 1977.

Health and Safety Guide for Hospitals, Division of Technical Services, Publications Dissemination, National Institute for Occupational Safety and Health, 4676 Columbia Parkway, Cincinnati, Ohio 45226.

Hospital Self Evaluation Form for Safety and Sanitation, Publication Number 105, Joint Commission of Accreditation of Hospitals, 875 North Michigan Avenue, Chicago, Illinois 60611.

Patient Safety Approach to Professional Liability. *American College of Surgeons*, July 1977.

The Reagan Report on Hospital Law. Medica Press, 1979.

Risk Management. A Self Evaluation Guide. Ohio Hospital Association—Research and Educational Foundation, 88 East Broad Street, Columbus, Ohio 43215.

Risk Management Manual, A Guide to Safety, Loss Control, and Malpractice Prevention for Hospitals. Publication Office, Federation of American Hospitals, Post Office Box 2451, Little Rock, Arkansas 72203.

Safety Guide for Health Care Institutions. American Hospital Association Catalog Number 1975, American Hospital Association, 840 North Lakeshore Drive, Chicago, Illinois 60611.

INDEX OF CASES BY STATE

COLORADO

CONNECTICUT

DELAWARE

DISTRICT OF COLUMBIA

FLORIDA

GEORGIA

HAWAII

NORTH CAROLINA

OREGON

OHIO

OKLAHOMA

PENNSYLVANIA

INDEX